1ST ED

NEW ENGLAND SEA TRAGEDIES

New England SEA TRAGEDIES

EDWARD ROWE SNOW

ILLUSTRATED

DODD, MEAD & COMPANY
NEW YORK / 1960

To my brother
WINTHROP JAMES SNOW
who years ago introduced me
to the fascination of Boston Harbor
when he took me ashore
at Governor's Island
for the first time

Library of Congress Catalog Card Number: 60-14102

*Printed in the United States of America
by The Cornwall Press, Inc., Cornwall, N.Y.*

Introduction

The average reader is usually fascinated by true stories of spectacularly successful struggles against death out on the billowy deep. None of us ever beholds with indifference the dangers which may beset our fellow man in trouble either at sea on a stormy ocean or approaching danger close to the rocky shore. Even though thousands of volumes of fiction have been written attempting to tell the sufferings or hardships of sailors, the true accounts of marine disasters as related by actual survivors are impossible to match.

The chapters which make up this book offer the reader a great range in time and location. They emphasize the part played in maritime disasters by New England sailors and ships on and off New England shores and in many other areas of the world.

Four different mysteries which were to have been included in this book as they involve the general subject of New England sea disaster will not be found in this volume. The story of the positive solution to Captain Joshua Slocum's strange disappearance at sea has been delayed because of the failure of expected information to arrive in time for publication.

The true account of the four chaplains on the *Dorchester* also must await a coming book for the same reason.

The story of the unfortunate disappearance of atomic scientist Richard H. Tingey of Quincy, Massachusetts, will be postponed for its inclusion in a book on New England sea mysteries on which I have been working for many years. Several other enigmas concerning the sea will be found in that volume planned for the future. Details concerning the Van Rie Boston Harbor murder not brought out in the court trial will also be in the book on New England sea mysteries.

My wife Anna-Myrle stayed up many late hours correcting manuscript and galley sheets for this book, and to her I owe my deepest thanks.

The following people also helped me in the preparation of this volume: Charlotte Bayley, Alton Hall Blackington, M. V. Brewington, Clarence S. Brigham, Mary E. Brown, Blanche Cummings, Leo Flaherty, Charles C. Gallery, Margaret Hackett, Marie Hansen, Ralph D. Hatch, John R. Herbert, Gordon Jenkins, Louise Kraus, Katherine Kuechle, Patricia R. Lynch, Laurence P. Macdonald, Alan Miles MacDougall, Mrs. Otis C. Nash, Robert I. Nesmith, S. J. Nevins, Frederick J. Quinn, Lawrence H. Rideout, Wendell P. Sargent, Ruth W. Shea, Samuel Shon, Erwin D. Smith, Dorothy Caroline Snow, Winthrop James Snow, Janet H. Sumner, Harriet Swift, Johanna von Tiling, Barbara Whitledge, Harold Winerip.

Generous assistance was given to me by the following institutions: The Bostonian Society, the Boston Athenaeum, the Boston Public Library, the Massachusetts Historical Society, the U. S. Coast Guard, the National Archives, the Harvard College Library, the Peabody Museum, the Essex Institute, and the American Antiquarian Society.

EDWARD ROWE SNOW

Marshfield, Mass.

Contents

Illustrations

I

Julian, the Poor Indian

This is the enigmatic story of a Cape Cod Indian, who through no fault of his own became a pirate and afterward a slave.

Julian, or John Julian, as he was often called, was born on Cape Cod shortly after the beginning of the eighteenth century. Taking an early interest in the sea, he quickly became familiar with its ways and before he was even fifteen he found himself performing the functions of a pilot.

Late in the spring of the year 1717 the notorious pirate Captain Samuel Bellamy obtained the services of the young Indian. He ordered the boy to go aboard the pirate chieftain's flagship *Whidah* * to guide her around New England waters.

Bellamy hailed from the west of England. In 1716, he journeyed to the West Indies in an attempt to raise a sunken treasure galleon, which proved unsuccessful. As a result he hoisted the Jolly Roger and sailed away in search of ships to plunder. Several months later he captured the *Saint Michael*, which had sailed from Bristol, and brought her into the harbor at Blanco. There he forced one of the captive men, Thomas Davis of Wales, to join the pirate band.

---

* Pronounced as in Ida.

Early in February 1717, Captain Bellamy reached the Windward Passage, located between Puerto Rico and Cuba. One day he sighted the London galley *Whidah* on her homeward-bound journey to England. Heavily loaded with a rich cargo of gold, ivory, and silver, the *Whidah* had just finished a very successful slaving trip, manned by a crew of fifty men under the command of Captain Lawrence Prince.

Pirate Captain Bellamy came upon the *Whidah* late one afternoon and gave chase, but it was three long days and nights before he closed the gap enough to fire a shot. Then to the amazement of every pirate aboard Bellamy's vessel, Captain Prince ordered his flag dipped in surrender. Bellamy went aboard the *Whidah* and found the galley to his liking. Giving the docile Captain the pirate ship *Sultana* in exchange, Bellamy transferred all his own belongings and crew to the *Whidah*, aboard which he found gold and silver worth today the equivalent of $1,000,000.

A few weeks later Bellamy was cruising in the *Whidah* off Block Island, when he overtook and captured Captain Beer's sloop from Newport, aboard which Indian pilot Julian was a crew member. After removing the cargo, Bellamy decided to let Beer have his vessel back. The other pirates voted against it, however, and the unfortunate skipper was set ashore on Block Island.

Later the same week Indian Julian noticed a small wine pinky, the *Mary Anne*, in the offing, and Captain Bellamy ordered the *Whidah* to overtake and capture her. Captain Crumpstey of the pinky was made a prisoner aboard the *Whidah*, and the *Mary Anne* joined the pirate fleet.

After a consultation with Julian, Captain Bellamy then ordered the setting of a northwest-by-north course, which was followed until noon on April 26, 1717, when a heavy fog set in, and the New England area was hit by an easterly gale which soon increased to a full hurricane. Losing sight of the remainder of his fleet in the storm, Captain Bellamy was forced to sail under bare poles. The wind steadily became more violent until by ten o'clock that night it was blowing the full strength of its fury.

Continuing to shape his course to the northward, Captain Bellamy was being driven closer and closer to the shores of Cape Cod, the very land where Julian was born. Knowing well what might lie ahead, the Indian remained alert through the terrible night.

Breakers were sighted, and the captain ordered his anchors let go. They failed to hold, however, and the great galley crashed against a sand bar offshore with terrific force. She slid over, capsizing almost at once. Most of the pirates were never to know that they were off the shores of Wellfleet, Massachusetts.

Julian and a shipmate Thomas Davis were able to get ashore in the bounding breakers and scale the bank of sand to reach the tableland, but everyone else aboard the *Whidah*, including Captain Crumpstey of the *Mary Anne* and Captain Bellamy himself, perished in the surf.*

Meanwhile, the pinky *Mary Anne* had crashed ashore ten miles to the south at the back of Stage Harbor, and the surviving pirates were soon rounded up by the local authorities.

Back in Wellfleet, Julian and Davis hiked across the sands to reach the residence of Samuel Harding, whom they asked to return with them to the scene of the disaster. By noon, more than a score of persons were removing supplies which had come ashore from the pirate wreck.

Shortly afterward, Justice Doane arrested Julian and Davis as pirates and put them in the local gaol with the seven survivors from the *Mary Anne*. The nine men were soon taken to Boston, where they were imprisoned in heavy irons.

During the summer Major John Quincy ** of Braintree was

---

* Of the 144 who lost their lives, the remains of 102 of them were later buried on the Cape Cod shore by Captain Cyprian Southack. He was on the scene to get the gold and silver cargo, but he failed to bring back any money at all, for just before the *Whidah* capsized, all her treasure had been placed in "one head," and was lost to the sea.

** After whom Quincy, Massachusetts, is named.

told of a young, attractive Indian lad who was incarcerated in the Boston gaol, and made plans to visit him. After viewing the red man and talking with him, Major Quincy decided to use his considerable influence to acquire the boy as a domestic slave.

A short time later Julian was released from the prison and made a slave of the Major. Accompanying his master to Quincy, the Indian became a part of the large household. Meanwhile, Thomas Davis had convinced the authorities of his innocence and was also released. The remaining pirates were soon tried and sentenced to be executed.

On Friday, November 15, 1717, the other survivors of the *Whidah* fleet were taken down to the Boston waterfront where North End Park stands today. There were seven of them, but only six were destined to be hanged. Julian was an interested spectator at the proceedings, for his master is believed to have thought it would make him a more disciplined servant.

One by one, as the condemned men appeared near the scaffolding, Julian recognized them. First to appear on the gallows was Simon Van Vorst, twenty-four years of age, from New York. John Brown of Jamaica, twenty-five, was next, and after him came Thomas Baker, twenty-nine, and the twenty-five-year-old Dutchman, Hendrick Quintor. Then followed Peter Cornelius Hoof, thirty-four, from Sweden and John Sheean, twenty-four, from Nantes. The seventh pirate, thirty-year-old Thomas South of Boston, England, was a ship carpenter who had been forced to join the Bellamy fleet the previous December. Evidence that he had been involuntarily impressed reached Boston just in time to clear his name, and he was allowed to go free at almost the last possible moment.

The others, in the order named, mounted the scaffolding erected between the rise and fall of the tide and were hanged. All except John Brown went to their death penitent and calm, but Brown broke out into "furious expressions with many oaths." Later he did read a prayer, but as the Rev. Mr. Mather stated later, it was "not very pertinently chosen."

Apparently the execution made a definite impression on the young Indian who had sailed the high seas with the six executed pirates, and in 1721 Major Quincy decided to have him accepted into the Christian church. On November 12 of that year, the Indian and all other members of the Quincy household were baptized, at which time the Major promised to give them a Christian education.

Between 1721 and 1732 Julian left the household of Major Quincy and became the property of a Mr. Howard of Bridgewater. Subsequently the Boston *Weekly News-Letter* printed an advertisement for the Indian as a runaway slave. This notice was seen by a Mr. John Rogers of Pembroke, while passing through Weymouth, Massachusetts, and he believed that he knew where he could find Julian, who was known in the vicinity because of his former association with Major Quincy. Rogers tracked the fugitive down on Monday evening, September 11, 1732, and taking him captive, he lodged with him that night at Braintree,* but the Indian escaped.

On Tuesday morning Rogers advertised a reward of ten shillings for the recapture of his prisoner, and another Indian volunteered to take Rogers to Julian's hiding place. Again the two set out for Rogers' home in Pembroke which was on the way to Bridgewater. They had walked about five miles when Rogers decided to go into a local tavern run by a Mr. Scot. He called for a dram, but they had none, and while they were discussing what liquor there was to drink, the Indian edged his way over toward the door. A moment later Mr. Scot saw Julian pass by the window and he told Rogers that his prize had escaped.

The harried captor ran out and catching sight of the Indian crossing a cornfield near the outskirts of Braintree, raced

---

* I am greatly indebted to City Historian William Churchill Edwards of Quincy, Massachusetts, for his substantial help in discovering certain details of Julian's career during the time the Indian resided in Braintree.

after him. According to the tavern keeper who was watching
at a short distance, Julian opened up his jackknife. "I could
tell what he was doing," said Scot later, "by the motion of
his arm."

When Rogers approached the Indian, Julian ran at him
and stabbed the white man in the left side "to the hilt," leaving a deep and open wound. Scot and a Negro ran to help
Rogers, after which they chased his assailant, who still had
the knife in his hand, until they finally subdued him. Scot
then tried to get Rogers to speak, and on the third attempt,
the victim answered, "I am either stabbed or wounded,"
which proved to be his last words. A widower, he died at the
age of forty-three, leaving three children.

The Indian now eluded his captors again, but several pur-
suers caught up with him and held him until the authorities
took him off to the gaol. At the inquest the coroner urged
that the prisoner be charged with murder, which was done.
He was found guilty and received a sentence of death at
the Supreme Court session held in Boston for the County of
Suffolk. On Thursday, March 22, 1733, the Indian who had
once served as a pirate was taken out to Boston Neck where
he was executed before a great assemblage of people.

As was the custom of the period, three broadsides were
issued to commemorate the occasion. The most effective one
was printed in Boston and sold at the Heart and Crown in
Cornhill. The broadside contains an admonition warning
possible buyers not to purchase "a foolish Paper printed, called
Julian's Advice to Children and Servants, [because] the said
Paper is false and spurious, and disowned by the said *Julian*
in the Presence of three Persons."

The text appears below, and it bore the title: "Advice from
the Dead to the Living; or, A Solemn Warning to the World,
Occasioned by the untimely Death of poor Julian, Who was
Executed on Boston Neck, on Thursday the 22d of March,
1733, for the Murder of Mr. John Rogers of Pembroke, the

12th of September 1732. Very proper to be Read by all Persons, but especially young People, and Servants of all Sorts."

This Day take warning young and old,
By a sad Sight we here behold,
Of one whom Vengeance in his Chase
Hath taken in his sinful Race.

Here we behold amidst the Throng,
Condemned Julian guarded strong,
To Gallows bound with heavy Heart,
To suffer as his just Desert.

Where we for Warning may observe
What cruel Murder doth deserve,
Also the sad procuring Cause
Why Sinners die amidst their Days.

Here now we have a lively View,
Of Cain's vile Action fresh and new,
That old Revenge is by Permit
Prevailing in our Natures yet.

* * *

And by his Master in his Youth,
Instructed in the Ways of Truth.

Was also taught to Write and Read,
And learn'd his Catechise and Creed,
And what was proper (as he saith)
Relating to the Christian Faith.

His pious Master did with care,
By Counsels warn him to beware
Of wicked Courses, that would tend
To his Destruction in the End.

When Twenty Years were gone and past,
By his Account he took at last
To Drinking and ill Company,

Which prov'd his fatal Destany.

No timely Warnings would he hear,
From kind Reproofs he turn'd his Ear,
Provoked God for to depart,
And leave him to an harden'd Heart.

Since he despis'd the Ways of Truth,
And good Instruction in his Youth,
God then withdrew restraining Grace,
And let him run his wicked Race.

*   *   *

So here we leave his pitious Case,
In tender Arms of sov'reign Grace,
Altho' his Crimes are great and sore,
Grace can abound and pardon more.

Now may the Congregation hear,
This awful Voice, and stand in fear,
And being timely warn'd thereby,
May do no more so wickedly.

FINIS

II

Colonel Winslow's Slave

The historic Winslow House in Marshfield, built in 1699, is well known to many residents of Massachusetts' South Shore. In the year 1703 a baby boy, named John Winslow, first saw the light of day in this house. In 1755, as a Colonel on an expedition to Nova Scotia, it was his unhappy task to supervise the removal of the Acadians and scatter them along the shores of what is now the northeastern coast of the United States. The story in this chapter, however, concerns a Negro slave of Colonel John Winslow named Briton Hammon, who had left the Winslow homestead on Christmas Day eight years previously.

Hammon had been given permission by Colonel John Winslow to take a trip down into the West Indies on a sloop belonging to Captain Howland of Plymouth, Massachusetts, which was scheduled to leave her home port the day after Christmas. Hammon was able to secure transportation that Christmas Day to Plymouth, where he soon found the sloop and went aboard her.

A short time afterward Captain John Howland set sail with the slave as a member of his crew. After a pleasant voyage of about thirty days, they arrived at the Island of

Jamaica, where the sailors unloaded a heavy cargo of New England commodities.

Five days later Captain Howland announced that the next port of call would be one of the islands in the Bay of Honduras, where they were to put aboard a great cargo of logwood. Arriving there, the crew worked hard and faithfully for the next two weeks. On May 25, 1748, with the last log aboard, the heavily laden sloop sailed for New England.

Two weeks later a terrible storm caught them between the shores of Florida and Cuba, and the sloop was battered about unmercifully. As soon as the wind went down, the crew attempted to repair the damage, but hardly had they put the craft back into shape than another great gale hit the area and the unfortunate vessel was smashed ashore on what has become known as Carysfort Reef, off Cape Florida.*

The reef was several leagues from land, and the sloop was not so securely grounded that she probably could not have been freed had the captain thrown his deckload overboard immediately. Writing of the incident years later, Briton Hammon tells us that Captain Howland was "advised, intreated, and beg' on, by every Person on board to heave over but only 20 Ton of the Wood, and we should have got clear." At that time, Captain Howland evidently thought more of the logwood than he did of his own safety, for he made an outright refusal to sacrifice his cargo.

His opinion changed after a rough night on the reef, however. At the end of the second day he was so frightened that he decided to abandon the vessel. Ordering the longboat hoisted out over the side, he asked volunteers to stay on board, as the small boat would hold only about nine people.

Not one person volunteered. Howland then announced that he himself would remain on the sloop, after which a

---

* It was here that the 28-gun *Carysfort* ran aground October 23, 1770. Although the ship was worked off by the skill of her master, the name Carysfort still identifies the reef. The lighthouse now at Carysfort Reef was completed in 1852.

passenger and one sailor agreed to stay with him while the other nine on board, including Hammon, rowed for the distant shore. Supplies and provisions were then loaded into the boat, including a sail for a tent, arms and ammunition, cooking equipment and water. It was decided that as soon as the boat reached shore, five sailors would get out, while the other four would row the long distance back to the sloop for the three who remained aboard.

In charge of the boat, the mate soon had the oarsmen pulling with a steady rhythm. Two hours later they reached a position half a mile from shore. Guiding the boat in toward the beach, the mate sighted what he thought were several rocks sticking up out of the ocean. As they rowed closer they saw the rocks change into canoes, and the survivors became apprehensive. A British flag flying from one of the craft, however, relieved their fears.

Taking up their oars again, they approached the strangers and counted twenty canoes in all. Then suddenly to their horror the sailors saw that these craft were manned by sixty hostile Indians who had used the British emblem as a terrible ruse.

After a quick skirmish the Indians overwhelmed the mate and the eight sailors, and took away all their supplies. A council of war was held, and the savages decided to split up. Eighteen of the canoes started paddling out toward the sloop, leaving two behind to proceed at a slower speed in company with the boat, the occupants of which were ordered to row back to the wreck.

Three hours later, a long time after the Indians had reached the sloop, the tired sailors came alongside. Hammon then discovered to his horror that the men left aboard had been killed. He learned later that the captain had resisted the marauders, who slaughtered him and the other two men almost at once.

The boat had been brought up to the port side of the wreck, but the Indians now directed the mate to have his men row around the bow and come up on the starboard side. As the boat was just passing under the jibboom, the mate, who was standing at the steering oar, gave a shout of terror.

"They are loading their guns to fire down on us," he cried. "My lads, we are all dead men!" Surely enough, a moment later the Indians began shooting their muskets into the boat.

Reuben Young of Cape Cod was the first to be hit. He died within a few minutes. Then two Plymouth men, Joseph Little and Lemuel Doty, were shot to death. A moment later Hammon, who had been watching his chances, slipped off the boat as though he also had been wounded. Diving under water, he swam rapidly away as far as he could. Coming up only to breathe, he finally reached a position several hundred yards from the place where the others were being killed. It was only then that he rested and breathed deeply.

He heard volley after volley being discharged at his companions in the open boat, and when the shooting stopped he realized that they must all be dead.*

A short time later Hammon was spotted, and one of the canoes caught up with him and pulled him aboard. Time and again an Indian slashed at Briton with a cutlass, and then the others tied him to the thwarts of the canoe, and started back to the Plymouth sloop.

By the time they reached her, the savages aboard had set her afire, and the hull was burning briskly. Raving and shouting, the Indians ran along the deck through the flames, which soon became too hot. They abandoned the craft, paddling out a few hundred yards to watch the fire roar through the rigging until the sloop finally burned right down to the water's edge. As it was nearly sunset, the Indians took a last look at the smoldering ruins, after which the entire assemblage of canoes started for the distant shore.

---

* They were Moses Newmock, a mulatto; John Nowland and Nathaniel Rick, both of Plymouth; Elkanah Collymore of Scituate; and James Webb of parts unknown.

Now the sole survivor of the entire crew, Briton began to wonder what his own fate would be, and why they were saving him. He soon found out, to his utmost terror.

A husky Negro, almost to the point of being fat, Briton was told by the Indians that they were taking him ashore for one reason only, to roast him alive. His captors had run out of meat, and of the entire crew he was the nicest morsel they had encountered.

All the way in the savages were explaining to Briton that the moment they landed he would be immediately roasted alive. Suddenly, while they were still a mile from their destination the Indians sighted a great fire blazing in the gathering twilight. Paddling faster, they landed on the beach and ran up to the conflagration, where they found a giant wild boar weighing hundreds of pounds roasting over a spit. Several of the warriors who were out hunting, had been lucky enough to kill the great animal.

Briton also was extremely joyous at the turn of events and listened happily as the savages explained that the boar would take his place at the feasts for at least the next few days. His bonds loosened at once, the prisoner was allowed to share in the banquet. From that moment on, because he had a dark skin like the Indians, he was accepted as one of almost equal rank. As the days went by and the Indians grew more accustomed to him, he was given greater liberties. In the daytime he could wander as he pleased about the encampment. Every night, however, he was placed under guard, and the sentries were alert until sunrise.

In this manner five weeks went by. Long before the wild boar meat had been all consumed, the hunters went out again and were able to return with several more animals. Briton soon had the feeling that his immediate danger was over. By this time the corn crop was ready for harvesting and the prisoner was allowed to eat his fill with the others.

One day, several months later, a Spanish schooner appeared offshore and sailed into the harbor where the Indian village

was located. In the Marshfield Negro's account of his experiences he tells us that Captain Romond of the schooner
was an old friend of his, who had been ashore with him in
Jamaica many years before. Briton's remarks follow:

"Captain Romond knowing me very well, weigh'd Anchor
and carry'd me off to the Havanna, and after being there four
Days the Indians came after me, and insisted on having me
again, as I was their Prisoner;—They made Application to the
Governor, and demanded me again from him; in answer to
which the Governor told them, that as they had put the whole
Crew to Death, they should not have me again, and so paid
them Ten Dollars for me, adding, that he would not have
them kill any Person hereafter, but take as many of them as
they could, of those that should be cast away, and bring them
to him, for which he would pay them Ten Dollars a-head.

"At the Havanna I lived with the Governor in the Castle
about a Twelve-month, where I was walking thro' the Street,
I met with a Press-Gang who immediately prest me, and put
me into Gaol, and with a Number of others I was confin'd
till next Morning, when we were all brought out, and ask'd
who would go on board the King's Ships, four of which
having been lately built, were bound to Old-Spain, and on my
refusing to serve on board, they put me in a close Dungeon."

There Briton was forgotten. He was confined for four
years and seven months, during which time he often made
application to the Governor through visitors who came to
see the prisoners. The Governor was never notified of Hammon's incarceration, and had no idea of what had become of
him.

One of those who visited Briton in jail was a Mrs. Betty
Howard, then a Havana resident. She had not paid much
attention to Briton, and had neglected to carry his message
to the Governor. The chance arrival of a merchantman from
Boston reminded Mrs. Howard of Briton's plight, and she
mentioned the fact to the captain. He, in turn, visited the

prisoner, and was able to secure his release from gaol the next day. Briton's own words continue:

"I lived with the Governor about a Year after I was delivered from the Dungeon, in which Time I endeavour'd three Times to make my Escape, the last of which proved effectual. The first Time I got on board of *Captain Marsh*, an English Twenty Gun Ship, with a Number of others, and lay on board conceal'd that Night. The next Day the Ship being under sail, I thought myself safe, and so made my Appearance upon Deck, but as soon as we were discovered the Captain ordered the Boat out, and sent us all on Shore—I intreated the Captain to let me, in particular, tarry on board, begging and crying to him, to commiserate my unhappy Condition, and added, that I had been confin'd almost five Years in a close Dungeon, but the Captain would not hearken to any Intreaties, for fear of having the Governor's Displeasure, and so I was obliged to go on shore.

"After being on Shore another Twelvemonth, I endeavour'd to make my Escape the second Time, by trying to get on board of a Sloop bound to Jamaica, and as I was going from the City to the Sloop, was unhappily taken by the Guard, and ordered back to the Castle, and there confined.

"However, in a short Time I was set at Liberty, and order'd with a Number of others to carry the Bishop from the Castle, thro' the Country, to confirm the old People, baptize Children &c. for which he receives large Sums of Money. He is carried (by Way of Respect) in a large Two-arm Chair; the Chair is lin'd with crimson Velvet, and supported by eight Persons. I was employ'd in this Service about Seven Months, during which Time I lived very well, and then returned to the Castle again, where I had my Liberty to walk about the city, and do Work for my self.

"The *Beaver*, an English Man of War then lay in the Harbour, and having been informed by some of the Ship's Crew that she was to sail in a few Days, I had nothing now to do, but to seek an Opportunity how I should make my Escape.

"Accordingly one Sunday Night the Lieutenant of the Ship with a Number of the Barge Crew were in a Tavern, and Mrs. Howard who had before been a Friend to me, interceded with the Lieutenant to carry me on board. The Lieutenant said he would with all his Heart, and immediately I went on board in the Barge.

"The next Day the Spaniards came along side the *Beaver*, and demanded me again, with a Number of others who had made their Escape from them, and got on board the Ship, but just before I did; but the Captain who was a true Englishman, refus'd them, and said he could not answer it, to deliver up any Englishmen under English Colours.

"In a few Days we set Sail for Jamaica, where we arrived safe, after a short and pleasant Passage.

"After being at Jamaica a short Time we Sail'd for London, as convoy to a Fleet of Merchantmen, who all arrived safe in the Downs. I was turned over to another Ship, the *Arcenceil*, and there remained about a Month. From this ship I went on board the *Sandwich* of 90 Guns: on board the *Sandwich* I tarry'd 6 Weeks, and then was order'd on board the *Hercules*, Capt. John Porter, a 74 Gun Ship, we sail'd on a Cruize, and met with a French 84 Gun Ship, and had a very smart Engagement, in which about 70 of our Hands were Kill'd and Wounded, the Captain lost his Leg in the Engagement, and I was Wounded in the Head by a small Shot.

"We should have taken this Ship, if they had not cut away the most of our Rigging; however, in about three Hours after, a 64 Gun Ship, came up with and took her.—I was discharged from the *Hercules* the 12th Day of May 1759 (having been on board of that Ship 3 Months) on account of my being disabled in the Arm, and render'd incapable of Service, after being honourably paid the Wages due to me.

"I was put into the Greenwich Hospital where I stay'd and soon recovered.

"I then ship'd myself a Cook on board *Captain Martyn*, an arm'd Ship in the King's Service. I was on board this Ship almost Two Months, and after being paid my Wages, was discharg'd in the Month of October.

"After my discharge from *Captain Martyn*, I was taken sick in London of a Fever, and was confin'd about 6 Weeks, where I expended all my Money, and left in very poor Circumstances; and unhappy for me I knew nothing of my good Master's being in London at this my very difficult Time.

"After I got well of my sickness, I ship'd myself on board of a large Ship bound to Guinea, and being in a publick House one Evening, I overheard a Number of Persons talking about Rigging a Vessel bound to New-England, I ask'd them to what Part of New-England this Vessel was bound? they told me to Boston; and having ask'd them who was Commander? they told me, Capt. Watt; in a few Minutes after this the Mate of the Ship came in, and I ask'd him if Captain Watt did not want a Cook who told me he did, and that the Captain would be in, in a few Minutes; and in about half an Hour the Captain came in, and then I ship'd myself at once, after begging off from the Ship bound to Guinea; I work'd on board Captain Watt's ship almost Three Months, before she sail'd, and one Day being at Work in the Hold, I overheard some Persons on board mention the Name of Winslow, at the Name of which I was very inquisitive, and having ask'd what Winslow, they were talking about? They told me it was General Winslow; and that he was one of the Passengers, I ask'd them what General Winslow? For I never knew my good Master, by that Title before; but after enquiring more particularly I found it must be Master, and in a few Days Time the Truth was joyfully verify'd by a happy Sight of his Person, which so overcome me, that I could not speak to him for some Time—My good Master was exceeding glad to see me, telling me that I was like one arose from the Dead, for he thought I had been Dead a great many Years, having heard nothing of me for almost Thirteen Years.

"I think I have not deviated from Truth, in any particular of this my Narrative, and tho' I have omitted a great many Things, yet what is wrote may suffice to convince the Reader, that I have been most grievously afflicted, and yet thro' the Divine Goodness, as miraculously preserved, and delivered out of many Dangers; of which I desire to retain a grateful Remembrance, as long as I live in the World.

"*And now, That in the Providence of that God, who delivered his Servant* David *out of the Paw of the Lion and out of the Paw of the Bear, I am freed* from a long and dreadful Captivity, among worse Savages than they; *And am return'd to my* own Native Land, to Shew how Great Things the Lord hath done for Me; *I would call upon all Men, and Say,* O Magnifie the Lord with Me, and let us Exalt his Name together! O that Men would Praise the Lord for His Goodness, and for his Wonderful Works to the Children of Men!"

General Winslow arranged for the return of Briton Hammon to Massachusetts, where he wrote out the above account of his truly remarkable experiences, in the year 1760, when he was very ill and feared that he would soon die. His passing, however, did not come until some time later.

III

Famine on the *Peggy*

Famine frequently leads men to do terrible things, and hunger and thirst at sea often dictate extreme measures which on other occasions would be unbelievably bestial.

In the year 1765, the American brigantine *Peggy*, under command of David Harrison, arrived at Fayal in the Azores. The captain disposed of her cargo, after which he took on board wine and spirits. Her loading finished on October 23, and the following day she sailed on a trip to New York.

Five days later, as the *Peggy* was far at sea, the wind suddenly shifted. Then began a series of violent storms, one succeeding another almost without interruption, which lasted through the entire month of November.

Battered day after day by the gales, the *Peggy* sprung her masts, both of which went by the board. All the sails, excepting one, were torn to rags. To add to the distress, several leaks were discovered in the hold.

With the coming of December the wind abated a little, but the waves were still mountainously high. The helpless vessel was soon driven out of her course. Destitute of masts, sails, and rigging, she was now in unknown waters and unmanageable, drifting to and fro at the mercy of the sea.

By this time the provisions were getting low, and one day when stock was taken the food was found to be practically exhausted. Early one morning a short time later, however, two vessels were sighted, and this brought cheer to the starving crew of the *Peggy*. Unfortunately the sea ran so high that Captain Harrison could neither successfully signal to the ships nor approach them, and they soon vanished. The disappointed seamen, who were now desperately hungry, fell upon the wine and brandy with which the ship was laden. They allotted to the captain two small jars of water, each containing about a gallon, and this comprised the remainder of their stock. Three days elapsed, during which time the men appeased the painful cravings of hunger by keeping in a state of intoxication.

On the fourth day a ship was observed bearing toward them under full sail. No time was lost in making signals of distress, and the crew soon realized that they were answered. The sea was sufficiently calm to permit the two vessels to approach each other, and the captains were able to communicate. The strangers seemed much affected by the account of their sufferings and promised them a certain quantity of biscuit, which would be sent aboard as soon as the captain completed a nautical observation which he had just begun and expected would take an hour. However unreasonable such a delay appeared to them, the famished members of the *Peggy*'s crew were obliged to accept it.

During the subsequent interval of anxious waiting, however, the strange vessel continually increased the distance between them. Then, to the extreme dismay of the starving crew, the captain of the other craft, regardless of his promise, suddenly crowded on all his sails and bore away. Despair and consternation overwhelmed the crew of the *Peggy*. Enraged, they fell upon the only animals that remained on board, two pigeons and a cat, which were killed, roasted and devoured. They gave the captain the head of the cat and he afterward declared that however disgusting it would have been on any other occasion, he thought it then an exquisitely delicious treat.

After this repast ended the unfortunate men then supported themselves by living on oil, candles and leather, but even these unusual delicacies were entirely consumed by December 28. From that day until January 13, they ate nothing at all.

For some time Captain Harrison had been confined to the bed in his cabin by a severe case of the gout. On January 13 the sailors went to him in a body, with the mate at their head. He reminded the master of the deplorable state to which they were reduced and then declared that it was necessary to sacrifice one of their number in order to save the rest, adding that whatever the captain might say they were going through with their plan.

Harrison, a tender and humane man, could not hear such a barbarous proposition without shuddering. He explained that by such an act as they contemplated they would forever be guilty of murder in their own eyes, and he commanded them to forget their plan.

But the captain had spoken to "deaf men." They answered with one voice that it was not important to them whether he approved of their resolution or not, and they had only told him about it out of respect. They stated that he would run the same risk as they did, adding that, in such a crisis of life and death, all authority was at an end. With these words they left him, and went up on deck, where the lots were soon drawn.

A Negro, who was on board and belonged to Captain Harrison, drew the unlucky lot. It is more than probable that those who arranged the macabre sweepstakes had planned that he would be the victim.

Then followed a terrible scene, more to be expected from a pack of wolves than from human beings. The Negro was instantly sacrificed, after which one of the crew tore out his liver and devoured it, without having the patience to cook it. The man was soon afterward taken ill, and died the following day in convulsions, with all the symptoms of madness.

Some of his comrades then proposed to keep the second man's body to live upon, after the Negro was consumed; but this advice was rejected by the majority, doubtless on account of the sickness which had carried him off. He was, therefore, thrown overboard, and consigned to the deep.

The captain, in spite of his gout, was just as hungry as the rest of the crew, but he managed to resist all the persuasions of his men to partake of their terrible repast. He made the most of the water which had been assigned him, daily mixing with it a small quantity of spirits, and this was the only sustenance he took during this whole period.

The body of the Negro, equally divided among the others and eaten with the greatest economy, lasted until January 26. Three days later the famished crew began deliberations as to their choice of a second victim. They again told the captain of their intention, and he gave his consent, aware that the enraged sailors would conduct the lottery anyway. They left it to him to fix upon any method he might think proper for the next awful draft. Harrison decided to write each man's name on a slip of paper, which he folded twice and dropped into a hat. He shook them together while the crew watched him in silence, their eyes fixed in terror on every move he made.

With a trembling hand one of them drew from the hat the fatal ballot, which he delivered to the master. Captain Harrison opened it and read aloud the name—David Flat. The unfortunate man on whom the lot had fallen appeared perfectly resigned to his fate.

"My friends," said he, "the only favor I request of you is not to keep me long in pain; dispatch me as speedily as you did the Negro."

Turning to the man who had performed the first execution, he said, "It is you I choose to give me the mortal blow. I desire one hour to prepare myself for my execution."

The victim's comrades began to weep, and decided to delay

the execution until eleven o'clock the following morning. Such a short reprieve afforded very little consolation to Flat, and the certainty of dying the next day brought his complete collapse. He was seized with a violent fever and became delirious. Several of the sailors proposed to kill him immediately, in order to terminate his sufferings. The majority, however, agreed that they should wait as they had planned.

At ten o'clock the next morning, January 30, the men had arranged a fire, on which they were to roast the limbs of the unfortunate victim.

A short time later, with less than a full hour remaining before the execution, all hands sighted a sail coming toward them, driven by a favoring wind. She proved to be the *Susan*, returning from Virginia to London.

She dipped her colors, indicating that she had seen the *Peggy*'s flag of distress, and soon one of her boats came alongside, carrying her master. When he heard the sad account of the *Peggy*'s crew the captain's eyes filled with tears. He lost no time in bringing them relief, first supplying them with the provisions essential for life and then with the materials necessary to put their vessel back in commission, after which he made an offer to convoy the *Peggy* to London.

Because they were so much closer to the English coast than to their destination, New York, Captain Harrison accepted the offer of escort to Britain. During this return two more of the *Peggy*'s crew died, but the others gradually recovered their strength. David Flat himself was restored to perfect health, after his close brush with death as a living sacrifice.

IV

Captain Woodard

One hundred and sixty-nine years ago David Woodard, or Woodward as some spell his name, left his pleasant home in the town of Braintree, Massachusetts, to journey to Boston, where he sailed within a short time aboard the *Robert Morris*, then under command of Captain Hay. The ship, owned by Thomas Russell of Boston, was bound for the East Indies.

Arriving in the Indies, David Woodard helped in the unloading of the cargo. Then, a short time later, Captain Henry Hubbard of another American ship in port, the *Enterprise*, offered him the position of first mate which was so attractive that Woodard accepted and transferred his belongings to his new berth. On Jan. 20, 1793, the *Enterprise* put out to sea.

Encountering contrary winds and a southerly current while passing through the Straits of Makassar, she made no progress at all for six long weeks, and soon the cook was running short of water and provisions. On the morning of March 1, Captain Hubbard noticed a sail four leagues, or twelve miles, away and ordered Mr. Woodard to take the ship's boat and sail across to the other craft for the purpose of purchasing necessary supplies. They were then sailing in three degrees south latitude.

Mr. Woodard took five seamen in the boat with him; two New Englanders, William Gideon and John Cole; two Englishmen, Archibald Miller and George Williams; and a Scot never identified by name. As they expected to reach the other ship in a short time, they took no water, food, or compass. They did have aboard an axe, a boat hook, two pocket-knives, a gun (but no bullets), and forty dollars.

Unfortunately, the moment that they left the vessel a strong squall came out from the land. Soon a heavy downpour set in which completely blotted out even their own craft from view, but they kept their course as best they could.

Hours later the rain ended, visibility improved, and Woodard sighted the other ship less than a mile away! It was not until after sunset, however, that they reached her. Going aboard Woodard was told that there was not the least bit of food or water to spare, as the vessel was in the same predicament as the *Enterprise*. With darkness falling, the *Enterprise* was lost to view, and Woodard was invited to spend the night aboard the ship with his men, an offer which he was glad to accept.

All that night the rain poured down heavily, with a full fresh breeze springing up from the south before dawn. When morning came, they found that the land bore in the same direction as it had the evening before, but there was no sign of the *Enterprise*. In desperation, Woodard climbed to the masthead, but could see nothing at all.

As the other craft, whose name has not come down to us, was bound for China, Woodard decided that the most prudent course was to leave the ship without further delay and sail in search of the *Enterprise*. The captain agreed to give him twelve cartridges for his gun, and he also received a bottle of brandy, but the strangers could spare neither water nor provisions.

Pushing away from the ship, Woodard and his men set a southerly course. Alternately sailing and rowing, the men saw no signs of any craft all day long. Toward evening they sighted a small island, on which they landed to get water. They built a roaring bonfire which they believed that Captain Hubbard might notice. Then about fifteen miles away, the captain actually did see the flames from his ship, but he did not associate them with Woodard, believing that the fire had been set by natives.

When morning came Woodard climbed to the top of the highest hill on the island, but the *Enterprise* had sailed on during the night, and he could see no sign of her. They had found neither water nor provisions on the island. Discouraged, they put out to sea again an hour after sunrise.

For six long days, because of a heavy prevailing southwest wind, they were forced to continue their course down the middle of the Straits. All they had to drink in that period was the single bottle of brandy.

When the wind ended, they had the Island of Celebes clearly in sight. A council of war led to an agreement that they would go ashore in search of water and provisions. Then they could proceed to Makassar, which they hoped was about three degrees to the south.

Rowing all day and night, they finally came close to the shore in the dark, but thought it would be prudent to wait until morning to land. Several proas, or native sailing craft, were then sighted. The sailors steered toward them with great eagerness, but on pulling alongside, found that the natives had armed themselves and were ready to fight.

Nevertheless, Woodard and his men were desperate for water and provisions, and regardless of the outcome, he shouted across to the natives that he needed food and drink. The Malays replied in sign language that they would sell them a little water and some provisions, and then they asked Woodard where his ship was. Woodard answered that she was quite a distance at sea. The natives then realized that he was at a disadvantage with his vessel so far away and with no weapons to speak of in the boat. The Malays brandished their cresses, or steel daggers, which were about two feet long, and ordered him to row ashore to a point of land.

All the way in Woodard kept asking for provisions, requesting a large quantity of either Indian corn or coconuts, but he was refused. Three of his men were so desperate that they jumped on board a proa and appealed for food; whereupon they were given four small ears of corn.

Woodard then gave the leader of the Malays a silver dollar, hoping to get some coconuts. Accepting the money, however, the chief still refused to give Woodard anything. Instead the savage jumped into the boat with another Malay. He pulled up Woodard's shirt in an attempt to find more money, at the same time holding his dagger drawn. Woodard grabbed his small axe to threaten the Malays, and finally forced them back to their proa and made them cast off the boat.

Just as the two craft drifted apart, the Malay chief reached for his pistol to shoot Woodard, but the weapon misfired. The white men then rowed desperately to reach the shore. Finally Woodard landed with one man and ordered the other four to stay in the boat. Soon afterward two proas came to anchor just off the beach and sent six armed men toward shore in canoes.

Suspecting the worst, Woodard ran to his boat and shoved her off, to avoid being massacred. Rowing desperately, the sailors soon covered a quarter of a mile. Keeping up a steady stroke, for they realized that they were rowing for their lives, they reached a point of land four miles away, where they landed out of sight of the proas.

Leaving one man, Cole, to guard the boat, the others went into the forest. They cut down three coconut trees and began to gather up the fruit. As they were working, Archibald Miller said that he would return to the boat and relieve Cole, who soon appeared. The men had just finished cutting down a fourth tree when they heard Miller give a scream of terror, which ended in a strange agonizing manner.

Rushing down onto the beach, they saw their boat several

hundred yards out to sea, crowded with Malays, but there was no sign of its guardian. Reaching the water's edge, Woodard called out for Miller, but there was no reply. Finally they gave up. Turning around to go back to the coconut trees, they then saw the dead body of their companion rolling back and forth in the surf. His throat was cut and several other knife wounds showed. Woodard and the four other survivors ran into the forest again, where they concealed themselves in the dry leaves for the rest of the day.

That night, after a council of war, they decided to leave the vicinity, traveling only in the darkness. Starting out at about eight o'clock, and taking a star for their guide, they walked about fifteen miles, but when morning came they found to their dismay that they were within a few rods of the beach from which they had started the preceding evening, having gone around a mountain instead of over it.

The next evening they again set out for Makassar, but this time they followed the beach. Continuing in this manner for six successive nights, hiding each day in the woods, they made good progress toward their objective.

Now thirteen days since they had left the *Enterprise*, they decided to rest. Exhausted and discouraged, they were faint from hunger. They had had no provisions for nineteen days, only now and then a little water in the hollow trees and a few berries when they could find them. Without shoes, their feet were sore, and their bodies were covered with scratches from briars and brambles.

The next morning they found a mountain by the side of a deep bay, and decided to stop there for the day. At noon they noticed scores of Malays fishing in the bay.

A short time later Woodard took a walk along the banks, where he found a yellowish-looking berry, about the size of a currant, hanging in little bunches. He ate a few and then filled his hat to take some back to his companions, who did not like them. Three of the men then began eating the leaves of a bush nearby.

That night, those who had eaten the leaves were attacked with violent pains in their bowels, vomiting time and again. In the morning, Woodard searched for water for them and brought back a small supply. He arranged for them to drink the water through a reed, giving each man three mouthfuls until the entire supply was consumed.

Realizing that they were then in no condition to continue their hike to Makassar, Woodard asked his group if they were willing to surrender to the natives. All except one man, Jim Cole, consented. Cole said he would rather die of hunger than be massacred by the Malays. Woodard, however, finally won him over. After hiding their weapons in the ground, they all walked down to the bay and prepared to give them-selves up, but upon reaching the shore, they discovered that the fishermen had vanished, and that the tide was high.

With difficulty they found a path, and walked away from the bay until they noticed three girls fishing in a brook. When the girls saw them, they scurried up the path and vanished. A quarter of an hour later three men came back by the same path and threatened the white men with their cresses. Other natives followed them.

Then and there Woodard realized that it was time to carry out his plan of surrender. Telling the others to hold back, he walked toward the Malays alone until he reached a position a few yards away, when he fell on his face and begged for mercy. Finally one of the natives put up his cress and knelt down toward Woodard, grabbing him by the hand.

About twenty savages now surrounded Woodard and com-menced taking off his clothes. They removed his hat, took away his handkerchief, and cut off the buttons from his jacket, believing them to be money. Woodard's four com-panions were treated in a similar manner. Thus, within a short time, the whites were completely at the mercy of the Malays.

Woodard begged for something to eat, and the sailors were given five green coconuts, after which the natives took them to a town called Travalla, where they were brought into the so-called "Judgment Hall" in the center of the village. Placed near the judgment seat, they were watched by a vast concourse of people, most of whom had never seen a white man before.

Half an hour later, the Rajah of the place made his appearance. He was six feet tall, straight and powerfully built. As he entered, the combination of weird costume and heavy paint made him resemble a madman. He flourished a large cress in his hand, the blade of which was bright and thirty inches long. His attire consisted of a pair of short breeches, a girdle around his waist, and a red handkerchief on his head.

Reaching a point about ten feet from Woodard, he stopped. The white man arose at once and went to meet him. The Chief did nothing but stare at him while he begged for his life. Woodard approached the Rajah, knelt down, and lifted up the Chief's foot, placing it on his own head as a token of submission.

The Rajah then sat down in his judgment seat and called his officers together for a consultation. After a decision was reached, he took five pieces of betel nut, which the natives chew instead of tobacco. He presented each of the white men with a piece of the nut, and then ordered that they be given extra coconuts. Woodard now felt relieved, for he knew the decision had been in their favor.

Sunset came, and the men retired to sleep. They rested until eight o'clock when supper was served to them in the Rajah's house. Their menu consisted of sago bread and peas, but the quantity was so small that any one of them could have eaten the entire meal. Finishing their food, the white men were again allowed to sleep. Later they were awakened once more, to be inspected by a new group of Malays who had been out of town and had not seen them before. After the visitors left, the whites slept peacefully until daylight, at which time a large group of women and children filed into the house, crowding every available inch, to see the strangers. They stayed there until noon.

The sailors were given no breakfast, but at lunch time they received an ear of Indian corn and a coconut. The same meal was given them at night, and for the next twenty days each man had lunch and supper of a coconut and an ear of corn.

One day a Mohammedan priest named Tuan Hadjee visited them. He could speak a few words of English, a little Portuguese, and some words of Arabic. Apparently he was an influential Malay gentleman. He had visited Bombay and Mecca, and had with him a certificate from Governor John Herbert of Balambangan on the island of Borneo. The paper, dated 1771, certified that Tuan Hadjee was a good and trusted man and empowered by John Herbert to assist all distressed Englishmen.

"Where did you come from?" asked Tuan Hadjee.

"We came from Bengal and lastly from Batavia," answered Woodard.

Tuan Hadjee then asked the Rajah what he would sell his prisoners for, but the Rajah said that he did not wish to part with them. Tuan then offered $100 in gold dust, but this was turned down. That ended the bargaining and the five white men were now kept closely guarded for the next month, after which they were taken into the woods two at a time to make sago bread, which is prepared from the crushed washed pith of the sago palm.

A few months later they were given permission to walk around town in the daytime, but each night they were carefully watched. One morning, after they had been at Travalla for about four months, they noticed their own boat pulled up on the beach but they were not allowed to approach it. The next time they returned to the shore, the boat had vanished. As Woodard realized that they would not be ransomed unless the Rajah received a large sum of money, he asked where the head priest was to be found and learned that he resided in the town of Dungally, eight miles away. Woodard then decided to escape there if he ever had the opportunity.

One day eight months after they had been made prisoners, a proa from Dungally arrived in Travalla to buy coconuts, and Woodard asked questions of the native sailors about their chief. A few days later the Rajah of Parlow, whose name was Tommy Ganjoo, requested that the white men visit him. Three days afterward they were in his presence, and he asked if they understood how to use a musket, which he showed them. Woodard answered in the affirmative, after which, for reasons never explained, he and the others were placed in a large drafty house.

A few days later Woodard caught a violent cold which turned into a fever. Ganjoo then had Woodard carried into a warmer house where a fire was kindled and rice prepared for him. The fever went down within a few days.

The Rajah now sent for the Commandant at the Dutch port of Priggy, located on the east side of the island, in another effort to ransom off the white men. When the Commandant arrived, he proved to be a Frenchman who had been working for the Dutch for thirty years and he showed no interest at all in the prisoners. He offered no money, clothes, or assistance to Woodard or his companions, and departed for Priggy a short time later.

Realizing that he and his associates were not to be sent away, Woodard again went to the Rajah. He asked permission to return to Travalla aboard a proa then about to sail for that location. The Rajah agreed but admonished the captain of the proa not to let Woodard visit Dungally, as he had heard that the priest there had been inquiring about the captives. The trip to Travalla began, but in the middle of the night they were becalmed right off Dungally, and Woodard was able to get a full view of the town and observed its location.

Arriving at Travalla, he decided that he had now gained enough knowledge of the Celebes coast to allow him to try to escape to Dungally. Day after day he begged for Indian corn, a portion of which he would conceal under his pillow. He also was able to provide himself with a bamboo spear. One night Woodard arose at midnight, took up his spear, and slipped out of the house. Reaching the shore, he stole a canoe but he had hard luck. The craft sank in five feet of water, and he was forced to return to the town. No one had missed him, however, and he now set out for Dungally by land. He reached his objective, scaled the fence around the town, and as the sun came up walked to the middle of the village where he sat himself on a log of wood.

A half hour later he saw a man coming out of a public building, who proved to be Tuan Hadjee's servant.

Revealing himself, Woodard was surprised by the man's outcry.

"Puta Satan," he shouted, which translated means "white devil."

Again and again the native screamed out against the sailor, and soon a crowd gathered. Woodard was then taken to his friend Tuan Hadjee, who questioned him about his plans. The priest gave him plenty to eat and brought him linen for a shirt, jacket, and pair of trousers.

Three days later the chief of Travalla sent for him, but Tuan refused to let him go. He explained that in three months they would take him either to Batavia or Makassar. Tuan also told him to write a letter to the four white men still at Travalla, and explained that the message would be given to them secretly. Five days later all his comrades arrived safely at Dungally.

After a week had gone by, Woodard and the others decided to risk a try for freedom. Their friend, Tuan Hadjee, had been called to another part of the island, and after he had left there would be no immediate hope for ransom. Day after day they went into the woods and made paddles to use for the canoes they planned to steal. Finally they were ready for the escape attempt.

At last the night came for Tuan Hadjee's departure. The old priest went down to the gate in the fence, on his way to the ship which would take him on his long sea journey, due to start at midnight.

The sailors followed the priest down to the gate, and after he was out of sight, they presented themselves to the guard, explaining that they were going with Hadjee to Sawyah to make sago. They were let out through the gate, which was then closed.

They reached the shore just as the priest started out to sea aboard his proa, and leaped into the nearest canoe to pursue him. When daylight came, the fugitives headed for the opposite shore to prevent being discovered. After hiding in the underbrush all day long, they set out again at night, but when they attempted to raise the sail, the canoe capsized. Towing the craft to shore, they bailed her out and started afresh.

Toward morning they were overtaken by a large proa. "Where are you going?" they were asked.

"We were with Tuan Hadjee, and are following him to Sawyah. We are not running away," Woodard explained.

As a result, the sailors were taken to Sawyah, where they were brought before Tuan Hadjee, who of course was surprised to see them.

"We were following you," explained Woodard, "and are very hungry. Could we have some rice?"

Hadjee soon provided them with a good meal of rice, but took the canoe they had stolen and sent it back to its owner at Dungally.

Tuan grew as fond of Woodard as of a son. One day he took him out in the Bay of Sawyah, where he actually granted an island to the Braintree resident.

Some time later Tuan brought the white men to Dumpalis, located some distance to the south of Sawyah. The priest then continued on business to Tomboo, which is south of Dumpalis and a few miles west of a gold mine on the island, leaving the white men behind. He promised to return in twenty days, but fifteen days later, Woodard believed that he had a chance to sail to Solom in the Philippine Islands, and he and his men went aboard the proa which was to take them there.

When at sea, however, the captain of the proa sailed straight for Tomboo, where he turned his passengers over to Tuan Hadjee. Crestfallen, Woodard admitted to the priest that he was attempting to escape, whereupon Tuan "spoke to me very roughly," as Woodard wrote later, and the old priest then made it a point to ignore the sailor for the next hour.

Woodard sat down on the ground, feeling very sorry for himself. Finally he burst into tears, at which the old man asked him the cause of his grief.

"This is not the way to treat an American," Woodard explained. "I have been guilty of no crime, and it is merely my desire to go home to my wife which makes me try to escape."

Tuan became so affected that he also began to cry.

"If I still have a mouthful to eat," he said as he clasped Woodard in his arms, "you will have your part of it."

The white men remained at Tomboo for ten days, after which they stole a pirate's canoe and started out for an island twelve miles away, where they landed at daybreak.

They then headed toward Makassar. After three days at sea, they encountered a strong wind from the south, and the waves nearly swamped them. When the blow subsided, they fell in with a proa, whose captain challenged them, but as there were only five aboard the native craft, Woodard decided to risk an attempt to escape.

They rowed into the wind, and the proa, after vainly trying to catch them, gave up and headed shoreward. The wind freshened again, and they decided to head for land, eventually reaching a beach near a place called Tranamare, located about thirty miles south of Travalla.

While the others were kindling a fire to cook rice, Cole went into the forest to get wood with which to repair his canoe paddle, which had broken. Suddenly he was seized by two Malays who escorted him back into the camp.

"To my great surprise I recognized them both," said Woodard. "One of them was the captain who had brought me from Parlow to Travalla."

When asked by the Malays what his plans were, Woodard took up his huge knife and a spear, and told the captain that he and his companions were determined to escape. Then, leaping up with the others of his group, he ran down to the canoe. They pushed off and were soon a distance from land, leaving the Malays undecided as to what action they should take.

Soon the canoe was far at sea. They ran into a squall, but weathered it, and darkness followed a short time later. For the next eight days they paddled south and were not bothered by the natives.

Then on the eighth day, they went ashore to get water. While there Woodard noticed three other canoes approaching the location where they had pulled up their craft. The white men pushed off at once, avoiding the strangers, and kept paddling all that day.

At sunset they encountered two canoes whose occupants were fishing. When asked for the distance to Makassar, the fishermen picked up their paddles and headed at once for the shore without saying a word.

Then in the distance Woodard sighted two proas, and they proceeded toward one of them. Hailing an old man on the deck, Woodard asked him where his captain was and soon the skipper appeared with a spear in his hand.

"How long will it take me to reach Makassar?" asked Woodard. The captain answered that it would be a month and a day, a statement Woodard knew was a lie. Realizing that he would get no reliable information, the New Englander started paddling again, whereupon the captain shouted for the natives on shore to send out a canoe in pursuit of the white men. It was an exciting chase, but three hours later

Woodard's crew had pulled out of sight of the native craft, whose paddles they had seen flashing in back of them in the moonlight for several miles.

At daylight, they observed two fishing canoes approaching them with one man in each. When the first came alongside, Woodard asked how far it was to Makassar, and was told that a proa could sail there in two days.

"This was joyful news," said Woodard later, "and it cheered up our spirits amidst all our distresses and fatigues." The sailors paddled away at once, and soon were helped by a favoring wind.

That evening, just as the sun was going down, they noticed a proa heavily manned by paddlers, approaching them rapidly. Soon several men grabbed the canoe and held it firmly. Thus Woodard and his men were again taken prisoners. The captors brought them ashore at a village called Pamboon. Again the white men were stripped of all clothes and belongings. Then they were taken before the Rajah.

The Rajah and his councilors asked Woodard many questions about where they came from and where they wished to go. Finally the Rajah asked if Woodard might be familiar with muskets. Realizing from previous experience that it was best to claim no knowledge of firearms, he did so, but his interrogator answered that "all white men understood" muskets. Woodard's reply was that soldiers did understand them but sailors did not as they were rarely used at sea. Evidently the Rajah was doing everything he could to induce the white men to stay, and his next approach was of a different nature.

"Would you like a beautiful wife, so that you can settle here and be one of us?" asked the Rajah.

"No, thank you," came the reply, "for I have a wife back in Massachusetts whom I love dearly."

In spite of this apparent rebuff, the Rajah sent his own wife to sit down beside Woodard. She informed the astonished American that she would enjoy becoming the mother of a white child. Then she called outside, and twenty other girls came in and surrounded him.

"Take your choice," she suggested. "Which one of all of us do you wish?"

"None," answered Woodard. "None at all!"

Getting up, he then went outdoors, where the natives brought him his supper, and the night passed uneventfully.

When morning came Woodard was told the Rajah of Pamboon had asked for him to report at once. In the presence of the ruler, the sailor made a strong plea that he should be allowed to go to Makassar.

"The Governor has sent for me," Woodard lied, "and if you detain me any longer, the Governor will send his armed proa here to get me."

Finally the Rajah agreed that he would send Woodard and his men to Makassar, and three days later they were taken to sea on the proa. Unfortunately, with his objective of freedom almost attained, Woodard came down with a violent fever and found that he could not even stand up to leave his bed. He was carried down to the shore, placed in a canoe and then paddled out to the proa for the ninety-mile journey to Makassar.

Three days later the craft stopped at the island of San Bottan, twenty-seven miles north of Makassar. Several days went by, and nothing happened. Still feverishly ill, Woodard told one of his sailors, George Williams, to go on shore and either steal another canoe or ask the Rajah of the island just what was delaying the expedition.

Finally the Rajah sent word to have Woodard and the others brought to his house, where they were fed some boiled rice. Eventually the Rajah agreed to have another proa made ready in which the white men could finish their journey to Makassar. Late that same afternoon they started out and reached their goal the following day, June 15, 1795, after two years and four months in captivity.

The five white sailors were taken to the Governor of

Makassar, William Pitts Jacobson, who was a native of Amsterdam. He noticed that Woodard's back was terribly sunburned, and had it treated with oil and then bandaged. Each of the white men was given a glass of gin, and later they received clothing and money. The Governor had them lodged in the sailors' hotel nearby.

Allowing Woodard two days to recuperate, Jacobson then requested that the Braintree sailor appear before him. When he reached the Governor's quarters, the latter ordered his personal tailor to measure Woodard for two jackets, two pairs of breeches, and a coat "made of nankeen." He was also liberally supplied with shirts, neck cloths, stockings, and shoes.

Finally came the day when Woodard and his sailors were to sail to Batavia. The Governor had written a letter to the General there, explaining the circumstances under which the fugitives had arrived at Makassar. It was then July 1, 1795, and they reached Batavia ten days later.

There, Woodard was presented to the General, who took his party to a hotel, and they were told to be ready to meet the Governor at ten o'clock the next morning. When he finally reached the Governor's quarters the next day, Woodard was asked where he would like to go, and his answer was Manila. His four companions obtained berths on the American ship *Betsey*, bound for her home port of Boston.

A few days later Woodard met an old friend, a Captain Sands, who was on the way to Bengal, and he accepted the position of chief mate on Sands' craft, the *America*, an American ship which sailed from Batavia July 20, 1795. She arrived at Calcutta September 20, and there Woodard met the same Captain Henry Hubbard, who had sent him out in a boat from the ship *Enterprise* to get water and provisions so long ago.

Hubbard welcomed him as from the dead, and told him that he had sent his wife in Braintree fifty dollars, explaining that Mrs. Woodard believed herself a widow. The Captain told Woodard that he was making a trip to Mauritius and offered him command of the *America* the moment they arrived there. Woodard sailed with him July 1, 1796, and the vessel arrived at Mauritius forty-two days later.

Now a captain in his own right, David Woodard, of the ship *America*, the former captive of the Malayans, sailed from Mauritius to the Isle of Bourvon, where he took on a cargo of cotton and coffee. After many other adventures, Captain Woodard arrived in the harbor of Cowes, England, on July 27, 1796. A vessel was then leaving for Boston, and Woodard dispatched a long letter to his wife and another to the owner of his ship.

Two weeks later, on a visit to London, Woodard learned that his good friend and benefactor, Thomas Russell, had died back in Massachusetts.

Returning to America as a passenger some time later, Woodard landed in Boston. He purchased a farm in the suburbs and left the sea for good. Many of his descendants live today in the United States.

African Adventure

A sailing master from the South Shore of Massachusetts, Captain Benjamin Stout, was aboard the ship *Hercules* when she left Sugar Roads, India, for England on March 17, 1796.

Because of a terrible corn famine in England, the *Hercules* carried 9,000 bags of rice to relieve the food shortage. She had a crew of sixty-four, which included Americans, Danes, Swedes, Dutch and Portuguese, but there were more lascars than all the whites put together.

Two and a half months later, while the *Hercules* was a considerable distance off the southern coast of Africa, a gale began to blow up from the westward. The *Hercules* was then in latitude 35° south, longitude 28° 40′ east. The storm became so severe that Captain Stout ordered the *Hercules* reduced to her mizzen staysail, and the intensity of the wind forced the ship to sail in this fashion for the next six days.

On June 7 the gale increased to hurricane force, and the sea in all directions was a mass of breaking waves and foam.

"Although bred to the sea from my earliest life," Captain Stout said later, "all I had ever seen before, all I had ever heard of or read, gave me no adequate idea of those sublime effects which the violence and raging of the elements produced, and which at this tremendous hour, seemed to threaten nature itself with dissolution."

It was an awesome sight. At one moment the *Hercules* was almost perfectly balanced on the crest of a mighty wave; a second later she was precipitated into an abyss where she wallowed helplessly and then the following wave raised her higher and higher until she seemed almost to touch the clouds. Relentlessly the gigantic billows came rolling in, and the wind terrified even the most experienced sailors. As night fell, the fearful aspect of the hurricane as seen by day was intensified. When midnight approached, the gale shrieked through the rigging of the ship in such fashion that it was impossible for the men to hear each other talk.

Shortly after midnight, the wind shifted, and the *Hercules* found herself caught in the trough of the sea. The violence of the storm struck the afterdeck of the ship, tearing away the rudder, starting the sternpost from the hauden ends, shattering the entire stern frame, and allowing the sea to pour into the hull. Captain Stout ordered the pumps sounded, but by the time they were functioning properly the water in the hold had risen to four feet.

Realizing that he would have to get at the leak, the captain ordered the rice thrown out of the run of the ship and overboard, but it was not until more than three hundred bags had been jettisoned that the leak was discovered. Sheets, shirts, jackets, bales of muslin, and other material were stuffed into the crack, but the leak continued at a steady rate, although the pumps were delivering fifty tons of water an hour. The men worked themselves at fever pitch to keep the vessel afloat.

By sunrise, the wind had moderated, but the great swell of the sea continued. It was then estimated that the *Hercules* was about two hundred miles from the southeast coast of Africa. Suspecting that in the crisis the lascars might attempt a mutiny, Captain Stout ordered the longboat put over the side, directing the second mate and three seamen, all heavily armed, to take charge of her.

"Shoot the first man who attempts to board her without my permission," the captain told the second mate. "Keep astern, but stay up with the ship off the larboard quarter until we anchor."

Stout now requested the first and third mates to report.

"Build a large raft," he ordered, and soon the lumber began to take shape.

When finished, the raft measured thirty-five feet long and sixteen feet wide. At this time the captain believed that there was little chance that the ship could make land. Knowing that only half of the crew could get into the longboat, he intended the raft for those who otherwise would perish.

As the final work on the raft was being completed, the carpenter left his task and presented himself to the captain.

"Please, sir, I implore you that we leave the ship right away."

"Get back to your work, carpenter; what's the matter with you? Get back to work!"

"Sir, the entire stern frame is shook and loosened in such a manner that we may go down at any moment."

The man then began to sob. The pleading tone of his words increased the terror of those who heard the conversation, and because of this the captain felt obliged to make an announcement that the ship was in no immediate danger.

The carpenter then returned to his post at the pumps, spurred on by a final admonition from the skipper that if he did not make the crew work harder pumping, Stout would personally throw him into the ocean. The carpenter resumed operations at the pumps again, and "exerted himself with a manly perseverance."

With the carpenter out of the way, several of the crew took it upon themselves to ask the captain that they be put ashore. It was then that Stout noticed one of the lascars coming up the gangway with a handkerchief in his hand.

"What have you got there?" asked the captain.

"I am going to make an offering to my God," was the reply. "This handkerchief contains a certain quantity of rice and all the rupees I am worth. Suffer me to lash it to the mizzen top, and rely upon it, sir, we shall all be saved."

Although the captain was about to order him back to the pumps, he decided that he might as well give in to the lascar's idea of salvation, and gave the man permission to climb to the mizzen top.

Thanking him profusely, the lascar climbed up the shrouds and reached the mizzen top. Fearless of all danger, he lashed the handkerchief to the mizzen topmast head, after which he returned safely to the deck below.

Secure in his knowledge that he had done everything he could with the longboat in charge of the second mate and the raft finished, Captain Stout decided to hold a consultation with his officers. All agreed that the ship probably could not be saved, but nevertheless it was decided to make some type of jury rig which might enable the *Hercules* to reach land, then almost two hundred miles away.

When this decision had been announced to the crew, all seemed to work with happier spirits. At first, however, the *Hercules* could not be headed toward land. Finally the captain made a rudder out of the topmast and fitted it into place, but it was found of little use without the help of the longboat, which was held athwart her stern to maneuver the ship into a heading toward shore. The wind at the time was from the eastward.*

In this way the *Hercules* made slow progress toward the coast. Shortly after nine o'clock on the evening of June 15 a great shout went up when land was sighted. As it was six leagues away, the captain considered anchoring, but then

---

* The reader may question as to why a cable could not have been got out that might have steered the ship in the fashion of a drogue, but it should be realized that by this time almost every able-bodied man was pumping and there were no sailors available who could be spared to make the drogue.

decided that the stern was so hopelessly shattered that it would be safer to attempt reaching shore as soon as possible. Ordering his second mate to come on board, Stout delivered the ship's register and all other important papers to him. Giving the mate water and provisions, he directed him to stand by in the boat until the ship was run aground.*

The captain then ordered the head sail set in order to get her pointed toward the shore, and the ship moved on steadily. Finally Stout headed her directly into the waves. The vessel ran about half a mile, and then struck a cluster of rocks with a grinding crunch. She slid over and settled heavily. Giant breakers took possession of the ship, each succeeding wave making it increasingly difficult for the men to hold on. Relentlessly, comber after comber thundered across the stricken hull.

Then a spectacular sea, higher than all the others, was sighted rolling in, forming a fearful, breaking crest. All aboard the vessel waited with apprehension. The mighty wave crashed against the *Hercules*, picking her up and carrying her more than a cable's length nearer the shore. The ship grounded again, and heaved to and fro with the dreadful surf. Each wave now made a complete breech over her. Soon the lashings which secured the raft began to snap apart, one by one, and not long after the spars and masts broke free and were carried away.

A large fragment of the raft remained, however, which one of the lascars, leaping into the waves, swam to and climbed aboard. Hardly had he gained temporary safety, when a wave swept in and capsized the raft, throwing him under it. A few moments later he came to the surface and again pulled himself aboard. Time and again the raft was pushed nearer the beach until finally it hit the shore and the man jumped to safety.

By this time darkness was falling. Fires were now noticed

---

* It was not ascertained until later that the *Hercules* was off the coast of Kaffraria, near where the river Infanta empties into the sea.

along the shore, lit by natives who had appeared armed with spears and accompanied by a large pack of dogs barking at their heels.

The moment he landed the lascar was seized by these savages. Twelve others in the crew now decided to get ashore, by whatever means they could. The others watched as the twelve launched themselves onto the spars. Eventually they reached land, but each man in turn was seized by the natives. Those who remained on board took shelter in the forecastle. Each sea crashed over them and there was no security anywhere on the ship.

All that night the survivors wondered what would happen to them. Some feared that they would be roasted alive by the natives, should they attempt to reach shore, and felt that they would be just as well off staying aboard, even though they would eventually drown. As the hours passed many plans were suggested, but nothing was agreed upon. By the time the sun appeared, most of the men had abandoned hope.

Looking shoreward, they were astonished at what they saw. As the sun illuminated the land, not a person was in sight. After a while, however, the various sailors who had reached the shore the preceding day appeared, and beckoned for those on the *Hercules* to follow them. The captain took particular notice of those who had landed safely, and studied them through his spy glass as best he could. After deliberating carefully, he decided to chance a journey shoreward.

"I immediately stript off my shirt," recorded the captain, "put on a short jacket, wrapt a shawl around my waist, in the corner of which I put a gold watch, and keeping my breeches on, seized a spar and launched into the sea. For nearly ¾ of an hour I preserved my hold and drifted toward the shore. Sometimes I was cast so near as to touch the rocks with my feet, then hurried away to a considerable distance; again I was precipitated forward and in a moment afterward carried off by the returning sea.

"At length a sudden wrench, occasioned by the swell,

strained both my arms and I was compelled to quit the spar. At this instant, although a considerable distance from the beach, a wave that was proceeding rapidly toward the shore bore me along, and in a few moments cast me senseless on the sand.

"My people, who were on shore, observed my situation; they ran down, and snatching me from the danger of the coming waves, bore me to a place of security. I was insensible at this time, but soon revived as they placed me near a fire and used every means in their power for my recovery.

"The first subject of inquiry when my faculties returned was, of course, the fate of my unfortunate crew; and I enjoyed the heartfelt pleasure of beholding them all around me, except those in the longboat and one who perished near the shore.

"I then addressed myself to the natives; but on this occasion I labored under the difficulty of not being understood. I knew nothing of their language and for some time endeavored to explain myself by signs. Fortunately there was a Hottentot present, who had lived with the Dutch farmers, and could speak their language. He served as an interpreter."

Actually the *Hercules* was wrecked relatively close to where the *Grosvenor* had been lost in 1782. Several of the natives told Captain Stout that they remembered the other craft and pointed to the exact location where she had been stranded.*

---

* Two ladies had survived the miseries of this dreadful event, and were residents in the interior of the country, uninhabited by Europeans.

Some years after the turn of the century several Englishmen heard of their survival. The *landdrost*, or head official, of Graaf Ragrel was deputed by the British government to pay a visit to the king of Kaffraria, for the purpose of ascertaining whether there were any survivors from the wreck of the *Grosvenor*. Finding there were two females, he succeeded in procuring an introduction to them. He saw them habited like Kaffre women; their bodies were painted after the fashion of the native inhabitants; and their manners and appearance were altogether "anti-European."

The *landdrost*, however, sought to obtain the women's confidence by a liberal offer of his best services to restore them to their country and friends. However, they were unmoved by his solicitations. They stated that they had

Worried as to what might happen to him and his fellow survivors Stout was told that the native nation where he had been shipwrecked was then at war with the white colonists. It was believed, however, that if the captain and his sailors could reach the Christian farms, they might be saved, but of course they could not be sure. Concerned over the fate of the ladies from the *Grosvenor*, Stout was apprehensive as to what might develop in the next few days.

That night the natives returned to their village, leaving the sailors to sleep under the sand hills without covering and without food. The fires which they kept burning were barely adequate to keep them warm until daylight finally came.

At dawn, the chief of the tribe appeared, bringing with him a bullock which was then killed to feed the survivors of the *Hercules*. The natives skinned the animal expertly, and then cut it up into lumps which they placed on the fire. Their method was to singe, rather than to roast the meat, after which the cooks began to eat it with the "highest satisfaction." Although the beast had been given to the sailors, the natives saw no reason why they should not eat most of it themselves. Nevertheless, the crew soon had more than they could consume for the moment.

As soon as the meal was over, Captain Stout noticed the longboat far out to sea. He also saw that the *Hercules* was going to pieces fast. A new gale seemed to be making up, and many articles soon began to wash up on shore. Among them was a huge cask containing sixty gallons of rum which rolled high on the beach, carrying enough liquor to intoxi-

---

fallen into the hands of the natives after they had been cast ashore from the wreck; that their companions had been murdered, and that they had been compelled to give themselves in marriage; that having affectionate husbands, children, and grandchildren, their attachments were bounded by their actual enjoyments.

Upon being repeatedly urged to depart with the *landdrost*, they replied that probably on their return to England they would find themselves without connections or friends, and that their acquired habits ill fitted them to mingle with polished society; in short, that they would not quit Kaffraria. After more futile efforts by the *landdrost*, the two women were left to their fate, if fate it was.

cate all the natives. Fearing the consequences of such an orgy the captain stove in the head of the cask and let its precious contents run out into the sand before the savages were aware of what they had lost.

An hour later one of the natives discovered the ship's compass which, attached to some of the wreckage, had floated ashore. Not knowing what it was, he brought it to his chief, who took it apart, and later appeared with the copper ring hanging from his neck as an ornament. The captain then gave the chieftain a pair of knee buckles, which he hung from his ears, thereby commanding even greater prestige from his followers.

Sitting at the base of one of the sand dunes as sunset approached, Stout now thought it was time to bring up the subject of their departure for one of the Dutch settlements. He requested a guide who would be able to accompany them through the deserts to the first Christian settlement. The chieftain agreed, whereupon the captain asked him when they could leave.

"When I consider that matter, you shall be made acquainted with my determination," was the only answer he received through the interpreter.

Alarmed at first by this reply, the sailors finally decided that they had no "just complaints for suspecting his integrity." That night they slept unguarded again under the partial shelter of the sand hills. It was agreed that sentinels should stand watch, and timbers from the wreck were thrown onto the fire at hourly intervals throughout the night.

At sunrise the next day they climbed the highest sand hill to see if the longboat might still be in sight, but she could not be found in any direction.

A short time later the natives began to approach the camp, many of them armed with assagais.* Others carried clubs

---

* An assagai is a slender, hardwood spear, usually tipped with iron and dipped in deadly poison. It is used by the tribes in South Africa for throwing or stabbing.

decorated with ostrich feathers. Their chief, wearing a leopard skin and still adorned with the captain's knee buckles at his ears, approached the sailors. He and Stout saluted each other in a friendly manner and the entire group went down on the beach, which was strewn with wreckage, for several additional parts of the ship had come on shore during the night.

One of the sailors picked up a hand saw and hid it in the sand, as he knew the natives would demand it. This was a valuable find and proved of great service to them later.

Believing that the chief wished to give an assagai exhibition, the captain asked if he would put on a show of skill in the use of the weapon, and the savage readily consented. The natives began their performance by placing a block of wood on the ground and then walking seventy yards away. Thirty of them began maneuvering toward the block. First they ran about ten yards, then fell on the ground immobile. A moment later they jumped up, divided, joined again, and ran back to the original starting place. Motionless for a moment, they then let fly a shower of assagais at the block and their aim proved remarkably accurate, for almost every spear hit the target.

All day long, following the exhibition, Stout hoped the chief would bring up the subject of their departure, but sunset and darkness came as before without a mention of it.

The next day at sunrise the worried captain again climbed to the top of the highest sand hill. Once more he scanned the ocean carefully for the sight of the longboat, but she was not to be seen. He realized that if she had not appeared by then, the chances were slight of their ever seeing her or her occupants again, and these forebodings proved to be all too true.

Two hours later, when the chief and his band of natives approached the beach, Captain Stout made it a point to ask that a guide be provided so that they could take their departure on the next day.

"A guide?" asked the chief. "I shall furnish you with two guides." These joyful tidings were delivered with so much frankness that the captain believed he had nothing to fear.

The chief had already anticipated that Stout would wish the interpreter, a Hottentot, to lead the sailors to the first Christian farm they might reach. Another member of the tribe, an expert in the terrain of the country, also agreed to join the party.

The survivors were then suffering from lack of water, and the captain asked the chief where they could find more.

"I will conduct you," he replied, "to a spring of excellent water. It is not far from this place and if you think proper, we will proceed directly to the spot."

Stout agreed, and after gathering up all belongings which would be needed on the long journey ahead, the whites started out with the chief and his natives for the spring. A walk of four miles westward through a delightful country took the group to a wooded area in the center of which was a hollow. Reaching the bottom, they found a gurgling brook, and every one drank deeply of the water, finding it delicious.

Resting from their hike, the men looked around and decided, from the remoteness of the place, that the natives were intending to massacre them there.

"We have been brought here," shouted one of the sailors, "to be killed."

The captain, however, had faith in the chieftain and did everything he could to quiet his companions. He succeeded in allaying their fears, and the sailors began to prepare wood for a fire. Using the hand saw, they cut down some dry trees and underbrush and soon a crackling blaze illuminated the unusual scene. Expecting that the natives would soon leave them, the sailors became alarmed when they did not start back to their kraal. Instead, the savages went to sleep, and the whites followed them with renewed confidence.

Early the next day "we were roused by the savages, as the sun appeared and we departed from this supposed Gol-

gotha in tolerable spirits," the captain wrote. "We had, however, consumed the last pound of our bullock before we had
left the sand hills, and our party began to dread an approaching famine. I mentioned the distress of my people to the chief,
and he promised to relieve us. We had journeyed but a few
miles when the natives told us we must remain where we were
that night. We accordingly set to work to procure firewood,
and had scarcely completed this necessary business, when the
chief presented us with another bullock. It was soon dispatched, skinned, cut into pieces of about four pounds each,
and we then proceeded to dress them as provisions for our
journey. This was a business of so much importance that
most of the day was spent accomplishing it.

"The night passed with less apprehension than before, and
when the morning came, we prepared for our departure."

The natives divided up the provisions so that each hiker
would carry his own stock, which amounted to about four
pounds of beef and some biscuit which had been brought
ashore from the wreck.

Finally came the moment for the actual departure. Captain Stout shook hands with the chief in farewell, whereupon
the native leader asked him to tell the colonists that the ship
had been lost at sea too far from shore to be salvaged. After
a last and "affectionate adieu," the survivors left the company of the natives on June 23 with the sun "well up."

All the hikers were unarmed, and it was feared that a single lion, leopard, or panther could destroy any of them.
Therefore, Stout reasoned that it was important that they
did not move until such time as these predatory creatures
would already have satisfied their hunger.

Only four in the entire party wore shoes, and even those
were in sad condition.

"As my feet were naked," said the captain, "one of the
sailors offered me an old pair of boots which he then wore,
but I refused."

At this time Stout was dressed in a short jacket, a tablecloth wrapped around his middle, a shawl over it, four shirts, a pair of trousers and a hat.

Traveling through a country of hills, dales, extensive plains and wooded areas, they then passed through a region where the grass reached an extraordinary height. After having journeyed about thirty-five miles, they began to get thirsty. Just before sunset the sailors discovered a brook where they decided to spend the night. The guides struck a light and set fire to a tree which blazed fiercely. They tried to discourage the party from sleeping there, however, saying that the area was infested with leopards. The sailors, on the other hand, were too weary to move on and slept in perfect safety until morning.

At dawn, however, they were aroused by the tremendous roaring of lions, and they decided to leave the vicinity, setting out along the bank of a small river. All that day they hiked, traveling about thirty miles. Again, just before sunset, they discovered a small rivulet that ran near the forest.

They built roaring fires to prevent the attack of wild beasts and when morning came they had been unmolested and were all ready to continue.

Around noon, however, a horde of natives, identified by the two guides as a "bad tribe" was sighted, and soon came up with them. Stout spoke to two of the women, who gave them a basket of milk.*

A short time later twelve native men armed with spears and dressed in leopard skins appeared, at which the two guides became frightened and ran away to the banks of the river, two hundred yards distant. One of the native Kafirs noticed that a sailor was wearing a knife over his shoulder. The savage made a snatch at the handle, but the owner scuffled with him, whereupon the assailant raised his assagai with an apparent intention of killing the white man. One of the native's comrades, however, diverted him from his purpose

---

* The baskets were made of twigs which had been woven so closely together that they held water and milk without difficulty.

just in time, and the two savages walked away from the terrified sailor.

Reaching the Fish River, the sailors forded it, and finally located their frightened guides standing a half mile away on the summit of a nearby hill. The two men told them how lucky they were and explained that they would all have been massacred if the main horde of the native ruffians, who were off hunting, had returned to catch them.

It was a beautiful sight which they gazed upon from the top of the hill, but they knew they should push on again through the forest. That night they camped again beside a brook, and when morning came started out once more in leisurely fashion toward their objective. All that day they passed through another delightful part of the African jungle.

They came upon some deserted huts, but the sailors who ventured into one of them paid dearly for their curiosity by emerging covered with fleas. Further on, however, they found a pleasant location in which to camp for the night, and estimated they had traveled thirty-five miles that day.

During the following day, many of their group dropped behind because of fatigue, while the captain and about half of the others continued on ahead. At intervals they set fire to the tall grass so that the stragglers would be able to pick up their trail.

Not one of the people left behind had appeared by the following morning, but the guides were almost certain that a Christian settlement, where they could all be expected to congregate, would be reached before sunset that same day. Finally they sighted a farmhouse, but it proved to be deserted, so they started out again. That night they built another roaring fire, around which they sat and talked over what might have happened to their missing shipmates.

They now had no food left to eat, and were barely able to stand erect. Furthermore, they were in real peril of an attack from the dangerous Boshishmen, who populated that section of Africa. Out of the sixty survivors who had departed from the beach thirty-six had dropped back, and after sunup, the other twenty-four decided to start out again for help.

Three hours later one of the guides shouted that he saw "a Hottentot attending a flock of sheep." They all hastened as best they could to the location of which the guide was speaking, and surely enough, some distance away they noticed a shepherd attending a flock of what appeared to be thousands upon thousands of sheep.

They approached the shepherd, who was frightened at first, but seeing that they planned him no harm, finally awaited their arrival.

"Can you tell us how to reach the nearest settlement?" asked the captain, and the stranger pointed out the way to a village which was then three miles distant.

An hour later they reached the farm of Jan Dupliesies, who, as he explained later, was a settler born in Holland sixty years before. Jan had six sons in his family, and they had all married. Together with their wives and children they made up a clan of about twenty people.

Stout explained in detail the shipwreck and their subsequent overland journey. Farmer Dupliesies was more than kind, and ordered his sons to harness eight oxen to a wagon and travel back over the path which they had taken in an attempt to find the stragglers. He also ordered a sheep killed and roasted for his guests.

Farmer Dupliesies was actually amazed that the native chieftain had allowed the sailors to leave the shore.

"They are such a horrid race," he explained. "Nothing is so gratifying to their nature as the shedding of human blood. I am amazed that you could travel so far without harm and reach my home."

The farm was surrounded by trees on which were hung the skins of lions, tigers, panthers and other wild animals killed nearby. The carcasses of two enormous creatures were seen lying near the door, and had the appearance of being recently destroyed. They were two rhinoceroses which the farmer's sons had killed the day before.

In the midst of an elaborate description of wild animals in general, Farmer Dupliesies was interrupted by a Hottentot servant who shouted that the wagon was coming back. When it appeared, the captain saw that twenty-three of his sailors were lying in the vehicle. They had given up all hope of being saved when they were found by the Dupliesies wagon in a dense wood. Thirteen others were still missing, and had probably died of exhaustion.

Now there were forty-seven sailors at the farm in various stages of weakness and fatigue. On July 2, after making careful arrangements to travel by easy stages to Zwellingdam, about two hundred miles east of Capetown, farmer Dupliesies loaded several wagons with the survivors, and they started out for the next farm thirty-five miles away, a ranch owned by Cornelius Engelbrock. The Engelbrock farm was relatively impoverished, but of what he had the owner gave them with good cheer. After remaining there overnight, during which time the poor farmer donated nine sheep, they started out for Zwellingdam again.

Day after day went by, and their average travel was about sixteen miles. The sailors' greatest trouble was getting bread and water, and they were often frightened by great packs of wolves. Once they came upon 14,000 deer in a drove. Nevertheless, from July 8 to July 16 the journey continued uninterrupted.

On the fourteenth day they had reached the settlement of an old blind man who had a large family, and apparently was comfortably independent. Upon hearing the captain's story, the host burst into tears and ordered a glass of brandy to be given to every member of the crew. Finally, after the drinks had been consumed, he addressed Stout.

"Now, Captain, I have a favor to ask of you," he began. "Pray desire all of your people to sing."

An American sailor volunteered to start the songfest, and

began singing one of his best songs. He was soon joined by the lascars, the Swedes, the Portuguese, and the Dutchmen, each group singing in their respective language at the same time. Finally, after several hours, the party broke up. Late that night the captain was given a sheepskin on which he slept in the farmer's cottage, but of course there was not room for everyone, and most of the men enjoyed their slumbers outside under the stars.

From July 17 to July 21 the survivors traveled a mountainous country, but on July 22 they arrived at Zwellingdam and were taken to the home of the chief magistrate, or *landdrost* as he was called. This gentleman gave them a hospitable reception and the next morning presented the captain with both a horse and a guide.

The group arrived at Stellenbosch on the fourth day after leaving Zwellingdam, and appeared at the settlement of Johannes Brinch. Two days later Stout and his men started out by horse for the Cape of Good Hope, where they arrived the following morning.

There the captain soon made the friendship of the skipper of an American craft then in the harbor. Of course no one sea captain could take on more than five or six seamen, and so it was that the surviving sailors of the *Hercules* were scattered aboard many vessels sailing to all points of the compass.

Finally came the morning when the American vessel of his friend was scheduled to return to Boston, and Stout, who was to sail aboard the ship, bade farewell to the men who had gone through such a tortuous experience with him.

Five months later Captain Stout landed in Boston. He later wrote of his experiences, describing the ordeals when his proud ship the *Hercules* was shipwrecked on the African coast, and it is this account which forms the basis of this chapter.

VI

The Corsairs

In the year 1948 I visited Newburyport for information concerning the area's history to be used in a book which I later wrote under the title *Strange Tales from Nova Scotia to Cape Hatteras.* During my wanderings that year around Newburyport I visited the historical society, where I met Miss Charlotte Bayley. She told me a weird story of how one of her collateral ancestors, Captain Samuel Bayley, had been captured at sea along with his crew and sold into slavery at Algiers more than a century and a half before.

She explained that it was customary in those days for the families whose relatives had been enslaved to raise money in various ways for their ransom, and sometimes they were forced to go from door to door soliciting funds to free their loved ones.* Unfortunately, Miss Bayley's Captain Samuel Bayley never returned to Newburyport, dying of the plague at sea after his release.

Her story impressed me, and I never forgot it. Ever since then I have been collecting material for a chapter on this

---

* It became a common trick for beggars to pretend that one of their relatives was a prisoner of the corsairs and that they were collecting money for his return.

little-known subject of American maritime history, the capture of American sailors by the corsairs of Africa.

Although most people scarcely realize it, enslavement of New Englanders in Africa was a common occurrence from the earliest times. In the year 1625 two ships "freighted from Plymouth" were taken by the Turks in the English Channel, and their crews sold into slavery. In 1640 John Winthrop wrote in his *Journal* of "one Austin, a man of good estate" from New Haven, who was taken by Turks with his wife and family to Algiers, where they were sold as slaves.

In 1671 there came "sad and heavy tidings" of the capture of Captain Foster and his son at sea. The two were taken to Sallee, on the African coast two hundred miles south of Gibraltar.

Three years later the scribe of the First Church of Roxbury, Massachusetts, recorded that "This Sabbath we had a public collection for Edward Howard of Boston, to redeem him out of his sad Turkish captivity, in which collection was gathered £ 12 18s. 9d. which, by God's favor, made up the just sum desired."

Not long afterward William Bowen "was taken by the Turks." Money was raised for his freedom, but he died before the sum was collected in full. The funds were subsequently used to "build a tomb for the town to inter their ministers."

In 1678 a ship from Charlestown was taken by a corsair to Algiers, and everyone aboard eventually died in slavery including Dr. Daniel Mason, a Harvard College graduate of the class of 1666, and James Ellson, mate of the vessel.*

The very next year William Harris, a "person of consequence" and a friend of Roger Williams, was captured at

---

* Dr. Daniel Mason, according to Sibley's fine history of Harvard graduates, had shipped aboard James Ellson's vessel as a surgeon. The son of Hugh Mason, a tanner of Ipswich, he was born in 1649 at Ipswich, where his father had become a freeman. Samuel Sewall mentions him in his diary on March 3, 1676-7. Captain Ellson also mentions him in a letter from Algiers of January 30, 1679.

sea and taken to Algiers. He was sold in slavery on February 23, 1679, and a $1,200 ransom obtained his freedom.

Samuel Sewall, writing in his diary on January 11, 1714, speaks of a Mr. Gee, who had a dinner given him "in remembrance of his landing this day at Boston, after his Algerine captivity." The first recorded escape from the African captors was made in 1788.

The corsairs kept accurate books of all their slavery dealings, and evidently considered the entire affair merely a matter of commerce to be conducted by businesslike methods. Prices asked at first were $6,000 for the ransom of an American sea captain, $4,000 for a mate, and $1,400 for a seaman. This market value placed on American sailors somewhat stunned the first United States representatives who had come to ransom their fellow countrymen from the schooner *Maria* of Boston. They had been prepared to pay a price of about $200 a person, but a compromise was eventually reached. Captured July 25, 1785, the crew was finally freed at the following rates: Captain Isaac Stevens of Concord, Massachusetts, at $2,000; Mate Alexander Forsythe of Braintree at $1,500; and the four seamen, James Cathcart, George Smith, John Gregory and James Hermit, all at $725 each.

The corsairs evidently made a practice of keeping peace with one important power while they plundered the craft of others. The English came away from one conference with hands far from clean, for in 1793 a one-year truce between Portugal and Algiers was suddenly terminated "through the influence of the English consul at Algiers" for the express purpose of "allowing the Algerines to cruise against Americans."

The Algerians now sent four frigates, three xebecs,* and a brig out through the Straits of Gibraltar searching for prey.

Not knowing what they were up against, the Americans continued to expand their commercial activities in the summer

---

* A three-masted vessel with overhanging bow and stern, lateen-rigged but often having square sails on the foremast.

and fall of 1793, and sent craft of various types across the ocean and into the Mediterranean. As a result, in the two months of October and November, 1793, eleven American vessels with 109 officers and men were captured and taken into Algiers.

The ships *Thomas* and *Hope* and the schooner *Despatch* were captured on October 8. Three days later the brigs, *George*, *Olive Branch*, and *Jane* were taken, while the schooner *Jay* fell victim the next day. On October 18 the ship *Minerva* was made a prisoner, followed five days later by the ship *President*. The final captures of this period were made on November 23, when the brigs *Minerva* of New York and *Polly* of Newburyport were taken at sea and sailed into Algiers.

Seaman John Foss of Newburyport kept careful notes of the capture and subsequent slavery of the Newburyport crew of the *Polly*. The captain was the same Samuel Bayley whose collateral descendant, Miss Charlotte Bayley, first interested me in this terrible business more than ten years ago.

Let us learn the story as John Foss wrote it.

"On Saturday the 27th of July 1793, I sailed from Newburyport in the State of Massachusetts, in the capacity of a Mariner on board the Brig *Polly*, belonging to the above mentioned place, Samuel E. Bayley, Master, bound to Baltimore, in the State of Maryland, expecting to take freight from thence for the Island of Tabago.

"On Tuesday the 6th of August, we were brought to by a French privateer, and permitted immediately to proceed on our voyage. Being then in sight of the Capes of Virginia, we took on board a Pilot and stood in for the Chesapeake.

"Wednesday the 7th of August, we entered the Capes and were 'till Saturday the 10th, before we arrived at Baltimore; and found, on our arrival, that the freight, which Captain Bayley expected, was embarked and sailed on board another vessel. Nothing particular happened, until Monday the 19th when we were ordered by the Captain to discharge the ballast, and were informed by him that he had agreed to take a freight for Cadiz.

"Thursday, the 29th, Paul Noyes, one of our mariners, was attacked with a severe fever, and continued on board until Monday, the 9th of September, when he was carried on shore, and put under the care of a woman, well qualified for attending sick people. I understand he died in a few days after our departure. Tuesday the 10th we sailed from Baltimore, bound to Cadiz; and on Friday the 13th we left sight of the Capes of Virginia. Nothing of any great moment occurred, until Thursday the 24th of October, when we fell in with and spoke two Brigs from Elsinore, bound to Barcelona. On Friday, the 25th, early in the morning we saw the same Brigs about two miles to windward, standing on their larboard tack, with the wind about E. N. E.

"We got our breakfast, and ate it in the greatest jollity, not apprehending any danger nigh, within 48 hours; As we judged ourselves to be about 35 leagues westward of Cape St. Vincent. But what a fatal day was this! How visionary our hopes! Our sprightly looks, and cheerful congratulations, and anticipations of reaching the port of our destination was soon turned into the most gloomy despair. Little did we think in the morning when we arose with nothing before us but Liberty and content, that before the Sun should reach his meridian altitude, we should be slaves to merciless Barbarians. This however, was the case. For at 9 A.M. we saw a strange sail bearing about E. N. E. and standing directly for the two Danish Brigs. We then discovered (with a prospect Glass) that she had boarded them; and that she had the English flag displayed at her peak. We then supposed her to be an English Privateer. She soon dismissed them, and bore down upon us. By this time we could see that she was a Brig; and discerned by the cut of her sails, that she was not an English vessel, although she had still the English flag flying; we then supposed her to be a French Privateer, hoisting the English flag to deceive their enemy.

"We immediately clued down topgallant sails, and hove to in order to wait 'till she came along side. When she came near enough to make us hear, she hailed us in English, asked from whence we came, and where bound; which was immediately answered by Captain Bayley. The man who hailed us was dressed in Christian habit, and was the only person we could yet see on her deck. By this time, the Brig was under our stern; we then saw several men jump upon her poop, to haul aft the main sheet, and saw by their dress and long beards that they were Moors, or Algerines. Our feelings at this unwelcome sight are more easily imagined than described. What dreadful perturbations! to escape was impossible; weapons of defense, we had none, we must therefore resign ourselves to the mercy of piratical sea-rovers.

"She then hove to under our lee, when we heard a most terrible shouting, clapping of hands, huzzaing, &c, And saw a great number of men rise up with their heads above the gunnel, dressed in the Turkish habit like them we saw on the poop. They immediately hoisted out a large launch, and about one hundred of the pirates jumped on board, all armed; some with Symitres and Pistols, others with pikes, spears, lances, knives, &c. They manned about 20 oars and rowed alongside. As soon as they came on board our vessel, they made signs for us all to go forward, assuring us in several languages, that if we did not obey their commands, they would immediately massacre us all.

"They then went below into the cabin, steerage, and every place where they could get below deck and broke open all the Trunks, and Chests, there were on board, and plundered all our bedding, cloathing, books, Charts, Quadrants and every moveable article, that did not consist of the Cargo, or furniture. They then came on deck, like a parcel of ravenous wolves and stripped the cloaths off our backs, all except a shirt and pair of drawers, (myself being left with no shirt at all.) The next day an old Turk, with an air of kindness, gave me an old shirt without sleeves, blaming those who had taken mine from me. It was soothing to find a spark of humanity in my barbarous master, who had but the day before mancipated and stripped us. This was the only Mahometan I ever met with, in whom I had the least reason to suppose the smallest spark of humanity was kindled.

"They having chosen a sufficient number of Algerians to take command of the prize, they ordered us all into the launch; and when they were all embarked, they rowed alongside their own vessel, and ordered us on board. We embarked accordingly, and were conducted by some of the sea rovers to the door of the poop, at which place we were received by a Negro man, who conducted us into the cabin; when we entered the cabin, we saw the commander of the pirates, sitting upon a matt on the cabin floor; who, with the help of an interpreter, asked us many questions concerning the vessel and cargo, the places of our nativity, and many others, as void of sense as he was of Philanthropy who asked them. He then informed us that he was an Algerine, that his vessel belonged to Algiers, that her name was *Babazera*, and his name Rais Hudga Mahomet Slamaia, and we were his prisoners, and must immediately experience the most abject slavery, on our arrival at Algiers, which we soon found to be true.

"Our embarrassments were still greater, when we found that they were Algerines, (for before we supposed them to be Moors) knowing that the Algerines used the most severity towards Christian captives, of any state in all Barbary.

"He then informed us that Charles Logie, Esq., British Consul at Algiers, had negotiated with the Dey for a truce with the Portuguese, for the term of twelve months, and before that time would expire, they would have a firm peace, and the Algerines could cruise in the Atlantic when they thought proper. He then told us we must do our duty as seamen on board his vessel; we told him we had no clothes, his people having taken everything away from us except what he saw on our backs, which was not sufficient for us to stand the deck with. He answered in very abusive words, that we might think ourselves well used, that they did not take them. And he would teach us to work naked, adding, 'now you are slaves and must be treated as such, and do not think that you will be treated worse than you really deserve, for your bigotry and superstition, in believing in a man who was crucified by the Jews, and disregarding the true doctrine of God's last and greatest prophet, Mahomet.' He then ordered us immediately to our duty. When we came out of the cabin, we saw the *Polly* just making sail, and standing after us, and that night we lost sight of her, and saw her no more until our arrival at Algiers.

"About sunset they brought us a dish of oil, olives, vinegar and some bread, and told us to eat heartily while we were on board, for after our arrival at Algiers, we would not be allowed such dainties. Although we were very hungry, we could eat but very little, considering the situation we were in, and not being used to such diet.

"When we sat down to eat, we were accompanied by three Dutchmen, whom we had not seen before. On asking them the particular of their being on board, they informed us that they sailed from Amsterdam, bound to Malaga, three weeks before, on board the ship *Hope* belonging to New York, commanded by John Brunham, and had been captured by an Algerine frigate within ten leagues of Gibraltar. And the frigate having taken several vessels, and having a great number of Christian captives on board, the Captain of the frigate being fearful lest they should make an attempt to rise upon the vessel, had distributed them on board the other Corsairs, which had not taken any prizes.

"After we had finished our supper they divided us (12 in number) into two watches and ordered us to stand the deck in our respective watches. It fell to my lot to have the first watch below, and as we went down they ordered us into the sail room to sleep, and shewed us the door. We were obliged to creep in, upon our hands and knees, and stow ourselves upon the sails in the best manner we could. We endeavored to get a little sleep, but could not, as our minds were filled with horror and dreadful apprehensions of the fate we might experience, and expecting additional severity at Algiers.

"We lay in this unhappy condition, bemoaning our hapless fate, until we supposed it to be past midnight, and could not conceive the reason that the watch was not relieved, as is customary among Americans and English. And being strangers to their manner of relieving the watch, supposed we had (innocently) neglected our duty; this made us very uneasy, fearing the watch had been relieved, and we not knowing it, they would inflict some corporal punishment.

"I then proposed to my fellow sufferers that I would go on deck in order to know whether they had called the watch or not; but they advised me not to go, adding, that if the watch was not called, they might treat me very ill for appearing on deck in the night, when my duty did not call me there, we then determined to wait 'till we were called, and to bear patiently our punishment if they inflicted any.

"We waited in this suspense for nearly an hour longer, when I resolved to go on deck by myself and know the issue: with this resolution I crept on my hands and knees to the sail room door, and on my appearance a Turk came to me, armed with a Scymitar & a pair of pistols, and made me to understand by signs, that he wanted to know where I was going.

"I answered him in the same manner, made him understand that necessity called me on deck. He then conducted me to the hatchway, and spoke to some person on the deck, in his own language, which I could not understand, and pointing with his finger, I found that I had permission to go up. I accordingly went on deck, and was received by another Turk, armed in the same manner, he asked me, in the French language, if I wished to go in the head, which I answered in the affirmative: as I understood some French, and could hold a tolerable discourse with him, I asked him if the watch was called, which he answered in the negative, and on asking him if it was not past twelve o'clock, he told me it was past two.

"On enquiring their manner of standing a watch, he informed me that they kept ten hours for one watch; and that it commenced at 8 o'clock in the evening and continued until 6 in the morning; then relieved and kept until 4 in the afternoon, and their dog watch was from 4 in the afternoon 'till 8, having only three watches in 24 hours.

"I then went below and informed my fellow-sufferers of what had passed, which gave them great satisfaction to think we had not committed an innocent offence, as we had feared. We then made ourselves as easy and comfortable as we could, considering the deplorable situation we were in. But could not sleep the remainder of the night, for by this time the vermin, such as lice, bugs, and fleas, had found their way to our apartment, and in such quantities that it seemed as if we were entirely covered with those unwelcome guests. However, we passed the remainder of the night in condoling our miserable condition, and in rubbing those vermin from our bodies in the best manner we could.

"At 6 A.M. we were surprised by three heavy knocks from the deck, and with such force, that it seemed as if they endeavored to knock the deck to pieces, and not hearing anything said, we could not imagine the meaning: We lay a few minutes, and were then called by a Turk, ordered on deck and informed, that that was their way of calling the watch. This office is generally performed by the boatswain, or one of his mates in the following manner; A large block is placed on deck near the hatchway and struck upon with a very large beetle, which makes such a horrid noise, as nearly sufficient to stun the brain of a strong headed person, and this was the cause of our surprise before mentioned. This being Saturday the 26th of October.

"We passed the Rock of Gibraltar on Monday the 28th and nothing of any consequence happened on our passage to Algiers; spoke several vessels, but none proved to be their enemies. We having a very fresh breeze from the westward, we arrived at Algiers on Friday the first of November.

"After they had brought their vessel to an anchor in the roads, they hoisted out their boats and ordered us to embark, and to lay ourselves down in the bottom of the boat; Having obeyed their commands, we were rowed on shore, and landed, amidst the shouts and huzzas of thousands of malicious barbarians. We were conducted to the Dey's palace by a guard, and as we passed through the streets, our ears were stunned with shouts, clapping of hands and other acclamations of joy from the inhabitants; thanking God for their great successes and victories over so many Christian dogs and unbelievers, the appellation they generally give to all Christians. On our arrival at the gates of the Palace, we were received by another Guard and conducted before the Dey, who after taking a view of us, told us he had sent several messages to our government, entreating them to negotiate with him for a peace, and had never received any satisfactory answer from them: That he was determined never to make a peace with the United States, in his reign, as they had so often neglected his requests, and treated him with disdain, adding 'now I have got you, you Christian dogs, you shall eat stones.' He then picked out four boys to wait upon himself in the palace, as follows, Benjamin Church, Benjamin Ober, Charles Smith and John Ramsey, and then ordered the rest of us to be conducted to the prison Bilic. When we arrived there, we found several other Americans, who landed a little before us, and they informed us that the Corsairs had captured ten sail of American vessels, and their captains and crews were chiefly in the same prison.

"After condoling our hapless fate, for a considerable time; a French priest came to us and enquired, if any among us understood the French language, and was answered in the affirmative. After conversing some time with the person who spoke French, he left us, and told us he should return in a few minutes. About half an hour afterwards he returned, and two Moors with him, who brought two baskets full of white bread, and he gave each man a loaf, weighing nearly a pound, which was a very delicious meal for us, we having eaten nothing during the day, it now being about 4 o'clock in the afternoon. He likewise informed us that it was a custom among those sons, of rapine and plunder, not to allow the slaves any kind of food on the first day of their landing, except one small loaf of bread at night. And what we then received, he gave us, out of his own pocket, and said if he was able, his charity would further extend.

"We thanked our kind benefactor, and he then took his leave of us. We then walked from one part of the Bagnio to another, not knowing in what part we might be allowed to remain. We wandered in this manner, bemoaning our deplorable situation, 'till about 5 o'clock, when we saw (according to the best of our judgment) about 600 men enter the Bagnio, all appearing to be in a more miserable condition than ourselves, with wretched habits, dejected countenances, and chains on their legs, every part of them bespeaking unutterable distress. I enquired of the prison-keeper, who those people were, and of what crimes they had been guilty, that they were loaded with such heavy chains. I was answered, that they were Christian slaves, had been captured in the same manner as myself, seeking an honest livelihood: A few minutes afterwards, we heard a man shouting out in a most terrible manner, and not understanding his language, made it sound more terrible. We were immediately informed by a man who understood the English Language, that all us (Americans) must appear in the third gallery. We made all haste up we possibly could, and as we entered the gallery we passed one at a time through a narrow door, on the side of which stood a task-master, and on the other side a Christian slave. The former had a large stick in his hand, and the latter a book, in which was written the names of all the Christian captives in that prison. The Christian asked each man his name, and then wrote it in the book, and as we passed, the

Turk gave each man a small bundle. On examining it, we found it contained a blanket, a capoot (which is a sort of jacket with a head) a waist-coat, made something like a frock, to draw over the head, it not being open at the belly, a shirt, with neither collar or wristbands, a pair of trowsers, made somewhat like a woman's petticoat, (with this difference,) the bottom being sewed up, and two holes to put the legs thro' and a pair of flippers. There was neither button, or button-hole on the whole suit. Such a suit excepting the blanket, of which they never get but one, is given to each captive but once a year."

Each man was given a small loaf of black sour bread weighing 3½ ounces. After their meal they lay down on the stone floor and went to sleep. The following morning at three o'clock the American slaves were ordered to go down into a large room where the jailers put a thirty-pound chain on each man's leg. Then they were driven down to the marine wharf where they were put to work. The daily procedure commenced with being awakened at dawn by the keeper, who called all the slaves to go to work in the nearby mountains. Some would drill holes, others would carry rocks away and still others carted the earth. The purpose of the project was to supply material for a pier being built down by the waterfront. If any slave fainted, the master would beat him until he got up.

Every night those who had disobeyed were punished. The slave was laid on his face with his hands and legs tied. Sticks slightly larger than an ox-goad were used and he was beaten upon his breech more than one hundred times for the most trivial offense. After receiving this punishment his ankles were lashed to a pole, which two Turks lifted up and then the offender was beaten on the soles of his feet.

On Fridays, a green flag, the favorite color of Mahomet, was hoisted from the mosque, and all slaves enjoyed a day of rest.

The food for their breakfast at eight o'clock in the morning consisted of a loaf of bread and a pint of vinegar. This meal was repeated at twelve o'clock. At supper they were given another loaf of bread, but no vinegar.

Punishment for escape attempts included the beheading of the leader, with his comrades receiving five hundred bastinadoes each. A chain weighing fifty pounds was fastened to each surviving man's leg for life, with a wooden block weighing seventy pounds attached to the end of that, which they were forced to carry on their shoulders when they walked to work.

If a Christian was seen in the company of a Mohammedan woman, he was beheaded, and the woman was put in a sack and taken a mile out to sea where rocks were placed in the sack with her and she was thrown into the ocean.*

Nothing of importance happened to the American prisoners until the eleventh of November when a messenger arrived from Colonel Humphreys, the United States Ambassador. His purpose was to get the Dey to confer with him. But the Dey answered that he could not be at peace with all nations at once, and that he had already captured ten American vessels and would probably take many more. Under the circumstances he would not make a peace with the United States.

On the twenty-ninth another prize arrived, and she proved to be the brig *Minerva* of New York, loaded with wine, oil, fruit, and marble, commanded by Joseph Ingraham, from Leghorn, bound to America. She had been captured by the Algerians on the twenty-fifth within seven or eight miles of Cape St. Sebastian.

Concerning the arrival of her crew, John Foss continues: "Seven more were now added to our number to participate in our distress, and partake with us the horrors of unspeakable slavery, and bemoan the loss of the blessing of liberty, dragging out an unwelcome existence of the slave on Barbary's

---

* While in Oran shortly after the North African invasion in 1942, I learned of another terrible torture meted out by the natives to Americans caught with Algerian women.

hostile coast, and to be persecuted by the hands of merciless Mahometans."

On December 23 the Swedish Consul, Mr. Skjölderbrand, told the Americans that an allowance from the United States would be given them. Each man would receive three dollars, each mate six and each captain eight, but the captors stole half of the money in every case. On December 29, 1793, the American sea captains wrote a joint letter to Colonel David Humphreys. They stated that they hoped the United States would take steps so that more of their countrymen would not be captured and made into slaves.

Colonel Humphreys answered them as follows:

Madrid, Jan. 12, 1794

I have been able to do very little to help you. I entreat you will be persuaded, my dear and unfortunate countrymen, that I would that my efforts were successful.

On February 1, 1794, several Americans caught smallpox, and the following died: Samuel Milborne of the ship *Minerva*, belonging to Philadelphia; Richard Wood, mate of the brig *Olive Branch* of Portsmouth, New Hampshire; John Mott, mariner, of the former vessel; and Thomas Furnace, cabin boy of the latter.

During the following April, when the slaves were working in the mountains, Joseph Keith and Peter Barry became tired and went to a spring to get a drink of water. They were caught and received one hundred bastinadoes each.

John Foss wrote: "On the 16th of November, 1794, a slave was employed in carrying timber upon his shoulder, and was stung by a tarantula spider on his left cheek; this being about three o'clock in the afternoon. He was obliged to work until night, his head having by this time swelled to a very large size. After work, he was sent to the hospital, where he expired the next day in the greatest agony. When he died, his head measured four feet one inch in circumference!

"In September of 1794 the Algerines captured 201 Corsicans who had been fishing off the shores of Africa. They were ransomed by the English for 12 hundred dollars each in March 1796. In July 1795 we received the joyful news that David Humphreys and Joseph Donaldson had arrived at Gibraltar from America and that Mr. Donaldson was going to sign a peace treaty at Algiers with the Corsairs. On Thursday, September 3, 1795, Donaldson arrived at Algiers with a white flag of truce flying from the polacre."

Negotiations began Saturday, September 5, at eleven o'clock and at twelve o'clock noon a peace treaty was signed. A twenty-one-gun salute was fired from the nearby castles of Fenelle and Cordalares, and the American flag was hoisted on the polacre.

The prisoners were all very happy but were informed that they could not leave until the ransom had been paid. John Foss was now told that he, Abiel Willis and Thomas Billings, must proceed at once to Mr. Donaldson's house and be his servants. On Friday the eleventh, Captain O'Brien was liberated by Mr. Donaldson and sent with dispatches for Mr. Humphreys, then in Lisbon.

The weeks went by, however, and nothing happened until the middle of January 1796, when Mr. Donaldson said that the money would reach Algiers within twelve days. When the middle of March came and no ransom had yet arrived, the impatient slaves heard that Mr. Donaldson had been ordered to go home.

More disappointments were to follow. On March 21, a brig arrived which proved to be the *Sally* of Philadelphia, commanded by Captain March. Aboard as a passenger was Joel Barlow, Consul General of the United States. At the same time a letter came from Humphreys saying that the money was not ready, and "impossibilities cannot be effected." A few days later Mr. Barlow obtained permission to take three months longer getting the necessary funds. On

April 1 Donaldson sailed ostensibly for the ransom, but the time went by and still no money came.

In the words of John Foss: "Joel Barlow then received a promise from Mr. Mackio Baccri (who was a Jew belonging to the Regency) that he would advance him one hundred and eighty thousand dollars, in the course of three or four days, which was just the sum required for the redemption of the American captives. The Dey (on being informed of this by Mr. Barlow) at first refused to let us go, because the money to pay for the peace had not arrived; however he at last consented to take it, and set us at liberty. On the 9th of July, we were informed by a letter from Mr. Barlow that we might expect to be at liberty within three or four days." Foss was told that the heart of Pharaoh "may be again hardened" but he hoped they would be free in three or four days. The taskmasters congratulated the slaves as follows: "*Sanzasidas droak imcbe il blaedic, ila kelp ou Romi.*" *

On July 10 at daybreak all the Americans were told to get ready to go to the Dey's palace, but nothing happened. On the 11th they were called out of the Bagnio into the street, and then they went to the palace. There each man received his *tiscara* or passport from the Dey.**

At nine o'clock all the Americans went aboard a ship belonging to Mr. Machio Baccri, which already had on board forty-eight Neapolitans. On the 12th they prepared the ship for sea, which was the very day Joseph Rogers of Salisbury, Massachusetts, died of the plague. On the 13th at five A.M. the ship sailed, but returned two hours later with a sick Neapolitan. She put out to sea once more and at four o'clock in the afternoon they lost sight of the Barbary coast. On July 15 Captain Samuel E. Bayley caught the plague and died two days later. He was given a very fine burial at sea, "in

---

* Which in English reads, "You unbelievers, now you are going to the country of Christian dogs."

** As was customary the sweeper of the palace at the time was liberated. He was a Venetian.

as decent a manner as our present situation would admit." On the 22nd all hands went ashore at Marseilles and were supplied with provisions by the American Consul.

John Foss later obtained a position as first mate on the ship *Fortune* of Philadelphia. Sailing in November for a cargo at Bona they were back at Marseilles on the 17th of the month. After a cruise to the island of Elba and back, Foss embarked as a passenger to Philadelphia, but was captured first by a Spanish privateer, and then by a French privateer, which in turn was boarded by two more Spanish privateers.

Finally he sailed as a passenger on board the schooner *Jay* of Edgartown, commanded by David Smith, and reached Boston on August 17, 1797. As soon as possible Foss took passage for Newburyport and arrived the same evening, having been gone four years and one month. Of the nine persons who had sailed on the brig *Polly*, only four returned: Michael Smith, Benjamin Edwards, Moses Brown and John Foss. The rest all died of the plague.

VII

Barbary Pirates Strike Again

After reading the foregoing chapter, which concerned the capture of the Newburyport vessel *Polly* and the imprisonment of her crew at Algiers, the reader might have assumed that with the ransom of the survivors and their return to Massachusetts the corsairs had given up their evil ways. Such was not the case, however. Year after year, the Barbary pirates continued to sell their victims in the slave markets.

Our present story begins some time before the War of 1812, when the corsairs were still exacting their tribute. And so it was that when Captain Alexander Boyle sailed from this country for the Mediterranean he knew that he might be molested after passing through the Straits of Gibraltar. This veteran New England sailor depended on the fast-sailing abilities of his ship, the *General Washington*, to avoid capture by pirates should they appear.

En route to the Straits of Gibraltar the *General Washington* had crossed the Tropic of Cancer "in an oblique direction," after which Captain Boyle steered directly for the island of Madeira. Purchasing water and fresh supplies there, he sailed again as soon as possible and proceeded at an average rate of nine knots to the Straits of Gibraltar. For the first few days Boyle saw no signs of the dreaded Barbary corsairs.

One morning, however, when prevailing winds carried them close to the African shore, they noticed several galleys a short distance away "running in and out." Becoming worried, Captain Boyle ordered the *Washington*'s course changed by two points, and eventually they were hull down and out of immediate danger.

After a speedy passage, they weathered Cape Bona-Silicia, which lay several leagues on the larboard, and then directed their course to Malta. Soon afterward the wind died away, and they made little progress, drifting on for some time with their sails flapping.

Suddenly during the night the lookout shouted that he could see a sail in the distance. It was not long before two large galleys crowded with men were observed approaching under both sail and oars. Without an instant to lose, the Yankees prepared for close-quarters combat. As was stated later, "each man resolved to fight to the last; but the ship not having a steerage way, they could not bring their guns to bear, except the bow-chasers, which were two six-pounders." The Americans fired their grape and canister, which killed and wounded many of the infidels. The survivors in the leading corsair galley then rammed the *Washinton*, carrying away her spritsail-yard. Swarming aboard the American craft, the invaders were repulsed after losses on both sides.

The galley, still entangled with the bow of the *Washington*, now swung broadside, thus enabling her to put aboard a greater number of men. The second galley then approached and rammed the *Washington* on the quarter. This maneuver made Captain Boyle divide his forces. The crew put up a gallant resistance, and a desperate struggle ensued. With men falling on both sides the assailants made a concerted rush on board, headed by their chief.

The corsair leader, stepping on the cathead, fired his pistol at the American mate, but fortunately missed. The pirate then started a saber blow, which the mate parried. Plunging at the corsair captain with a short boarding-pike, the mate thrust it through his opponent's body, and the infidel fell back dead into his own galley. But the rest of the *Washington*'s crew who were defending the quarter had lost so many of their brave companions that they began to give way. The corsairs, enraged at the fall of their chief, attacked the Yankees with such fury that the surviving New Englanders were obliged to retreat. Gaining the shelter of the hatchway, they fled below. As resistance was now of no avail they asked for quarter, which was finally granted.

Ordered to come on deck one by one, the Americans soon had their hands tied behind their backs, after which they were sent below again. They then heard a great confusion among the pirates, and learned that the first galley which had attacked them was in trouble. It appeared that when boarding the *General Washington*, the galley had started a plank forward, and otherwise injured her bow. Managing to stop the leaks by hard work at the pumps, the corsairs had then stuffed matting into the break. Now the vessel was sinking again, but unfortunately the corsairs were able to make further emergency repairs, and the crisis was at least temporarily over.

The savages then divided their prisoners between the two galleys. It was the fate of the mate to be put on board the vessel which had been damaged, where he was immediately recognized as the person who had killed the corsair captain. Inhumanly driven to the chains and lashed like a dog, the hapless prisoner was then reviled and spit upon by the piratical crew, but he realized that he would have to submit to their cruel treatment without protest.

As the weather still continued calm, the two galleys took the prize in tow. To accomplish this maneuver, the corsairs were obliged to triple-man their oars. The prevailing currents ran against them, and the strain on the oars was so great that the rowers soon dropped from exhaustion one by one. The chains of the captives were knocked off, and they were told to start taking the places of the regular oarsmen.

For several hours the poor Americans toiled with all strength, constantly lashed by the whips of their captors. Providentially, a breeze sprang up and grew so strong that it was neither necessary nor safe to continue rowing. The men were ordered to lie on their oars, which proved a great relief to the unfortunate sufferers from New England. As the evening approached, the sky turned to a heavy overcast, and the wind soon developed into a violent gale. The night became exceedingly dark, and they lost sight of the other galley and the tow. The storm increased to hurricane force and the leaks began again. In spite of all their efforts the water continued to rise, and soon it was apparent that the galley was about to go down.

The corsairs now began to clear their boat and hoist her out. When she touched the water half the crew got in, leaving the other corsairs and the prisoners to take their chance in the sinking vessel.

Those on board watched the boat push away and vanish. In a few minutes, the waves made a complete breach over the leaky vessel, and a quarter of an hour later she sank.

The mate of the *Washington* could swim remarkably well, having had great practice in the early part of his life. Striking off alone, he started in the same direction as the waves, hoping they would soon wash him ashore. After what seemed an eternity he realized that he was beginning to tire, and soon feared that all his efforts were fruitless, particularly as the sea showed no signs of subsiding.

Suddenly something struck him, and he grabbed at the object, which proved to be one of the galley oars. Grasping this support, he clung desperately to it, and finally was able to rest by locking his hands around it. The oar enabled him alternately to rest and swim as his strength would allow. Nevertheless, the constant battering of the sea took its toll, and he began to lose consciousness. Then a high breaking wave caught him and smashed his body across a jagged rock, and the shock of the blow aroused him. Getting to his feet in waist-deep water, he noticed that the seaweed on the rock was long and heavy, and he clung to it for the moment. Then another great wave drove him over some smaller rocks, severely bruising him. Picking himself up, the mate crawled and scrambled over the rocks until he reached a point above the fury of the sea. Resting for a time, he then found that he had enough energy to climb up the craggy shore until he was safely beyond the reach of the waves. Exhausted, bruised and cold, his senses at last became numbed, and he fell into a heavy deathlike sleep.

It was noontime before the penetrating rays of the sun awakened him. At first he stared with horror and surprise at the surrounding landscape. The storm had ended, but the waves were still lashing the shore. He saw with sadness the mangled bodies of many of his poor shipmates, stretched breathless on the beach. In the first agony of his feelings he burst into tears, which gave him some relief. Then, summoning all his strength, he removed the corpses above the tide line and covered them with seaweed.

Having paid this last tribute to his deceased companions, he began to feel the want of nourishment, for he had not eaten for more than two days. Walking along the shore he discovered a number of shellfish which had been thrown up by the gale, and he ate them hungrily. He was also well supplied with water as the rain which accompanied the storm had filled many cavities in the rocks. He did nothing for the remainder of the day and the greater part of the next night but think about the disaster and the situation in which he now found himself. Toward the break of dawn he became more composed, and even somewhat reconciled to his fate. He indulged a hope that God, having delivered him, might suffer him to breathe his last in quietness on the rock. Death, he decided, was preferable to slavery among such barbarous infidels.

For the next three days, he remained on the rock, comforting himself with having escaped the barbarians. Toward the end of the third day he climbed to the highest part of the rock, and there in the distance he saw a sail approaching. As it drew nearer he discovered it to be the sister craft of the corsair galley which had gone down under him. On nearing the rock, the pirates noticed several pieces of the wreck, and hoisted out their boat. Rowing around under the lee, they landed.

As soon as he saw the galley, the mate had endeavored to find a hiding place, but his search proved in vain, as the rock afforded none. It was about six hundred yards in circumference and almost entirely covered with coarse sand and shells, except at the summit where he found the rain water. As a last resort, he crawled to the water's edge, and stretched himself full length on his face, pretending to be drowned. But when the pirates began to explore the beach, they noticed the orderly mounds of seaweed, obviously piled up by human hands, and discovered the bodies of the unfortunate Americans. Knowing that a survivor was probably still alive in the vicinity, they renewed their search until at last they discovered the mate stretched out on the beach.

Rolling him over, the corsairs found that he was not only warm but breathing. They shook him, and then began to beat and to kick him. Finally he gave up the pretense of being dead, and was immediately conveyed out to the galley, where the corsairs questioned him about the wreck. Just before he was interrogated he noticed several of his former companions from the *Washington* serving aboard the galley. The man who acted as interpreter was a Portuguese renegade, who had long been in the service of the corsairs and could speak English pretty well.

As soon as the pirates had been told all the particulars about the lost vessel, they steered the galley for Tripoli. The mate then learned from the interpreter that it had been agreed between the two galleys to make for a small island in the

Gulf of Mahomet if they became separated. They had touched there, but finding neither the other galley nor the tow, they had gone in search of them and had found nothing until they came upon the mate and the bodies of his shipmates.

As they made their way to port, the survivors of the American vessel had mingled feelings of relief to be alive and distress at the melancholy fate of the other members of the crew.

The harbor of Tripoli, where they eventually lay at anchor, had a narrow channel which opened on a basin capable of accommodating several vessels. The town was surrounded by high walls which were strengthened in many parts with bulwarks and other fortifications. There were only two entrances, one on the north by the haven, and the other on the south by the mainland, each secured by forts.

Four days after their arrival, accounts reached Tripoli of the loss of the *Washington* and all hands on board, except three. The pirates, insufficiently skilled in either naval tactics or the American mode of rigging, had been unable to manage the ship, which was thus left to the mercy of the storm, and soon dashed to pieces on a rocky lee shore.

The disappointment and rage of the infidels when they heard of the loss was great. To have so valuable a prize suddenly snatched from their grasp was a calamity which sorely upset them. The galley was soon in an uproar and not even Mahomet himself escaped the verbal lash of the corsairs.

The captives were brought ashore and sold to the highest bidders without distinction. The mate was purchased by a Jewish merchant, who let his slaves out for daily hire to drag stones used to repair the town walls damaged by the recent storm, particularly the sections which lay next to the sea. This employment lasted a considerable time, and proved overwhelmingly difficult. The immense weight of the pieces of rock which he had to drag, encumbered as he was by his chains, was more than his reduced strength could bear. Whenever he attempted to rest, he was instantly lashed by the whip and had to resume his back-breaking toil.

At length the work on the wall was completed and the merchant, having no further use for the mate, sold him to an immensely rich native merchant. Here he had menial duties, carrying water, taking merchandise to warehouses, and performing all manner of dreary tasks. At other times, he attended the merchant and his daughter on their frequent excursions into the country, where he guided the mule on which the lady rode. Sometimes he attended his young mistress to the mosques, where a service called *sala* was performed five times a day.*

The mate observed that the men of the land shaved all their hair off with the exception of a lock which they grew on the crown of their heads, by which they believed that Mahomet would pull them into Paradise. Some young men cut off the whole beard, reserving only two large mustachios. Those, however, who were "stricken in years" wore their beards long and cut round. They used turbans made of red wool, wound up in a piece of cotton five or six yards in length. At their girdles they wore three knives, two large and one small, which were fitted in silver scabbards adorned with turquoise and other stones, often of great value.

At first the mate did not have a chance to notice the women, but he soon learned that they were clothed almost like the men, except for a fine linen cloth on their heads instead of a turban. The rich, he discovered, often wore five or six pendants in each ear, with jeweled bracelets on their arms. Before they would go into the streets to walk, they covered themselves with a cotton cloak, which hung down to their feet. The women corsairs would often tie a string of pearls on their foreheads, and wore a fine kerchief before their eyes, so that they would not be known as they passed in

---

* The mate's costume may be of interest. He wore next to his skin a linen frock and drawers, over which was fastened with great gold or silver buttons a loose coat of cloth of silk, which hung almost down to the knees. The sleeves extended only to the elbows.

the streets. The mate found that they were very particular in beautifying themselves, not only painting their eyebrows and eyelids black, but also dying their hair, using burnt antimony.

As the mate had many opportunities of traveling abroad, he several times met with some of his shipmates, particularly those who had been sold to the planters or farmers who lived a short distance from the town. He was nearly always certain of running across one or more of them on market day, as they carried the produce of the country in to be sold. On occasions of this kind they lightened their hearts by sympathizing with one another.

By his steadfast behavior and attention to business the mate soon gained the confidence of his master, who frequently took him on trips. On one of these occasions, the merchants were summoned to an auction sale of slaves who had formed the crew of a Portuguese polacre just brought into the harbor. The crew of the polacre had made a desperate resistance, which occasioned the death of their captain and half the crew; the survivors seemed to be young and healthy men and therefore brought a good price in the market. The mate's master and two other merchants bought six of the youngest, and the mate was ordered to conduct them to the prison where it was found necessary to lodge them until the following morning.

Early the next day, the mate was ordered to convey the six men to his master's house. For that purpose he waited on the head gaoler, who accompanied him into the prison. On approaching, they found the outer gate wide open. Walking toward the second gate, the first object which they saw was the body of the undergaoler, lying dead. Alarmed at the sight, they hastily withdrew to the outer gate, and shouted for assistance.

With several officers, they entered the prison, where they soon discovered that the six men they were hunting for had made their escape. As none of the ships or boats was missing from the harbor, it was evident that the runaways were lurking somewhere on shore. A careful search was begun along the coast. The fugitives were found on the evening of the third day, hidden among the rocks close to the sea, waiting for an opportunity to seize the first boat they could find.

The prisoners were brought back and taken immediately before the caliph. After a short examination, the ringleader was condemned to be executed the following day. On occasions of this sort, it was usual for all slaves to witness the exhibition, in order to impress them with its lesson. Accordingly, the mate was on hand when the proceedings began. At the appointed time a great concourse of people assembled, and the mate found himself with the opportunity to meet and chat with six of his shipmates and countrymen.

About an hour after he arrived, the workmen finished the platform where the unhappy culprit was to suffer.* As soon as the victim had ascended this platform, he was ordered to climb the ladder placed against one of the posts. The executioner then thrust a large iron hook, attached to a strong chain, into the palm of one of his hands and by that means hung him to the cross beam. The ladder was then placed on the other side, and a similar iron hook fastened to a chain was then driven through the sole of his foot. The Portuguese captive lingered long in the most insufferable torments, until a merciful death finally released him from the barbarity of the infidels. This torture was designed to reduce to a minimum all attempts at escape by the Tripoli slaves.

The experience had an opposite effect on the mate of the *Washington* and his six fellow sailors, however, and the Yankees resolved to seek the first opportunity of fleeing North Africa. The following day they received orders to attend the execution of another wretch who was doomed to undergo the same horrible ceremony. To behold such an-

---

* On top of the platform were two large posts or supports of wood, with a heavy crossbeam connecting them, bearing some resemblance to a gallows.

other revolting exhibition was almost too much, but they could not overlook the chance it afforded them of carrying out their own scheme.

Accordingly they assembled at an earlier hour the next morning. One of them proposed that they should attempt their escape as soon as possible. He explained that he was usually employed in gardening around his master's house, which was situated five miles from Tripoli, except when sent to town with the produce of his labor. He was well acquainted with a small creek nearby at the mouth of which were two or three small huts occupied by fishermen, who always moored their boats at night close to their huts. They kept a large dog chained on board in order to guard them, as they slept on shore.

The American proposed to poison the dog that evening, in order to prevent his giving an alarm. At first this seemed a sensible plan of escape, but on further reflection the idea of seven men rushing into an open boat without food, water or necessities of any kind did not promise much hope of success.

The mate thereupon suggested, that as it was then the last of August and the approaching fifth of September was the festival of the prophet Mahomet, in celebration of which great preparations were being made, each man should save a certain portion from his allowance of food every day, and deposit it in a secret place. The feast of the prophet would be a general holiday and there was no doubt but that all classes of people would be absorbed in their religious duties. It was equally certain that the fishermen would come to Tripoli on that day, giving the sailors a greater hope of escape.

They decided on a place at some distance from the town where they would all meet. Each promised, meanwhile, to save all the provisions he could to contribute to the general supply.

As they laid their plans the execution of the unfortunate Portuguese seamen was getting under way. He seemed to bear his fate with less resignation than his predecessor, and

David Woodard, having lost his ship, the *Enterprise*, finds himself with five men in a small boat at the mercy of the treacherous Malays. (Chapter IV)

At the height of the gale which crippled the *Hercules* in 1796, a lascar crewman tells Captain Stout that he is going to lash an offering to the mizzen top to propitiate his God.

(Chapter V)

No sooner had they gained the African shore from the stranded *Hercules* than the crew were seized by savages. (Chapter V)

The ill-fated *Margaret* of Salem capsized in 1810 during an Atlantic gale, never to be heard from again together with the thirty-one persons remaining aboard. *Courtesy of The Peabody Museum of Salem.* (Chapter VIII)

The luxury steam ship *Arctic* goes down after a collision off the Grand Banks en route from Liverpool to New York in 1854 with a heavy loss of life. *Courtesy of The Peabody Museum of Salem.* (Chapter IX)

Top: The Rhode Island pirate Albert W. Hicks, whose execution on Bedloe's Island was a gala affair attended by 11,000 witnesses aboard a flotilla of gaily bedecked craft. Bottom: The oyster sloop *E. A. Johnson* aboard which Albert Hicks climaxed a life of crime with his atrocious murders. (Chapter XI)

The execution of Captain Nathaniel Gordon, the only American slaver ever to pay the extreme penalty for his crimes. (Chapter XII)

The author (center), with Robert W. Morse (left) and Gerald Aycrigg (right) of Mystic Seaport, examines an ancient wreck uncovered on the beach of Kennebunk, Maine, which may be the remains of the sloop *Industry* which sailed from Cushing, Maine, in 1770 and was never sighted again. *Photo by George Stevens.*

(Chapter XX)

Top: The Government sloop *Hazard*, bearing a message from the new monarch George I in 1714, goes down with all hands off Minot's Rock. (Chapter XXII) Bottom: The last photograph of the *Don* which disappeared on an excursion from Dyer's Cove, Maine, to Monhegan Island. (Chapter XX)

One of the early North Shore marine disasters occurred in 1682 when Captain Horton's vessel grounded on Winthrop Bar in Boston Harbor with the loss of seven lives and a valuable cargo of silver. (Chapter XXI)

In 1858, the British bark *Vernon* dramatically grounds during a heavy blow near Little Nahant on the shore of Massachusetts Bay. *Courtesy of The Peabody Museum of Salem.*
(Chapter XXI)

The final moments aboard the 300-ton ship *Gertrude-Maria* which was wrecked in 1793 on a ledge among the Cohasset rocks. (Chapter XXII)

Clinging to the wreckage of the mackerel schooner *Maine*, survivor Alfred Wood signals desperately to the ocean packet *Hibernia* which had rammed them off Boston in 1846. (Chapter XXII)

The schooner *Agnes R. Bacon* is a total loss after running ashore near Beetle Rocks on Marshfield Beach during an 1885 hurricane. *Photo by L. B. Howard.* (Chapter XXIII)

Carried off course during a fog in 1889, the brig *T. Remick* piled up on the beach in front of Mitchell's Hotel, Scituate. (Chapter XXIII)

Disabled during her efforts to rescue the tug *M. Moran* in a blizzard of March, 1960, the Coast Guard Cutter *General Greene* was stranded on Spring Hill Beach, Sandwich, Massachusetts. (Chapter XXIV)

the executioner was obliged to force him to submit to his terrible fate.*

By sunset the victim had ceased struggling, and was dead. The people now began to disperse, but the mangled corpse was left to hang until a certain hour the next day, it being the rule that the bodies of those who suffered in this way should be exposed for a definite period in order to make the punishment more impressive.

On the evening of September fifth the conspirators met at their appointed rendezvous, and proceeded with all speed to a point on the shore previously agreed upon. Boldly entering the huts, they found only two old women and a little girl on the premises, the men having gone to the *sala* at Tripoli, as they expected. The women were alarmed and fell on their faces on the earth, praying for mercy, while the child ran toward the door. The mate picked up the little girl and held her in his arms while his companions began to soothe the old women with repeated assurances that no harm would come to them. The sailors did decide to secure them with cords, however, and after tying them up, the fugitives searched for supplies and found some black bread and dried fish, after which they hastened to the boat.

It occurred to the mate that the dog which was chained to the boat might prove disagreeable, so he thought it advisable to take the girl with him in his arms, in order to calm the animal. The child, however, was very unwilling at first to go with him, until he quieted her with hugs and kisses. He entered the boat first, and asked the girl to speak to the dog, which she succeeded in pacifying. He released the boat and as soon as it was in deep enough water, he threw the dog overboard.

---

* It was supposed that the two who died actually committed the murder of the undergaoler; but as there was no fair trial, this was only a matter of conjecture, for the judges of this arbitrary government sentenced whom they pleased. When they thought it expedient that an example should be made they selected for that purpose those who were the least serviceable to their masters, or with whom their masters were most willing to part.

Returning to shore, he put down the girl and told her to return to her friends and set them free. Then the Yankees pushed the boat out into deep water again. The dog swam to shore and joined the child, who remained for some time where they had left her, watching their craft start for sea. The little girl seemed very pleased at being able to assist them in their escape.

Fortunately, they discovered a nine-gallon cask of water in the boat, which proved to be of considerable service to them. They had to row several miles before finding a breeze, but at length they were able to spread their sail and shape a course for Malta, where they arrived exhausted twelve days later, having performed the rare feat of escaping the corsairs!

At Malta they found a ship bound for England, on board which they were given passage in return for their services. Nothing remarkable occurred during the voyage, and after spending several weeks in England they hired on board a craft which took them across to Boston.

In spite of the excitement and consternation they caused with the story they told on their arrival in New England, it was many years before an American craft could sail in the Mediterranean without fear of capture by the Barbary corsairs. Three treaties, the Tripoli Convention of 1805, the Tripoli Treaty of 1806 and the Algiers Treaty of 1815 were necessary before American merchantmen and sailors could sail off the shores of Africa in relative security.

VIII

The *Margaret* Meets Disaster

The ship *Margaret* was built at Salem, Massachusetts, in the year 1800. Ship-rigged, she was registered at 295 tons.*

One of the first ships from the United States ever to visit Nagasaki, the *Margaret* made a voyage there in 1801. In the next few years she entered harbors in many far-flung countries of the world, and finally sailed under Captain Fairfield's command to the Mediterranean.

After his return from his final voyage on the *Margaret*, Captain Fairfield wrote a dramatic account of his terrifying experiences, and the reader may now step back through the years a century and a half to the story written by Captain William Fairfield after his arrival at Marblehead:

"We sailed from Naples, homeward bound, on the 10th of April, with a crew, including officers, of fifteen in number, together with thirty-one passengers, making forty-six in all, men and boys.

"We passed through the Gut of Gibraltar the 22d of April; nothing of moment occurred until Sunday, 20th May, when

---

* The *Margaret* was first owned by the Derby interests, after which the Crowninshield family acquired her. Captain William Fairfield then became half-owner, and was her master when she sailed on her final voyage.

in latitude 40, north, longitude 39, 30, west, having strong breezes of wind at southeast and east southeast, and rainy weather. At 10 A.M. took in royals, top-gallant studding-sails, fore and mizzen top-gallant-sails, jibs, stay-sails, and main-sail. At meridian wind and weather continued as before-mentioned.

"At one P.M., on the 21st, the foretopmast studding-sail halyards parted, the studding-sail fell overboard, filled with water, and carried away the studding-sail boom.

"We took in lower studding-sail spanker, and mizzen top-sail, by which time it became squally, and we immediately clewed down fore and main top-sail, and let fly the sheets— the wind shifted in an instant from east southeast to southwest, and although the helm was hard to weather, we could not get the ship before the wind."

The great vessel heeled far over, and then, in spite of everything Captain Fairfield and his men attempted to do, she capsized!

"Every person on board the ship being at this time on deck, reached either the bottom or side of the ship, and held on. We secured an axe, and immediately cut away the weather lanyard of the shrouds, masts, and longboat, which being done the ship righted, being full of water, her hatches off, chests, water-casks, etc., drifting amongst the wreck; the guns, anchors, caboose, and every article on deck, we hove overboard to lighten the ship, and endeavored to clear the wreck of spars, riggins, etc., which lay beating against her to winward; but our efforts were in vain, the starboard lanyards of the shrouds being deep under water, and fast to the ship, and the sea making a continual breach over her; during this time the longboat lay beating among the wreck of spars, etc., bottom up, the pinnace being wrecked entirely to pieces except her keel, and about three streaks of the boards of her bottom lay in the same situation as the longboat, and the stern boat lying at a small distance from the

ship, full of water, with her gunwales torn off, butts started
and stern about half stove in.

"It was with the utmost difficulty that we bailed her out,
and kept her so far free as to enable us to get a rope fast to
the longboat, by which we hauled her alongside the ship,
turned her over and found her to be badly stove, her gunwales and stem broken entirely off, her wood-ends and garboard streak open, and large holes in her bottom, so that we
found it impossible to bail her out, and we were under the
necessity of upsetting her again in the sea, with the hope
of being able to stop a part of the holes in her bottom, which
we in part effected by driving the butts together and by
putting canvass, etc., into the largest holes in her bottom;
after which we turned her over again, and by continual bailing with every bucket, etc., which we could procure, we
were enabled to keep her from sinking, still keeping under
the lee of the ship."

Daylight soon ended, and an approach to the *Margaret*
was attempted by pulling on the line.

"By this time, when the boat being hauled near to the ship
for the purpose of getting canvass and oakum to stop the leak,
as many men as could reach the longboat jumped into her,
and finding the boat would be again sunk if we remained
so near the ship, we were obliged to veer the boat to leeward
of the ship at the distance of fifteen or twenty fathoms, being twelve in number in the boat. We had not been in this
situation but a short time, before one man jumped from the
ship into the sea and made for the boat; we took him in,
but finding that all on board were determined to pursue the
same plan, we were obliged to veer the boat further off. We
stated to those on board the ship our situation, which was
also evident to them, as it required all our exertions to keep
the boat from sinking.

"During the night, we lay with a rope fast from the ship
to the boat, and under her lee, when the people on board the
ship being exceedingly anxious to get into the boat, (which

had they effected we should all have been inevitably lost,) kept hauling the boat towards them; we then bent on another rope, and veered out as they hauled; but finding they were determined to sink the boat by getting into her, we were obliged (after stating repeatedly to them our situation) to tell them, that provided they persisted in getting into the boat, we should be obliged, though very reluctantly, to cut the rope and leave them; after which they desisted from hauling the boat towards the ship.

"At this time, we were thirteen in number in the longboat, and two men in the stern-boat lying under the lee of the ship, continually bailing to keep her from sinking, which augmented our number to more than could with any degree of safety attempt to leave the ship, in the longboat, in the shattered condition she was then in.

"Monday morning,—moderate breezes and sea tolerably smooth; at which time the people on the wreck were about half of them on the taffrel rail, and the remainder on the bowsprit and windlass, every other part of her being under water continually. They kept entreating us to take them into the boat; we then told them our determination was to continue by the ship while she kept together, and that the boat was not in a situation to leave them, unless they attempted to come into her; but if any of them once made the attempt, we should be under that necessity, notwithstanding our wretched situation, having no compass, quadrant, or any instrument whatever by which we could direct our course, nor a single drop of fresh water in the boat, and two men continually bailing; all of which circumstances were known to them."

About this time, according to Captain Fairfield, casks of brandy and other articles of the cargo were drifting from the wreck. The captain retrieved the mizzen top-gallant sail, two spars, five oars, one cask of oil, one drowned pig, one goat, and one bag of bread. Those still on the *Margaret* hove across a gallon keg of brandy from the ship. The captain then fixed a sail for the boat from the mizzen top-gallant sail. Unfortunately, those thirty-one persons still aboard the ship began to realize that if they stayed aboard the ship they would eventually drown.

"It being now about 11 A.M. the people on the wreck were determined to get into the boat, and began by jumping into the sea. Seeing their intention, we veered the boat further from the ship and they again returned to her, after which we repeated to them our determination to continue by them so long as the ship held together, but if any other person attempted to come into the boat, we should that instant leave them, notwithstanding our desperate situation.

"At this time they had secured on the wreck, two quadrants, two compasses, one hogshead of water, bread, flour, and plenty of provisions, as they frequently informed us; but they would not spare us any of these articles unless we consented to come alongside the ship with the boat, which had we done, we should have been sunk in an instant, as they were prepared to jump, having oars, chests, etc., ready for the purpose of the taffrel rail.

"Notwithstanding they knew our determination and the impossibility of our taking them into the boat, they still persisted in trying to get into her, and one of them jumped into the sea and made for the small boat, which lay veered to the leeward of the ship, which he reached; but finding we would not take him into the longboat, he returned to the ship with the small boat.

"As they were now all determined to pursue the same plan, we were under the painful necessity of cutting the rope by which we were fast to the ship, and row and sail from them for the preservation of our lives, in the hope of falling in with some vessel to relieve us, which was almost the only hope we had left, being about four hundred miles distant from the nearest land, and in the desperate situation before stated. At this time, it was about meridian, with moderate wind from the southward and westward; we made our course as nearly east as possible, for the island of Corvo or Flores, and the last we saw of the ship she was lying in the same situation as when we parted from her.

"We continued our course to the eastward, having the winds variable from S.S.E. to N.W., and two men constantly bailing; steering in the night by the stars, when to be seen, and in dark cloudy weather by the heaving of the sea, and in the daytime, by judging from the bearing of the sun, when to be seen, and when not, by the best of our judgment. For four days we continued in this situation without seeing any vessel; but on Saturday, 26th of May, at one P.M., to our great joy we espied a sail, which proved to be the brig *Poacher*, of Boston, Captain James Dunn, from Alicant, who took us on board and treated us with every attention and civility."

Captain Fairfield finally reached Massachusetts on board the *Poacher*, and after his arrival in Marblehead decided to record the experiences, which appear in this chapter. Nothing was ever heard again from the *Margaret*, or from the thirty-one persons whom he left aboard the ship when he sailed away from them that May day in 1810.

IX

The *Arctic*

There are some stories, long suggested, that must await the assemblage of certain elusive details before they can be told in full, and such an account I offer you now.*

When Sir Anthony Brown, Knight of the Garter, centuries ago took possession of Battle Abbey and Caldray in the British Isles, awarded to him by Henry VIII for services rendered, the monks are said to have placed a curse upon him and his descendants for his act of evicting them, vowing that fire and flood would always follow his family.

A direct descendant of Sir Anthony, Mrs. S. Fahs Smith of York, Pennsylvania, has collected information which would indicate that the curse, if curse it was, actually did influence the lives of many of Sir Anthony's descendants. Most of this chapter concerns the terrible affair of the steamer *Arctic*, on which Mrs. Smith's father, Charles Mitchell, sailed in the year 1854.**

---

* Walter Ehrenfeld of York, Pennsylvania, deserves special mention for help in making much of this chapter possible.

** Mr. Saylor, the husband of Mrs. Smith's aunt, Laura, was drowned about the year 1870 when getting off a ship at Charleston, South Carolina. Aunt Laura died from taking poison by mistake in 1872. Two of Charles Mitchell's nieces died by drowning when passengers on the S.S. *Champion*

Charles Mitchell had taken his sister Caroline with him to London, and they were planning to return aboard the *Arctic* on her fateful voyage. On the night before they were to sail, Caroline had a terrifying nightmare. She decided that her dream was a warning not to sail on the *Arctic* and Charles Mitchell agreed to cancel her passage. As he was getting anxious to see the other members of his family, however, he sailed without her and the decision to do so almost cost him his life.

The *Arctic* was launched on January 28, 1850, at the East River yard of William H. Brown. She was the third of four wooden-hull, paddle-wheel steamships of the New York and Liverpool United States Mail Steamship Company, usually referred to as the Collins Line. She was capable of breaking the transatlantic record of the period, and did so on her February 1852 crossing. On the average, all the Collins liners were making much faster crossings than the Cunarders.*

The *Arctic* was such a beautiful ship that she soon became the talk of two continents. In *Harper's* magazine for June 1852 we read that "never did there float upon the ocean a more magnificent palace." John S. Abbott, the writer of the article, speaks of the main cabin with its carcel ** lamps, highly polished satin wood and rosewood, and beautiful mirrors. He also mentions the "stained glass, silver plate, costly carpets, marble center tables and pier tables, luxurious sofas and arm chairs." He goes on to describe a "profusion of rich gilding giving an air of almost Oriental magnificence to

---

which collided with another craft en route to Charleston around 1878. In 1900 Charles Mitchell's nephew, a Mr. Bramwell of Flushing, New York, was sitting on the shore at a resort in New Jersey. Handing his watch to his fiancée, he went into the water, swam out and was attacked and eaten by a shark. Burwell Smith's yacht was lost off Cuba in 1947.

Some years ago when Caldray Castle was rented by Americans two women were drowned in the sea there.

* The 284-foot *Arctic* had a crew at full complement of 140 people.

** A mechanical lamp, named for its inventor, B. G. Carcel, in which the oil is pumped to the wick by clockwork.

a room 100 feet in length and 25 in breadth."

It was indeed a remarkable ship, about which Congressman Barry of Mississippi later said: "If they had spent in life-boats for that vessel the money which they spent in ginger-bread ornaments and decorations, there might have been hundreds of valuable lives saved."

The *Arctic* left Liverpool on her ill-fated voyage for New York September 20, 1854, with more than two hundred and fifty passengers. Among the passengers were many of wealth and distinction. The wife, son, and daughter of Mr. Collins, owner of the line, were aboard, and the Duc de Gramont was one of the distinguished names on the passenger list. Captain James C. Luce, commander of the ship, had with him his crippled eight-year-old son who, it was hoped, would benefit from the sea voyage.

New Englanders aboard included a Bostonian, Mr. A. Stone, and his family. Frederick W. Gale from Worcester, Massachusetts, together with his wife, child, and servant had been traveling in Italy and had lived in Florence for some weeks. A young married couple named Lang came from Massachusetts. Mrs. John Childe and her daughter were from Springfield. Benjamin W. Copes, his wife, and child were said to have been aboard, as well as "R. S. Williams & Lady" of Salem. Mrs. Howland and her son, relatives of Dr. Williams of Boston also made the fatal trip together with M. M. Day, his wife and daughter of Salem.

A week at sea passed and there had been no bad weather. The Collins liner reached the Grand Banks and all aboard were expecting to arrive at New York three days later on September 30. On September 27 it was calm and hazy. Occasional low-lying fog moved into the area. Although a sailor was often stationed in the forecastle head to blow on a horn at intervals, Captain Luce did not consider it foggy enough for this precaution.

At noon the captain took his observations for latitude. All who had entered the ship's pool for guessing the day's run were anxiously awaiting the announcement of the ship's position, but Luce never was able to finish making his calculations. A few moments later the lookout in the bow gave a shout of alarm, and almost at once the officer of the deck told the man at the wheel to change the course "hard to starboard."

"I rushed on deck," said the captain later, "and just got out when I felt a crash forward and at the same moment saw a strange steamer under the starboard bow. In another moment she struck against the guards of the *Arctic* and passed astern of us. The bows of the strange ship appeared to be cut off literally for about ten feet. Seeing that in all probability she must sink in a few minutes, after taking a hasty glance at our own ship and believing that we were comparatively uninjured, my first impulse was to try to save the lives of those on board the stranger."

Immediately Captain Luce ordered two of the *Arctic*'s lifeboats lowered. His Chief Officer, Robert J. Gourlay, and six seamen got aboard the first in order to row over to the other vessel and see if help might be needed. Almost at once, however, Captain Luce heard that the *Arctic* herself was seriously in trouble. Later it was found that the craft with which the *Arctic* had collided was the 200-ton French steamer *Vesta*, on the way back to France from the island of Miquelon with 197 fishermen and sailors aboard. She suffered appalling damage, but still was able to stay afloat.

In the bowels of the *Arctic* the collision had not been felt at all. No one in the engine room realized what had happened when they received the signal for "full astern." A few minutes later, however, Chief Engineer J. W. Rogers saw an ominous flow of black bilge water beginning to swirl around the engine bed plates. He opened the bilge injector at once, allowing the giant jet condensers of the main engine to suck water from the bilge. In spite of this the flood continued to gain and soon Mr. Rogers realized that the *Arctic* was doomed.

In addition to water pouring into the engine room, it was also coming into the ship through several holes in the *Arctic*'s bow, the largest of which was more than five feet long and eighteen inches wide. No less than a thousand gallons a second were swirling into the hull.

Captain Luce now ordered a sail passed over the bow to cover the leaks, but it was found that a large part of the *Arctic*'s stem and her broken iron anchor stock prevented a snug fit. Carpenter George Baily then volunteered to go over the side in a boatswain's chair to attempt stuffing pillows and mattresses into the holes, but by the time they began to lower him, the *Arctic* was so far down by the head that the operation was abandoned as impossible.

Inside the hull Boatswain Thomas Wilde was also desperately attempting to plug up the leak. When the water reached the cargo, however, he realized he could do nothing more.

Captain Luce was now faced with a terrible decision. Should he keep on in his attempt to stop the leaks, or put all efforts toward a mad dash for the nearest land, fifty miles away at Cape Race, Newfoundland? He finally decided on the latter alternative. By this time Gourlay's lifeboat had disappeared in the fog, and the steamer *Vesta* had also vanished. Luce believed at the time that she had already gone down.

Now occurred one of the terrifying incidents of the disaster. The *Arctic* had just begun her desperate dash for shore when a horrifying scream pierced the air. Coming out of the fog, directly in the *Arctic*'s path, was a lifeboat which had been launched by the *Vesta*. Before anyone could do anything, the boat was caught under the *Arctic*'s paddle wheel, and eleven men were ground to pieces, with only one of the twelve occupants saved. Nevertheless, realizing he was gambling with hundreds of lives, Captain Luce sent his sinking ship through the icy seas, ordering his officers to stop at nothing. The survivor, hauled aboard, proved to be François Gajoick, a French-Canadian fisherman. He was so frightened

and incoherent at first that he could not even give the name
of his own vessel.

Meanwhile, in the *Arctic*'s hold, the sea water was rising
higher and higher, although the steamer continued her mad
pace toward land. When the water reached the ash pits and
the bottom grates, one by one the lower fires were extinguished, and the firemen soon were forced to flee topsides
to save their own lives. The paddle wheels, however, continued to turn rapidly and more vital progress toward Newfoundland was made. Later, the upper fires went out as well,
and this was the beginning of the end. Finally, the paddles
began to slow down, and then, with a last indecisive churning,
they stopped. As Alexander Crosby Brown in his masterful
story of the loss of the *Arctic* says, "the ship's doom was
sealed." *

Only an hour had passed since the two craft had come
together. The *Arctic* had made at the most fourteen miles of
her course to safety, and Captain Luce's gamble had failed.
During that time, however, the skipper had developed other
plans for saving the women and children in the five remaining
lifeboats. But, when the paddles stopped, uncontrolled panic
broke out. A group of men leaped into the stern boat and cut
her loose at once. A description of what happened on the
next lifeboat, written by a passenger, Mr. F. DeMaeyer, follows:

"The boat was then ordered to be lowered, but before let-
ting it down to the water, the passengers were placed in it
to secure it against seizure of the ship's crew. Twenty-five
passengers, of whom eighteen were ladies, and among them
Mrs. Collins, were placed in it, when one rope at the stern
end of the boat gave way, hanging it by the bows and pre-
cipitating all into the ocean except two men (one of them
was Thomas Stinson, officer's steward) and Mrs. Craig, who
clung to the boat. The lady was again taken on board the

---

* *The American Neptune*, October 1954, p. 237.

ship, and the boat with the two men in it was immediately
put afloat. As soon as it was on the water a rush was made
for it, passengers and crew together jumping from the ship,
some falling in the water and others into the boat."

All but one of the remaining lifeboats were taken over by
mobs of men and cut adrift. In the last boat the Chief Engineer placed a group of fifteen and rowed it out to a position
near the *Arctic*.

Captain Luce now decided to make a raft on which many
of the survivors could find refuge, and he gave all the women
passengers life preservers. Along with examples of cowardice
among the men, there were many instances of courage and
even heroism. A young apprentice engineer, Stewart Holland of Washington, had been given the task of firing the
signal gun at minute intervals. This he did continuously until
the ship sank beneath him. His last act was the final firing of
the gun as he was engulfed by the sea.

When the raft was almost ready, an alarm went around the
ship that the *Arctic* was about to go under. This created a
terrifying rush for the raft, during which Captain Luce almost tore the shirt off Fireman Patrick Tobin's back, attempting to restrain him.

"It was every man for himself," said Tobin later. "Life
was as sweet to us as life to others."

At 4:45 that afternoon the stern dipped under the water
and the bow rose in the air and the ship began her fateful
plunge stern first.* George Burns remembered "one fearful
shriek . . . but the most terrible noise of all, which drowned
other sounds, was the ship's own death moans as air trapped
below made its final escape through the smokestack with an all
but human-sounding wail, awful to hear."

Captain Luce, holding his little boy, went down with the
ship, but floated up to the surface. Then after struggling

---

* This was the moment depicted in Currier's lithograph, after a sketch by
James Smith. The lithograph was published the same year and appears in
this volume.

with his child in his arms, he was sucked under for a second time. When he came to the surface once more, he had a terrible moment in which he could not find his son, but then he, too, reappeared. The captain later reported:

"A most awful and heart-rending scene presented itself to my view; women and children struggling together amidst pieces of wreckage of every kind, calling on each other and God to assist them. Such another appalling scene may God preserve me from ever witnessing—I was in the act of trying to save my child again when a portion of the paddlebox came crashing up edgewise and just grazed my head and fell with its whole weight on the head of my darling child. In another moment I beheld him a lifeless corpse on the surface of the waves."

Although the raft had been put together in the best possible way under the circumstances, it was not a perfect job. Seventy-two men and four women went on board it after the *Arctic* went down, but only one person, Peter McCabe, managed to live through the following twenty-six-hour ordeal. Later, from the sanctuary of Sailors' Snug Harbor on Staten Island, New York, McCabe made the following statement:

"I swam to the large raft which had about seventy persons clinging to it. The sea, though not strong, was rough, and the waves, as they dashed over it, washed away a portion of its living freight. I shall never forget the awful scene. There we were, in the midst of the ocean, without the slightest hope of assistance, while every minute one or more of our unfortunate fellow passengers were dropping into their watery grave from sheer exhaustion. Those who had life preservers did not sink, but floated with their ghastly faces upwards, reminding those who still remained alive of the fate that awaited them.

"In the midst of this, thank Heaven, I never lost hope, but retained my courage to the last. One by one I saw my unfortunate companions drop off; some of them floated off and were eaten and gnawed by fishes, while others were washed under the raft and remained with me till I was rescued. I could see their faces in the openings as they were swayed to and fro by the waves, which threatened every moment to wash me off. The raft at one time was so crowded that many had to hold on by one hand. Very few words were spoken by any, and the only sound that we heard was the splash of the waters or the heavy breathing of the poor sufferers, as they tried to recover their breath after a wave had passed over them. Nearly all were submerged to their armpits, while a few could with great difficulty keep their heads above the surface. The women were the first to go. They were unable to stand the exposure more than three or four hours. They all fell off the raft without a word, except one poor girl who cried out in intense agony, 'Oh, my poor mother and sisters.'

"When I was about eighteen hours on the raft there were not more than three or four left. One of these gave me what appeared to be a small map, but which I understood him to say was a sort of title deed to his property. In a few minutes after I took it, he too unloosed his hold and was added to the number that floated about the raft.

"I endeavored to get the paper into my pocket, but found this impossible on account of my cramped position, so I placed it between my teeth and held it there till I was overwhelmed by a wave, when I lost my hold of it, and it was washed away. Another, who had an oiled silk coat on, called on me, for Heaven's sake, to assist him as his strength was rapidly failing and he must fall off if not relieved. As he was about four or five feet from me, it was difficult to reach him, but after considerable exertions I succeeded in doing so and helped him with one of my knees until I became quite faint, when I was obliged to leave him to his fate. Poor fellow, he promised me if he ever got to New York alive he would reward me well. He clung with terrible tenacity to life, but he too dropped off in his turn. I was now left alone on the raft;

not a solitary being was alive out of seventy."

McCabe was eventually rescued by the ship *Huron* of St. Andrews, New Brunswick, bound for Quebec.

Henderson Moore, one of the passengers, had watched several others jump overboard from the *Arctic* into the water to get a place on one of the lifeboats. He was picked up by a lifeboat which had about fourteen people aboard at the time. The second mate in charge of it told him that "the captain had given him orders to drop astern and pick up passengers overboard.

"We soon drifted out of sight of the steamer," Moore explained later. "After laying on our oars a few minutes, we went towards the steamer, being directed by the sound of her bells. While approaching her we fell in with another boat containing twenty-five persons in charge of the purser. Including those picked up, our boat now contained twenty-six persons in all, under the direction of Mr. Baalham. The boats being together, put it to vote and appointed him captain of both. We had at first six oars and the purser's boat three. We broke one of our oars and gave the purser one, which left us only four.

"We then headed for Cape Race, supposing it might be about a hundred miles distant, being guided by the wind and the sun which shone out for a few minutes. The compass taken on aboard failed to traverse and was of no use owing probably to the fact that Francis' lifeboats are made of iron. After pulling in company with the purser's boat all that night and the next day and night or until about one o'clock A.M. on the Friday following, we discovered land and which we reached about 4 P.M. the same day and landed at Broad Cove, a little bay and the only one within several miles where it was considered safe to effect a landing and providentially a fisherman's hut was found near the spot where we obtained some crackers and water, the first we had tasted after leaving the ship, as we had taken neither water nor food in either boat."

The first lifeboat to leave the *Arctic* vanished completely and was never heard from again in any way. Probably it did not survive the bad weather which set in on the first of October.

The *Vesta* arrived at St. John's, Newfoundland, on September 30 just before the weather turned bad. At the time of the collision she had launched two lifeboats, one of which was run down by the *Arctic*. The other boat had returned to the ship, and its occupants were taken aboard again. Captain Duchesne of the *Vesta* had ordered one hundred and fifty mattresses stuffed behind the bulkhead and fastened with timbers. The foremast was cut away; and the vessel set out for St. John's under "small steam," according to the *Illustrated London News*.

One of the strangest consequences of the *Arctic* tragedy, according to Alexander Crosby Brown, was the case of a Mr. Fleury of New Orleans who had supposedly perished on the liner. His young wife mourned for him and then married his chief clerk, by whom she had three children. Meanwhile Mr. Fleury, who had been taken aboard a whaler after the disaster, was then wrecked on an island from which another whaler saved him. He finally arrived at New York, where on October 4, 1860, he wrote a letter to his wife. The necessary adjustment was made, but the details have not come down to us.

Thirty-five years later, writing his notes on wrecks and rescues, Captain Robert Bennett Forbes, of Milton, Massachusetts, stated that "the principal cause of great loss of life in this case was the want of sufficient boats and a want of due organization for such an emergency. If the *Arctic* had no more boats than the *Baltic* in which I made a passage, not over two hundred persons could have been put into them with any chance of safety, even in smooth water.*

Estimates as to the number saved and lost aboard the *Arctic*

---

* Forbes later stated that the abolishment of flogging as a means of punishment might have contributed to the low morale among American seamen.

indicate the confusion common to this sort of statistics. The reader may decide for himself. Kennedy in *Steam Navigation* lists 87 saved of 365 on board. Angas in *Rivalry on the Atlantic* says that 86 survived and 322 were lost. The U.S. Government says 305 disappeared. John G. Dow estimates that 106 were saved and 283 lost. Alexander Crosby Brown compiled a list of 83 saved from the *Arctic*: four officers, 57 crew members, 22 passengers; and one fisherman from the *Vesta*. Of course, the eleven men in the *Vesta*'s lifeboat must be added to the casualties.*

No disciplinary action was taken against any of the survivors of the *Arctic*, some of whom had cowardly fought other men and even women to gain seats in the lifeboats. Nevertheless, many of the surviving crew members decided to remain in Canada until the episode was dimmed by the passage of time and they would be able to return home quietly, without attracting attention. Alexander Crosby Brown tells us that when Mr. W. W. Gilbert, a member of the New York Stock Exchange, arrived in New York alive and well, there was an "indescribable chill which ran through the entire community." In his own defense Gilbert said that he had gone to secure and hold seats for the lady members of the Brown family, and the inrush of the crew prevented him from getting out again. When he told his story it was believed that all witnesses who could contradict him had gone down with the ship. Later, George F. Allen, to the astonishment of all his friends, was picked up alive at sea. Unfortunately, he did not confirm Mr. Gilbert's story, but what Allen did say was never made public.

When the crash had come, Charles Mitchell had been able to take momentary comfort in the realization that his sister

---

* Rev. Henry Ward Beecher, in a sermon preached October 15, 1854, said: "Oh, what a burial was here. It was an ocean grave. The mists alone shrouded the burial place. No spade prepared the grave, no sexton filled up the hollowed earth. Down, down they sank, and the quick returning water smoothed out every ripple and left the sea as if it had not been."

Caroline was not aboard, but then the task of keeping alive occupied all his thoughts. He reached the ship's railing and grabbed a rope, from which he lowered himself and then jumped the remaining distance into the icy sea. Temporarily stunned by the fall, Mitchell was revived by the shock of the freezing water, and when he came to the surface some distance from the *Arctic* he noticed a lifeboat.

Feebly, he attempted to swim toward it, and on coming alongside was grasped by those aboard and hauled to safety. Minutes later the fog enveloped them, and they drifted away from the sinking ship. It was discovered that there were neither rations nor water aboard the lifeboat. There was no compass, and they were now adrift about forty-five miles from the nearest shore, with no means of determining direction. During the next day, because of their intense thirst, two of the men gave in and drank sea water. Both died within the next twenty-four hours.

Two days later the fog lifted enough to allow the occupants of the lifeboat to see about a mile around them. Soon a schooner was sighted, but it sailed away without observing them. Then a brig came into view, but it also disappeared.

One of the crew then noticed what he believed was a land bird flying overhead, and assuming that it disappeared in the general direction of the shore, the occupants of the lifeboat started rowing after it. Hours later they landed at a small fishing village, Broad Cove, Newfoundland, twelve miles north of Cape Race. They were followed shortly by another lifeboat from the *Arctic* which appeared offshore.

Charles Mitchell, because of his immersion in the icy waters, was taken to the hut of a fisherman, where he had to remain for "a month before he recovered sufficiently from his exposure so that he could leave his benefactors and return to Charleston." *

---

* I have been permitted to quote from the pen of Mrs. S. Fahs Smith, in recording the story of Charles Mitchell.

X

Tragedy out of New Bedford

At seven o'clock on the morning of July 21, 1857, a voyage began from a New Bedford wharf which was to be long remembered in the annals of that Massachusetts whaling community.

The ship *Junior* sailed out of New Bedford harbor, but a dense fog forced Captain Archibald Mellen to anchor off Dumpling Rock, and it was not until the following noon that the weather had cleared enough for the *Junior* to get under way again. Her eventual destination was the bowhead whaling grounds of the Sea of Okhotsk, which lie north of Japan, off Kamchatka on the east coast of Asia.

Early in the voyage trouble started as a result of the terrible food served to the men. The second mate's watch included Cyrus Plumer, who had been hired as boatsteerer-harpooner, Richard Cartha, Charles F. Fifield, William J. Herbert, Cornelius Burns, and John Hall. Plumer seemed to be the ringleader of the group, and when the food became so bad that the men grew ill, he and the other men from his watch raised their objections.

Twenty-four-year-old Cyrus Plumer soon became the idol of young William John Herbert, who was seventeen. During the long night watches Plumer told the lad of his thrilling adventures of former trips, and Herbert was fascinated. Plumer related how he had caused so much trouble aboard the whaler *Daniel Wood* that they had shipped him home on another ship, the *Cleon*, as an undesirable seaman. Still later, aboard the whaler *Golconda*, he had stolen a boat and deserted with a small group of followers off the east coast of South America. As the nights went by Herbert came to look upon Plumer as his great hero, and soon Plumer knew that he could count on at least one loyal supporter.

One noon the bread and meat were found to be so vile, filled with maggots and smelling terribly, that every seaman aboard complained. Plumer announced that he would eat the filth no more and would lead a protest in person to the master of the *Junior*. Leaping to his feet, Herbert shouted that he would join Plumer if he wished to protest to the captain, and several others announced their willingness to follow.

The trouble all centered on three old molding casks of bread left over from a former voyage, and a great amount of beef which had been purchased in the Sandwich Islands. None of the food was fit for human consumption.

In lodging their complaint, however, Plumer and his group went over the head of Chief Mate William Nelson, thereby making an enemy of him. Nevertheless, the following afternoon the boatsteerer walked aft with his followers and respectfully offered an oral protest to Captain Mellen. The master of the whaling vessel made it a point to inspect the bread and meat, after which he decided that the mate should "save it for the hogs."

Watching what was transpiring, Nelson, by this time, was boiling with rage. As the seamen started forward after their interview with the captain, the chief mate walked up to Plumer.

"Mark me well!" he began. "If you have anything to talk about after this say it to me or you'll be sorry you ever came aboard the *Junior*." Nothing further, however, happened at the time.

The weeks went by. On September 25, Trinidad was sighted and passed. A terrible storm broke shortly afterward, and soon a bad gale had developed. Higher and higher the waves built up, and when the blow was at its worst a giant sea swept across the deck, carrying the brick trygear and all other equipment over the side. Later another great billow brought green water cascading along the slanting deck, and the forward lifeboats were swept overboard.

Around midnight, when the gale was still at its height, the chief mate shouted across at Jim Hutchins to go aloft and cut away the foretopsail. The shrieking wind drowned out the command, and Hutchins never heard it. Another sailor who had been near Nelson relayed the message, but by this time the chief mate thought that Hutchins was willfully disobeying him. Crossing the sloping deck, he grabbed the sailor by the nape of the neck, smashed him in the face, and threw him against the mast. Hutchins received a bad cut, and a stream of blood ran down his cheek.

"Next time learn to jump when I give you a command," shouted Nelson. "Get aloft!"

Hutchins carried out the order, but soon all the sailors knew about the encounter. A few hours later Plumer and Herbert again headed a protest committee which for the second time bypassed the mate and appealed directly to Mellen. Stepping out from his little group, Plumer respectfully addressed the skipper.

"Sir, it is the mate. He just beat up Hutchins."

The captain considered Plumer's statement for a moment. "I am told that Hutchins refused duty. What about it?"

"That, pardon me, sir, is not quite true. Hutchins didn't get the command at once, and when he started aloft the chief struck him."

But Captain Mellen was adamant. "Plumer, return forward.

Don't come aft again unless you have some real grievance. That will be all."

The long voyage to the whaling grounds continued, and the weeks went by. Late the following November Cyrus Plumer was standing by his daytime watch at the wheel when he noticed a giant albatross, larger than he had ever seen. It was flying just above the *Junior*. Soon Plumer was paying more attention to the bird than to his helm. Then, without warning, the slatting of sails on a poorly steered course echoed around the ship. Plumer still was absorbed in the effortless gyrations of the albatross and made no effort to correct his mistake.

A moment later Nelson reached the wheel. He smashed Plumer on the jaw, after which the helmsman let go of the wheel completely and began to wrestle with his superior officer. The two men rolled to the deck in their struggle, and Plumer's head struck the wheelpost, stunning him temporarily.

While the boatsteerer was recovering, the chief mate leaped to his feet and started kicking the prone man with his heavy metal-tipped boots. The other sailors later agreed that Nelson would have broken Plumer's back but for the fact that the captain arrived on the scene and stopped the slaughter. Plumer recovered his senses a moment later and was told to resume his post at the wheel.

The following morning the captain called the crew aft. The sailors noticed that he wore a holster, from which a great pistol hung. When all the men had assembled the master began talking slowly.

"You all know what happened between Mr. Nelson and Plumer yesterday when Plumer was negligent at the wheel. Now any member of the crew, according to the law of the sea, who strikes an officer is guilty of insubordination and shall be duly punished. My mates will now carry out the punishment. Mr. Lord, Mr. Smith, seize the troublemaker and secure him to the rigging!"

The mates went forward and grabbed Plumer, who turned

purple with rage. He did not struggle, however, as they led him across to the main shrouds. An angry murmur came from the crew, but no one openly rebelled against what they knew was going to take place. The boy Herbert could not believe what was happening to his idol, but Plumer became a bigger hero than ever with his stoic acceptance of what followed. The first mate stood gloating nearby, and had prepared two long pieces of tarred-rope yarn. The two other mates held Plumer's hands high in the air, so that they barely touched the slanting main shrouds at a point seven feet above the deck.

Nelson climbed the ratlines and secured the tarred rope to Plumer's thumbs. He threw the other end of each line up and over a ratline suspended ten feet above the deck.

"Ready," he exulted. "Now hoist!"

The two mates lifted the yielding body off the deck, while Nelson pulled the ropes taut and secured them to a lower ratline. Plumer had now been hauled so high into the air that only his toes touched the deck. All his weight was on his thumbs, between the first and second joints.

The other mates returned to a position between the captain and the port rail, as the moment for the execution of the sentence arrived.

"Mr. Nelson," ordered Captain Mellen, "give boatsteerer Plumer twenty lashes with the rope's end. Let the crew understand that this is a merited punishment for insubordination and a warning to others in the crew that they must respect the ship's officers!"

The rope's end, a cat-of-nine-tails, was now removed by the overanxious chief mate from the brine in which it was soaking. As the first swish of the lash echoed across the deck and curled itself around Plumer's bare back, Herbert cried out in anguish. Again, again, and again the rope bit into the defenseless sailor, until the full twenty lashes had been administered.

"You may cut the boatsteerer down now, Mr. Lord," commanded Captain Mellen. Plumer, his bleeding back streaming blood, staggered forward and down into his steerage berth. The other sailors could hear him muttering quietly to himself, "I'll get even; I'll get even!" There the incident ended.

Hours later, as time for the midnight change of watches came, a little group of sailors surrounded the boatsteerer. Herbert was in his usual position at Plumer's side. Suddenly Richard Cartha stood up.

"How long must we put up with this?" he demanded. "I think I'll desert as soon as we get close to Amsterdam Island. It's been done before."

"You are right," said Plumer. "It has been done before, and I have done it, but now I have a much better plan. On my last voyage five of us took a whaleboat from the *Golconda* while off South America, and I'll never try that again. We were captured and put in prison. We could take over this ship, instead of deserting. It's much safer."

"There's a word for that act," said Cartha, "and it is mutiny at sea! I'm willing, but punishment is worse if we are caught. We've got to work out our plans carefully!"

"We can work them out much easier than you think," said Plumer. "It could take place in this coming watch. Let me think. Yes, I have it. We'll have Hall climb up on the windward rail. Fifield can be forward of the foremast, watching me for my signal, and for anyone else who might come along.

"Now, here's the plan. I'll give the signal by leaving the rail to start walking as though I might be getting a drink from the mainmast water cask. Hall is to hacksaw through the flying jib sheet and make it appear to break. Then he'll jump down, throw the blade over the side, and shout out that the sheet has parted.

"I can just see Mr. Lord hurrying forward to check the trouble. As he passes the foremast Fifield will knock him unconscious and bind and gag him. When this has been done we'll go below and surprise the other officers. The *Junior* will then be ours!"

Thus it was planned that before dawn the mutiny would be carried out. Hatchets, mallets, and knives were picked up and secreted in handy hiding places as the hour of attack approached. Just before the appointed time Fifield took a cooper's mallet and stood behind the mainmast. Hall hid in the bow where he could be ready to saw the jib sheet at the moment when Plumer began to walk toward the water cask.

Meanwhile, young Herbert was on duty at the wheel. The second mate strode up to the boy and started a conversation. "Have you ever been sailing in the Indian Ocean before?" Mr. Lord asked the lad, and Herbert told the mate that it was his first experience. A short time later the mate started across to the taffrail and looked at the wake. Then he began walking forward.

Suddenly an unexpected event occurred. The fore topgallant sheet parted with a snapping twang, which was heard all over the ship. The efforts to repair it threw the schedule for the mutiny completely off. The sheet was secured, and the revolt was abandoned for the time being.

On Friday evening, November 16, dark skies appeared, and another attempt at mutiny was planned. The moment arrived, and this time Hall successfully hacksawed the jib sheet. When it snapped off the noise brought Second Mate Lord sprinting up to the spritsail yard, where he stood to direct the securing of the jib. He had acted too fast for Fifield to strike him as he passed.

Plumer was very upset at this second failure.

"What happened this time?" he asked Fifield.

"The mate was too quick for me. If I had hit him while he was standing on the yard, he'd have pitched overboard to his death. Now I didn't promise to kill him, so that's the story."

"I'd have knocked him overboard myself, if I'd realized you didn't have the nerve to do it," the harpooner replied.

Another encounter of a minor nature between officers and crew occurred on November 30, 1857. Four months and more had gone by since the *Junior* sailed away from New Bedford harbor. They had not caught any whales, and as there was comparatively little to do in the second mate's watch, Plumer decided that he would hide until he really was needed. Crawling under the carpenter's bench, he was soon sound asleep.

Unexpectedly, Mr. Lord appeared on deck, where he heard stentorian snores coming from under the bench. Dipping a bucket into the brine tub on deck, Lord threw the odorous contents full into Plumer's face.

"Jump out from there and stand by so I can get you when I need you," Mr. Lord shouted at the spluttering, strangling harpooner.

"Wait and see. I'll get you for this," cried Plumer, who rolled out from under the bench and went forward. Nothing further resulted on either side at the time, and Captain Mellen took no action when informed of the incident the following noon.

Christmas Day found the *Junior* off the coast of Southern Australia, in the Great Australian Bight. The ship kept a northeast by east course that day, with strong southwest winds blowing. When the sun set the sail was shortened to main topsail and foresail. The wind veered to the south, increasing in intensity.

As was his custom, Captain Mellen treated each member of the crew that evening to a small glass of spirits because of the Christmas holiday. Plumer accepted his share without comment.

Then, as the hour grew late, the officers went to their quarters. Midnight approached. Just before the watch was changed, Plumer woke up young Herbert.

"Now is the time you have to decide whether you are a man or a boy," he admonished the youth as he awakened him. "By dawn we'll be masters of the ship!"

Ten minutes later the watch was changed, and Plumer

made his final arrangements. He strode over to the man at the wheel, Charlie Harrison.

"Keep quiet tonight, Harrison. If you hear anything, stay where you are. There will be trouble and if you make a stir, I'll have to shoot you. I mean it."

Harrison nodded his head but said nothing.

Plumer then called his fellow mutineers around the deck pot.

"This job must go through tonight without fail! We are going to take the ship. It is all up to you, Fifield. You crossed us up before. How about now?" Plumer looked at Fifield questioningly.

"Yes, this time I'll go through with it."

"Well, here is the plan. Take a hatchet, and don't let anyone in the cabin up on deck by the companionway door. Order Stanley to stand by the mizzen hatch and prevent anyone from coming up there."

Just then Herbert appeared on deck with a hatchet. Plumer, Hall, Cartha, and Burns went over and joined the lad. Plumer now led his group down the ladder through the mizzen hatch.

The crisis was at hand. The boatsteerer had a heavy whaling gun held in the bend of his arm and carried a pistol in his belt. Hall was armed with a whaling gun and a cooper's axe. Burns and Cartha had jammed pistols into their boot tops and carried boarding knives. This left only three men of the watch on deck: Harrison at the wheel, Fifield guarding the cabin door, and Stanley on watch at the mizzen hatch.

The moment Plumer reached the lower deck, he sent young Herbert to see if anyone might be awake in the forecastle, but the lad came back with the word that all were sound asleep. Plumer spoke again.

"We can't just bind the officers and then take over the ship, for just as long as one of them is aboard we are in trouble. No one likes to kill, but we'll have to do it for our own protection. I'll take care of the captain, and Herbert can back me up. Cartha takes the second mate, and I'll let Hall manage Nelson. Burns, your job is the third mate. We'll all fire our guns together."

Five minutes later Plumer and Herbert had reached the officers' messroom. Frightened at the prospect of physical violence, Herbert backed himself up against the bulkhead. Plumer then made his way slowly into the after cabin. The other mutineers joined Herbert in the messroom.

Plumer stood at the entrance to the captain's stateroom. Meanwhile, in his nervousness, young Herbert reached out and touched Cartha. Just then Plumer shouted "Fire!"

Three heavy detonations deafened the mutineers. Hall's shot wounded the first mate, but when Herbert threw his hatchet at the injured man to finish the job, it still failed to kill him.

At the signal Cartha struck with his knife at the second mate, but the officer grabbed the blade and deflected the point from his body. Cartha then dropped the knife and fired his pistol into Mr. Lord's left breast. Lord jumped up and tripped over the third mate, who had collapsed across his bunk, blood streaming down his body. Burns had struck him such a blow with the boarding knife that he died within a few minutes.

Captain Mellen, in spite of being shot, leaped from his bunk. Plumer hit the master twice with the hatchet, after which the captain died almost at once. Thinking now that all the officers had been killed, the mutineers scrambled up on deck.

"They're all dead," shouted Herbert, more to himself than to anyone else. Two officers, however, were still alive. Mr. Lord, the second mate, crawled out of the main hatchway, while Chief Mate Nelson was even then attempting to put out a fire caused when the blast aimed at him ignited the furnishings.

Nevertheless, Plumer had won. He was now in control of the *Junior*. The boatsteerer sent Herbert forward to awaken the sailors not on watch. He told the boy to explain to the others that if anyone came aft armed he would be severely dealt with. Herbert first awakened William Marlatt, shouting, "You're wanted up on deck!"

"It isn't my watch. Get out of here!"

"The ship's been taken. Plumer is in command!"

Marlatt and the other seamen soon dressed and reported on deck to Plumer, who explained that he was now in charge. There were no audible complaints.

Second Mate Lord was found still alive hiding below decks. Put in irons, he was taken to the forecastle. Later Plumer attempted to get Lord to navigate the ship for him, as the mutineers had a plan to sail to Cape Howe, formerly a desolate section of Australia, and then being used as an Australian prison camp. Lord was not an accomplished navigator, however, and Plumer realized he needed help.

Late that afternoon Nelson called up through the companionway that the smoldering fire, set by the flash of the mutineers' guns, had again broken out and was filling the cabin with smoke. Several men smashed in the skylights and lowered buckets of water to the deck below and the blaze was finally extinguished.

Plumer revealed a peculiar trait of his own when he asked for volunteers to dispose of the two dead bodies. "I can shoot a man but I can't touch him after death," he explained. "For some reason it seems to bother me."

Steward Hugh Duff, who had no part in the mutiny, volunteered for the gruesome task. Carrying the relatively light body of Captain Mellen, who was a small man, up the steps and out on deck, he placed the remains near the taffrail. Plumer ordered a grindstone attached to the captain's body, after which the late master was lifted up over the side and dropped into the sea.

Duff had more trouble with the body of Third Mate Smith, but with the help of others he finally was able to bring it up on deck where Plumer ordered several turns of a chain secured around it, and the third mate followed Captain Mellen into the sea.

"That's better," muttered Plumer to Herbert after the incident ended. "Dead bodies always bother me, and I don't quite understand it."

The voyage continued without incident for the next few days. Nelson was still hiding away below. When the morning of the fifth day following the mutiny arrived, Plumer sent Marlatt down to find the chief mate and ask him for a truce. He wanted to offer Nelson his life for navigating the *Junior*.

By now Nelson's wounds were bothering him severely, and the mate was agreeable to accepting any sort of compromise. He consented to be navigator if they would clean and bind his injuries, and the agreement was carried out.

On January 3, 1858, Cape Howe was sighted off the starboard bow twenty miles away, and Plumer became excited. Ordering the *Junior* hove to, he glanced around the deck.

"Everyone aft for a talk," he bellowed.

"Now I must decide what we should do," Plumer began. "You all know we could burn the ship here and now, but I have decided to allow Nelson to sail to New Zealand and let us land in Australia. If you officers give me your sworn word to let us alone and sail to New Zealand that's all there is to it. I have a Bible here, and I know that you, Nelson, are a Bible man.

"Do you two officers agree to kiss the Bible and say that you will sail to New Zealand after we leave? Is it agreed?"

Plumer held up the Bible. The two officers stepped forward and kissed the Holy Book one after the other, each promising in turn to carry out Plumer's plans for the *Junior* and sail her to New Zealand.

Two hours later Plumer had the two whaleboats over the side loaded with enough supplies to last them for some time. Ten men voted for going in the boats to Australia, making four oarsmen and one boatsteerer for each craft. They included Plumer, Herbert, Cartha, Hall, Burns, Harrison, Rike, Carroll, Brooks, and Stanley. All others were to remain on the *Junior*.

With a final warning to Nelson to sail the *Junior* to New Zealand, Plumer pushed off with his party in the two whaleboats. Within an hour they were tiny dots on the horizon. Nelson had plans of his own, however, and soon hoisted aloft distress signals which could not be misunderstood.

Five days later, on January 8, 1858, the brig *Lochiel*, under the command of Captain John Haddon, was sailing in the Sea of New Zealand. Far in the distance he sighted a vessel and soon had his telescope trained on the craft. To his amazement, he read one of the rarest signals ever displayed at sea. Not only was the American flag flying union down, but fluttering from the craft's mizzen were two flags "P" and "C." The combination of P, a blue square with a white center, and C, a white pennant with red in the field, stood for the awesome message "ASSISTANCE WANTED, MUTINY."

Captain Haddon ordered the course changed at once and headed for the vessel in distress. An hour later he was close enough to read the words, "Junior, New Bedford," on her stern. The two ships soon hove to.

Lowering a boat, Captain Haddon rowed across to the whaler, where he was invited aboard to make an inspection. He met Mr. Nelson and Mr. Lord, both of whom were still suffering from their wounds. He went below to find evidences of a recent fire in the cabin, and noted bullet holes in the bulkheads and bloodstains on the deck.

Mr. Nelson explained that the mutineers had killed both the captain and the third mate and thrown them overboard. They had then left the *Junior* in two whaleboats with others who had chosen to go with them. He told of how both he and Mr. Lord had kissed the Bible and sworn to sail to New Zealand.

"Never mind your promises to a mutineer. They are better broken than kept," admonished Captain Haddon. "Now you'll be in serious trouble if you don't follow me right into port. I don't expect that you'll make the same speed, but if you don't show up in Sydney within a few days I'll have to suggest to the officials that you are implicated in the mutiny as well. All I have is your word, you know, that things happened as they did."

Nelson and Lord realized then that they were suspect unless they sailed for the nearest port, Sydney, at once, and so they agreed to follow the *Lochiel*.

Captain Haddon returned to his brig and two hours later his craft was hull down. Reaching Sydney, Haddon made official notification to the authorities of the mutiny aboard the *Junior*, and the entire coast was soon alerted for the possible landing of the mutineers.

Three days later the *Junior* sailed into port. The harbor police went aboard immediately and conducted a thorough investigation. When the mutineers were not discovered anywhere on the mainland, it was agreed that they must have perished either at sea or at the hands of natives ashore.

Actually, Plumer and his group had encountered rough weather. Both boats had swamped, but by hard bailing the men again had the situation in hand. Finally they reached the island of Gabo, a short distance off the Australian coast, and went ashore.

There a native told them how to reach Ninety Mile Beach, a desolate part of the mainland. After many hardships the ten men landed on the Australian coast itself, where they found conditions very unsatisfactory for their plans.

Disagreements sprang up at once, and the party decided to separate. Plumer, Herbert, Harrison, and Brooks thought that safety lay to the east, while Cartha, Burns, and Hall headed the other expedition westward, which was to end in death for two of the mutineers.

The whaleboats separated. Plumer soon reached a point of land where he noticed a small hut. Beaching the boat, the sailors entered the cabin, which they found empty, and stole two pistols and other supplies. Hiking toward a road, they came to a clearing in a great forest, where they camped for the night.

Before daylight they were awakened by the sound of chopping. When it grew lighter, they saw a gang of Australian convicts wearing leg irons, cutting down trees about a quarter mile away. The prisoners were closely guarded by constables and soldiers.

All that day the Americans lay hidden in the woods. Occasionally bullock teams carrying logs would pass them, headed for either Sydney or Eden. Plumer decided to capture one of them and use it to escape inland.

When darkness came two of the drivers bedded down near the Americans for the night. Plumer's group overwhelmed the two men, robbed them of a handful of nuggets, and left them bound and gagged. The drivers were not discovered for four days but eventually recovered from their experience.

Plumer and his group finally reached a tavern, where they found the waitresses charming companions. Soon the *Junior* sailors were engaged in drinking each other under the table.

The boatsteerer became interested in a buxom barmaid, and she proved talkative. She told him of the exploits of certain great Australian desperadoes who had visited the tavern in months gone by.

Not to be outdone, Plumer explained that he himself didn't mind "killing a man," and admitted that he had just finished certain unusual adventures at sea in which men had been killed. Identifying himself as a Captain Wilson, he indicated that he was looking for a girl to marry.

As the barmaid appeared greatly impressed, Plumer went on to explain that he was now tiring of the sea and would like to give up his career as an American whaler, settle down to a gentle life of bushranging in Australia, and raise a family. What Plumer did not realize was that at that very moment the entire constabulary of Australia had been alerted for American whalers who might be the mutineers from the *Junior*.

Suddenly the girl got up from the table. When she failed to return in a reasonable length of time Plumer wondered if he had told her too much. Frightened and anxious to leave, he vainly attempted to awaken his three comrades from a drunken stupor, and then realized they were too far gone and that he would have to try to escape alone.

Running to the front of the inn, he saw the barmaid coming up the street with two constables, heading for the tavern. Plumer rushed through the hall and out into the back room, where he crawled through an open window and got away. A moment later the constables entered the building and arrested the three drunken men. Three hours afterward Plumer returned to a barber shop nearby, where he had his beard shaved off to disguise his appearance.

A few days later he fell in with a gang whose purpose it was to rob the brig *Splendid*, then lying at anchor in the harbor with the equivalent of $50,000 in gold aboard. The robbery came off successfully. Plumer took his share of the loot to a nearby boarding house, where he was arrested for not being able to explain where he had found the gold. Within an hour he was lodged in the same jail where his three companions had been taken.

Alarming news came from Howard Whittier, the American consul at Sydney. Cornelius Burns and John Hall had been hanged as *Junior* mutineers at Port Albert. This made four from the *Junior* who would never see New Bedford again.

Mate Nelson wrote a letter to the New Bedford owners of the *Junior*. He explained how he had brought the whaler into Sydney on January 12, 1858, after the mutineers had abandoned her. He reported that out of the original crew only thirteen remained to stand by him.*

* On February 10, 1858, the Sydney *Morning Herald* carried the list of those aboard the *Junior* when she had sailed from New Bedford on the pre-

Plumer and his three companions were eventually placed with four others from the *Junior* crew who had been captured. The Australian authorities looked upon the eight sailors as possible mutineers. All were put aboard the *Junior* in a specially built lockup made of hardwood bars and iron, which occupied most of the after cabin area. The men were listed as Cyrus Plumer, Richard Cartha, Jacob Rike, Charles H. Stanley, Adam Cannell, Joseph Brooks, Charles Fifield, and William J. Herbert.

The journey back to America was uneventful at first, but thoughts of mutiny and seizure of the *Junior* again were very much in the minds of the four original mutineers. William Herbert devised a plan for getting out of the cells and murdering all the officers. He wrote out the plot in great detail and passed the directions through an aperture in his cell to the one occupied by Plumer.

The harpooner was clever enough to roll the message tightly and conceal it in a lock of his hair * until the proper time came to pass it on to Cartha, whose cell was across the aisle on the starboard side of the vessel. Plumer misjudged a guard's conversion to the mutineers' way of thinking, and when Plumer asked him to relay the message across to his companion, the guard took it instead to Captain Gardner, thereby saving Gardner's life, for this time the plan involved throwing all the officers overboard after killing them. Thus the second *Junior* mutiny failed before it began, and no other incident occurred on the long trip.

After crossing the ocean the eight sailors were brought into

---

ceeding July 21. They were Captain Mellen, 1st Mate William N. Nelson, 2d Mate Henry Lord, 3d Mate John Smith, steward Hugh Duff, harpooner Cyrus Plumer; Joseph Venn, William Sampson, Joseph Brookes, Adam Cannell; Herman Graff, cooper; Jacob Reke, carpenter; John Enos, Charles Harrison, John Lewis, William J. Herbert, David Carter, Antoni Ludwig, Charles F. Fified, William H. Marlatt, Henry Collins, Charles H. Stanley, J. W. Hutchins, Henry Mason, Charles H. Mansfield, Cornelius Burns, Frank Stafford, William H. Cartha, Owen Duffy, Henry Lynch, Sam Howard, William Paine, alias John Hall, and Manuel Larrador, the cabin boy.

* Many sailors during the 1840s to the 1880s braided their hair, wearing it flat on the top of their heads.

Boston on August 21, 1858, and lodged in the Charles Street jail. It was soon decided that only Plumer, Herbert, Cartha, and Stanley were actually mutineers, and the other four men were freed. The trial of the remaining prisoners was set for the October session of the Federal Circuit Court.

Tremendous interest developed in the proceedings. Benjamin Franklin Butler was assigned as lawyer for Cyrus Plumer's defense, and was to be assisted by Attorney Charles F. Chandler. F. F. Heard was chosen with F. W. Pelton to serve for Cartha. Thornton K. Lothrop and John Quincy Adams were assigned as lawyers for William J. Herbert. J. H. Prince and Samuel W. Quincy were appointed the attorneys for Charles H. Stanley.

The trial began on Monday morning, November 8, 1858. By then newspapers in many parts of the country were including stories of the *Junior* mutineers. In addition to the tens of thousands of words which were recorded by the court stenographer after the trial began, other tens of thousands of words were published in scores of papers all over the United States.

Early in the case an important document was introduced, a statement written by William J. Herbert and signed by five of the six mutineers a few hours after the mutiny:

Lat. 37° 58′ S, Long. 166° 57′ E
Friday, December 25, 1857.

This is to certify that we, Cyrus Plumer, John Hall, Richard Cartha, Cornelius Burns, and William Herbert did, on the night of the 25th of December, take the ship *Junior,* and all others of the crew are innocent.

The captain and third mate were killed and the second mate was wounded and at the time was taken prisoner.

The mate was wounded in the shoulder with balls from a whaling gun and at the time we fired, we set his bed on fire and he was obliged for fear of suffocation to take to the lower hold where he remained until Wednesday afternoon; we could not find him before, but then made a close search and found him; we promised him his life and the ship if he would come out and he did so; since he has been in the ship he has been a good officer and has kept his place; we have agreed to leave him a great part of the crew, and he has taken an oath not to follow us, but to go away and not molest us. We shall stay about here for some time, and if he attempts to follow us we shall go on board and sink the ship. If we had not found Mr. Nelson the ship would have been lost.

We have taken two boats and ten men and everything we wanted. We did not put Mr. Nelson in irons, because he was wounded, but kept a strict watch over him. We particularly wish to say that all others in the ship but the five aforesaid are quite innocent of any part of the affair.

Witnesses:	[signed] Cyrus Plumer
Hugh Duff	John Hall
Henry T. Lord	Richard Cartha
Herman Graff	Cornelius Burns
	William Herbert

Ship *Junior*, New Bedford, Massachusetts, U. S.

Why the names of Stanley and Fifield were not included in the signatures has never been satisfactorily explained. It is true that the two in question did not go below, but Fifield guarded the companionway and Stanley the hatchway that Christmas night, and apparently were in the mutiny.

On November 9, 1858, United States Counsel Milton Andros, the Assistant District Attorney, opened for the government.

In his address to the jury he stated plainly and clearly what the charges were, the murder of Captain Archibald Mellen on the high seas aboard the whaling ship *Junior*, then owned by citizens of the United States, to wit: David R. Greene, Robert B. Greene, Dennis Wood, and Willard Nye, all of New Bedford.

"The case to be proved," stated Attorney Andros, "is not one of manslaughter or any minor degree of crime but one of downright absolute murder and if the government does not prove this in its fullest degree, it will prove nothing.

"After a long contemplation of their crime the boat's crew of which Plumer was boatsteerer was called to relieve another gang and Plumer coming up on deck said, 'By God, this is Christmas night.'

"Plumer then ordered Fifield to call Stanley, and the latter came with a whaling spade to guard the hatchway, and Fifield was set to guard the companionway . . . Plumer, Cartha, Burns, Herbert, and Hall * then went into the steerage."

Andros then gave a twenty-five-minute speech on how each man behaved in the actual crime of murder, but the moment he started to explain what happened after the murder Benjamin Franklin Butler leaped to his feet and objected. Butler's reason was that "what was done after the alleged murder was not competent to be described in the government's opening."

His objection was overruled, and the speech continued.

The testimony of Henry Mason, who has not figured in the story as yet, was given on Monday, November 13, 1858.

A seaman on the *Junior*, he explained how he had been awakened on the night of December 25, 1857, by young Herbert, who told him the ship had been taken. Mason dressed and went on deck, where he met Cartha at the forecastle scuttle.

" 'Come up on deck, all of you!' Cartha told me. 'If you stay here it will go hard with you.' I went aft as far as the tryworks, and heard Burns tell Cartha to call all hands on deck, and tell them he would shoot them if they did not . . . Plumer said to us that if we obeyed him we would fare the best. He had taken the ship and he wanted us to obey him the same as we had the officers."

As the bodies were later brought on deck he heard Plumer say, when the grindstone was attached to Captain Mellen's body, "Go down to Hell and tell the Devil I sent you there!"

---

* Andros made the point later that neither Burns nor Hall had been arrested. As we have explained, they had both been hanged in Australia, but word of this had not reached Boston when the trial began.

Mason explained that Plumer then armed himself with a double-barreled fowling gun. Cartha had a revolver; Stanley and Herbert both had double-barreled guns.

From then on, according to Mason, the following men took their meals in the cabin: Plumer, Burns, Cartha, Stanley, Herbert, Brooks, Graff, Rike, Hall and Sampson. They had, of course, previously eaten in the forecastle.

Plumer acted as the captain, with Sampson and Brooks the mates. All the whaling gear that would sink was then thrown overboard and the wooden portions were cut up into firewood.

Also brought out in the testimony was the fact that after the bodies had been thrown into the ocean Plumer ordered seaman Ludwig to search for the remains of the first mate, whom Plumer thought had been killed. Ludwig, overcome while searching in the smoke-filled cabin, located a body "hard fast to a rope." Pulled up on deck, it was found to be that of the ship's dog. This provoked the merriest laughter among the murderers.

The trial lasted for nineteen days in all. Finally, the last bit of evidence was recorded on Tuesday, November 30, 1858. After several hours' deliberation, the jury announced that it had reached a verdict. The foreman declared that they found Plumer guilty as charged of murder, and the other three defendants guilty as charged of manslaughter.

While Plumer had been awaiting trial in Boston, news reached him of the execution in Auburn, Maine, of two men, Peter Williams and Abraham Cox, who were hanged for killing the officers aboard the *Albion Cooper* while at sea. He had also been told of the execution in Australia of his two companions in mutiny, John Hall and Cornelius Burns, and now was getting worried about his own fate. He still thought that if he played his cards correctly, he would escape hanging.

On December 11, 1858, the day came for the sentence. The clerk of the Federal Court in Boston was instructed by

Judge Nathan Clifford to call Cyrus Plumer for sentencing. From the Circuit Court records we read what then took place:

"Time was allowed by the Court for the preparation of Counsel therein and the said motions were set down for hearing and afterward at the same term the Counsel of said Plumer moved the Court for leave to withdraw the said motions for new trial and arrest of judgment.

"And said Cyrus Plumer, otherwise called Cyrus W. Plumer, having been brought into Court, and being enquired of personally asks that such leave be granted and the said motions be withdrawn.

"Whereupon the Court doth grant him leave to withdraw the said motions, and the same are accordingly waived and withdrawn by said Plumer. Said Plumer is then asked if he has anything to say why judgment of Death should not be pronounced against him."

The statement of Plumer follows:

I am asked if I have anything to say why the sentence of death should not be passed upon me. I object to death because I am not guilty of the death of Captain Mellen. His blood does not rest on my hands. . . .

The firing of weapons was accidental and arose from a derangement of the plans agreed upon. The shot that I fired in the dark . . . didn't hit or wound Captain Mellen. Captain Mellen died from hatchet wounds inflicted by another person. . . .

That person was Charles Fifield, whom I generously, but unwisely, screened from suspicion, assuming his crime, that he might be protected from others in the crew who might do him harm. . . .

I object secondly and strongly because the real culprit, the most guilty person . . . was . . . Mate Nelson, the First Officer of the *Junior*.

Thirdly and lastly I object to the sentence of death being passed upon me . . . because after I was invested with authority, I saved the lives of Mr. Nelson and Mr. Lord, the First and

Second Officers of the ship. The other mutineers would have killed them. . . .

[Plumer now made a statement strangely similar to that of the infamous Captain John Quelch, who in 1704 had been hanged as a pirate.]

Let the sentence of death be passed and executed and hereafter, whenever any man finds himself in a position similar to which I found myself on the morning of December 26th in 1857, he will remember that dead men tell no tales and will be tempted by remembrance of my fate to use his authority not to preserve but to destroy life and property. . . .

These are my reasons: guiltless of bloodshed; led into crime by intrigue and complicity by an officer of the ship; and preserving life and property after the ship's mutiny for these I claim I ought not to die.

But before God who is my judge . . . I declare that I believe all that I have uttered, and everything that I have implied in what I have uttered is the truth. On that truth I object to the sentence now to be passed.

[signed]   Cyrus W. Plumer

The statement of Cyrus Plumer did nothing at the time to save his life. When the reading of his words were concluded, Judge Nathan Clifford stood up to give the sentence. Plumer was also standing, pale and rigid.

"Cyrus Plumer," began Judge Clifford, "you have fully replied as to why you believe that judgment of death should not be pronounced against you. No good cause appearing, and all matters having been fully heard and understood by the Court, you are now adjudged guilty of felony.

"Cyrus Plumer, you are to be taken back to the place from whence you came and there remain in close confinement until Friday the 24th of June next, and on that day, between the hours of eleven o'clock in the forenoon and one o'clock in the afternoon you are to be taken to the place of execution and be hanged by the neck until dead, and may God have mercy on your soul!"

The three other mutineers were then given sentences of a

little more than six years each. The four men were led away, one to await death and the others to spend their next few years in prison.

Powerful forces were now unleashed for the saving of Plumer's life. As the time for execution neared, a stay of sentence for two weeks was obtained, thus changing the execution date from June 24 to July 8, 1859.

Letters in the daily papers suggested the signing of petitions for changing Plumer's sentence to life imprisonment. The law offices of John A. Andrew, later to become the Civil War Governor of Massachusetts, were thrown open for the reception and signing of such petitions.*

This was not the first time, nor was it the last, that a sympathetic public allowed itself to be whipped up into a frenzy of activity to save a guilty man from execution.

Within a few days 5,000 signatures on a petition were sent to President James Buchanan. Ralph Waldo Emerson came out publicly for sparing the murderer's life.

A 7,200-word petition written by William J. Herbert from the Charlestown State Prison was published in the Boston *Journal* on June 24, 1859. An excerpt from this remarkable document follows:

> I do not believe that there was a thought of murder in the mind of any one that went into the cabin December 25, 1857. Hall (who was drunk) fired his gun . . . and the force of the explosion put out the lamp. This firing was quite unexpected by any of us and that, together with the lamp going out, threw us all into confusion, and rendered our plan useless.**

Two Boston papers, the *Journal* and the *Courier*, took opposite sides in the controversy. The *Journal* declared that "it seems impossible that any human being can be so cold-blooded and ghoul-like as to seek to make this man's peril

---

* A typical day's mail to Andrew's offices included 204 signatures from Danvers, and 611 from Worcester.

** The statement was witnessed by Gideon Haynes, Warden of Massachusetts State Prison, and two other officers of the institution.

greater than it is and his fate more horrible, but the Boston *Courier* seems to be thirsting for the blood of Cyrus Plumer and descends to the contemptible artifice of sneering at those acting in his behalf. . . .

"Let the *Courier* and its malignant hatred of whatever is generous and human pass. It is hoped that the President will grant Plumer a reprieve."

The *Courier* rebuttal was quick to come, emphasizing justice.

"That he ought to be hanged if ever a murderer ought to be hanged admits of no reasonable doubt. This opinion is not likely to be weakened by misrepresentations of editorials.

"The case of Plumer is that of a scoundrel who secretly crawled into the Captain's cabin and who, without warning or caring whether his victim was ready to meet his Creator, fired upon him and killed him . . . with language that could come only from the mouth of the most abandoned desperado. The murders of the Officers of the whaleship *Junior* were as atrocious as any we have ever heard of."

Down in New Bedford the general sentiment was in favor of the hanging of Cyrus Plumer. Few petitions were signed there for the saving of his life. Wives and mothers of men who sailed the high seas recognized the terrible acts that Plumer had perpetrated and felt that crimes of murder and mutiny should not go unpunished.

To do everything they could for the saving of Plumer's life, a delegation from Massachusetts visited Washington to impress the President with the importance of the case.*

Meanwhile, as the execution date of July 8 grew near, thousands of persons made plans to witness the hanging of the condemned man, but they were doomed to disappointment. President James Buchanan, who by this time had re-

---

* There were those who claimed that Cyrus Plumer was a cousin of the famous Senator Charles Sumner, who was caned in the Senate in 1856. Plumer seems to have had friends who helped him more than they would have if he had been a man without some connections.

ceived more than 21,000 signatures protesting the execution of Plumer, commuted the sentence on July 6 to life imprisonment. The commutation officially reached Boston just a few hours before the execution was scheduled to take place.

In explaining why he saved Plumer's life, the President stated that

> ...it does appear that Cyrus Plumer saved the life of the Chief Mate, Mr. Nelson . . . and it is doubtful if Plumer was more guilty of murder than the other mutineers sentenced to life imprisonment . . . and whereas ten members of the jury which tried the case have earnestly besought me to commute the sentence . . . therefore let it be known that I, James Buchanan, President of the United States . . . do commute the death sentence pronounced upon said Cyrus W. Plumer to imprisonment for life at hard labor in the State Prison of Massachusetts.
>
> [signed]   James Buchanan

The day after his commutation reached Boston, Plumer was baptized by the Rev. Dr. Lathrop. He was then given his cell in the State Prison, where he was expected to spend the remainder of his life.

The Civil War came. Benjamin F. Butler served as a general under the command of General Ulysses S. Grant, and later, when his superior officer became President of the United States, Butler decided that he could make a plea for pardoning Plumer.

And so it was that in the spring of 1874 papers were sent to Washington asking for the release from Charlestown State Prison of a man who had spent fifteen years behind the walls of that venerable correctional institution. Cyrus W. Plumer had aged considerably, and the Warden said that Plumer's health was very poor.

On July 24, 1874, fifteen years after the prisoner had been scheduled to hang, President Grant issued an unconditional pardon to Cyrus W. Plumer, and the next day he walked out of the Charlestown State Prison a free man.

XI

A Rhode Island Pirate, Hicks

In the year 1940 I followed an interesting clue concerning a pirate who at one time had lived in Quincy, Massachusetts. The trail led across to Jerimoth Hill in Rhode Island and finally back to Massachusetts, where I was later able to interview the pirate's great-grandson. William Johnson, alias Albert Hicks, was as famous a buccaneer in his generation as Blackbeard was in his.

For reasons which may become apparent as the story unfolds, I was sworn to secrecy after my interview, at which time I was given the pirate's signed confession. I promised that during the lifetime of my informant, who was even then approaching the Biblical three-score years and ten, I would not reveal his relationship to this unusual tale.

My source of information is now dead. For twenty years I have kept my word, and now there is no further need for secrecy. As I write these lines, I have at my side the confession of the pirate ancestor of my friend.

* * * * *

The sloop *E. A. Johnson* sailed from the foot of Spring Street, New York City, on Thursday, March 16, 1860, to obtain a cargo of oysters in Deep Creek, Virginia. On board were Captain George E. Burr, First Mate William Johnson, and two brothers, Oliver Watts and Smith Watts.

The sloop was put ashore near Tottenville, Staten Island, for carpenter work which was completed late Saturday afternoon. At high tide Sunday morning, after the vessel was floated and her sails hoisted, she proceeded out to sea. Reaching Gravesend Bay on Sunday afternoon, she remained there waiting for a fair wind until sunset Tuesday, when she set out again.

The next morning, while the schooner *Telegraph* of New London was sailing in the lower bay between Romer Shoal and the West Bank, her captain sighted the *Johnson* and hailed her. Obtaining no answer he came closer and was amazed to see no one on the deck. When he went aboard he found evidence of a collision, but all the crew had disappeared. The bowsprit had been carried away and was even then floating alongside, still attached to the hull by the stays.

The captain of the *Telegraph* reported the strange case to the captain of the steamer tug *Ceres,* and the latter went aboard the *Johnson.* He decided to put a tow line on the derelict and take her into port, and there the entire affair might have ended.*

However, when he went below for a careful check, he was shocked to find that the cabin bore signs of a terrible struggle, and there was evidence of a body's having been dragged out through the companionway. Blood remained on the rail and over the side, although it was apparent that an attempt had been made to wash it off. The floor of the cabin was still wet, and a pail of water stood near the bloodstains. Other evidence all pointed to the commission of a crime in the cabin.

Realizing that he might have a murder mystery on his hands, the captain of the *Ceres* brought the *Johnson* up to the slip at the foot of Fulton Market, and soon the entire

---

* Twenty-two years later a similar discovery was made at sea—the *Mary Celeste.* See my *Mysteries and Adventures Along the Atlantic Coast.*

waterfront was aroused by the story. During the day multi-
tudes visited the vessel. Eventually it was found that the craft
had been chartered by Daniel Simmons and Edward Barnes,
both of whom lived at Keyport. When reports of the sloop
and the possible murder appeared in the local press, it attracted the attention of Captain Nickerson of the schooner
J. R. Mather.

Captain Nickerson recalled that he had been sailing his
craft *Mather* from New York to Philadelphia and had collided after midnight on March 21 off Coney Island with the
sloop in question. The maneuvers which he was forced to
make on approaching the *Johnson* indicated that there was
no one at the wheel.

After the collision there had been no cry from the deck of
the *Johnson*. No attempt had been made to disengage the
sloop from the schooner, and in the darkness there was no
indication at the moment that any human even existed on
the sloop. Later, however, the schooner captain saw a dark
form aft and felt sure that some person was then on board.
This unknown man was subsequently observed to lower a
boat from the stern and leave the sloop. The yawl in which
he reached shore was found adrift the next day off Staten
Island. There were two oars, a right boot, a tiller, and part
of an old broom in the boat.

On further investigation George Nedlinger, the hostler
at Fort Richmond, located just to the south of the place
where the boat was found, said that around six o'clock on
the morning of the collision he had seen a man land from the
boat. He described him in such a manner that the authorities
agreed that it must have been First Mate William Johnson.

After inquiring in the vicinity, the policemen found that a
man answering Johnson's description had "made himself conspicuous at the Vanderbilt Landing, where he had indulged
freely in oysters, hot gins, and eggs," before crossing to New
York on the seven o'clock boat.

While the investigation was proceeding, the sloop, then lying at the Fulton Market slip, was visited by hundreds of people every day. Later in the week Mr. Selah Howell of Islip, Long Island, part owner of the *Johnson*, went aboard her. He told of eating supper in the cabin with Captain Burr and First Mate William Johnson on the evening before the vessel left the city. He stated definitely that he suspected Johnson of being the murderer.

Shortly after Howell made his accusation it was discovered that Johnson had gone aboard the Fall River steamer with a woman. The police trailed him to a house in Providence, Rhode Island, where they apprehended him. He was brought back to New York by Captain Smith and Officer Nevins of the New York police. Their statement follows:

"We arrived at Stonington on Thursday and made inquires for a sailor man, his wife and child. We heard of several women and children, but they did not answer the description. Mr. Howard, the Baggage Master, arrived on the Boston night train. He gave us information of a man, woman and child who stopped in Canton, Massachusetts. In Providence we called upon Mr. George Billings. We drove around the city to all sailor boardinghouses, but could not get a satisfactory clue. A deck hand on the Fall River boat remembered a sailor and a little sore-eyed woman and child who came up to him. They asked him if he knew any quiet boardinghouse in a retired part of the city where they could go for a few weeks. He referred the sailor to a hackman, who took him off to a distant part of the city. The hackman was soon found. It was then arranged by us that the hackman should go into the house and pretend that two of the three quarters which he had been given were counterfeit. He went there, but the man was not in."

Arrangements were then made for a descent upon the house at two o'clock on Saturday morning, at which time First Mate Johnson was captured.

"I searched him," said officer Nevins, "and found in his pocket the silver watch since indentified as Captain Burr's, also Burr's knife, pipe and two small canvas bags which were used by the Captain to carry his silver. In his pocketbook was $121.00. I didn't take his wife's baggage, and I felt so bad for her that I gave her $10 of the money. The poor woman. As it was, she cried bitterly, but if she had known what her husband was really charged with, it would have been awful. I told him to let me see his hands. He turned up his palms and said, 'Those are sailor's hands.' I said, 'Yes!' I told him I really did not want him for counterfeiting. He replied, 'I thought as much.' I told him what he was charged with and he cried out that he had never been on the sloop. I don't think his wife knew anything about it."

After the prisoner was brought back to New York, a man with whom he had lodged, John Burke, identified him at once as the person who, with his wife and child, had lived at 129 Cedar Street. Then Johnson was asked if he knew Captain Burr. He said he never had known him and had never sailed in the vessel which Captain Burr commanded.

Nevertheless, the net was rapidly closing on the man who called himself William Johnson. On the following Sunday afternoon Charles LaCoste identified Johnson as the person who had, on the preceding Wednesday at eight o'clock in the morning, purchased coffee and cakes from him. At the time Johnson had a ten-dollar gold piece to pay for the six cents worth of coffee and cakes which he ordered. Time and again Johnson was identified by various people who had helped him on the route from his Cedar Street home to the boat.

The first article to be shown at the police station was Captain Burr's watch, which the prisoner claimed he had had in his own possession for three years. Mr. Henry Seaman, an old friend of Captain Burr's, recognized the timepiece at once. Then Selah Howell identified the prisoner as the man who ate supper with Captain Burr and himself on the sloop the night before she sailed.

On Sunday morning Johnson's wife arrived in New York

from Providence. When taken down to the cell where her husband was locked up, she charged him at once with being a "bloody villain."

"Look at your offspring, you rascal. Think what you have brought on us. If I could get in at you, I would pull your heart out."

Johnson gazed calmly at her. His reply was a quiet one. "Why, my dear wife, I have done nothing. I'll be out in a day or two."

The trial of the First Mate, whose name was now announced officially as Albert W. Hicks, began on May 14, 1860. Mr. Dwight, Assistant United States District Attorney, made the opening statement for the Government:

"You are empannelled to try the issue between the United States and the prisoner at the bar, charged with robbery upon the high seas. Robbery committed upon the high seas or in any basin or bay within the admiralty maritime jurisdiction of the United States is defined by the Act of Congress passed in 1820 to be piracy, and punishable with death . . .

"The defendant, under the name of William Johnson, had shipped as First Mate on the sloop *E. A. Johnson*, owned at Islip, Long Island. . . . On the Monday following his being brought here Johnson was examined before a United States Magistrate, he was indicted, and is now brought before you for the offense of robbery on the high seas.

"It is a question of great interest which involves the performance of a terrible crime. He has been called upon to give an account of these men with whom he was and who are no doubt already dead; but he still disclaims any knowledge of them or of the vessel upon which they were.

"That, gentlemen, you will judge of in this trial. You will say whether he is guilty of the terrible crime. Whatever may be the result to him, and whatever the punishment, I have no doubt that your verdict will be in accordance with the law and the facts."

On the fifth day of the trial, Mr. Sayles, Jr., counsel for

the prisoner, cited Chitty's *Criminal Law,* which said that "the piracy must be distinctly proved to have been committed on the high seas, or the defendant is entitled to an acquittal," and asked the jury to "elevate your minds above outside prejudices. A supposed tragedy has been committed in the lower bay and the Government has undertaken to show by circumstantial evidence that this is the man who perpetrated it."

The trial went on to its conclusion and on the sixth day Judge Smalley charged the jury. He told them that without question the case was clearly within the jurisdiction of the Court, the occurrences have been taken place in the harbor.

The people in the closely packed courtroom watched the jury retire at 10:36 that morning. They were out seven minutes when they returned, at which time they announced that they had agreed upon a verdict. The prisoner was directed to stand up and he did so, exhibiting almost no emotion at all. In a voice scarcely audible to the listeners Foreman Bernard McElroy announced that the jury had found Hicks guilty of the crime.

Hicks meekly held his hands out for the handcuffs, and the leg irons were placed on him shortly afterward. Later a motion for a new trial was argued and denied. The sentence of death was passed upon pirate Hicks, and the date of his execution was set as Friday, July 13, to take place on Bedloe's Island.*

Although Albert W. Hicks had apparently evidenced very little interest in the trial, after his sentence he showed considerable anxiety and seemed to abandon the hope which had supported him.

When urged to make a free confession of his crime, he at first stoutly denied that he had anything to confess. Finally on June 13, 1860, just one month before his scheduled execution, he called for Lorenzo de Angelis, an official he had

---

* Where the Statue of Liberty stands today.

met at court. In the presence of another witness, Hicks made
the following statement:

"I have long believed that I am the Devil's own. He has
done very well for me for so many years. He has been by me
all my life at sea and on shore, in storms. Even on the battle-
field he has protected me from danger, but I now call on him
and he doesn't answer me. My past is a great horror, my
future one of dreadful fear. I have a heavy weight in my
heart and I feel that if I don't tell my secrets, I will go mad.

"I was born in 1820 in Foster, Rhode Island. My father
was a farmer and I was the next to the youngest of seven sons.
I worked on the farm until I was fifteen. I never hoarded
money but only used it to gratify my passions. I often
dreamed of the chests of gold and silver which were buried
by pirates and robbers in our neighborhood, but my father
compelled me to work. One night I left home, reached
Providence and then went to Norwich, Connecticut.

"I stole a package of goods at the Norwich depot, but
could not sell the laces and silks which I found inside, and
decided to return home with them. My parents were very
angry with me and I didn't let them know where I had been.
When a pedlar stopped at the house later I sold him the laces
and silks. One night I was arrested at my father's home for
having stolen the laces and silks. I was sentenced to eighteen
months imprisonment in Norwich jail."

Hicks escaped from jail after three months and went to
Plymouth, Quincy, Salem, and Gloucester, where he obtained
work. Six weeks later, however, he was recaptured, taken
back to Norwich and put to work in the prison with a ball
and chain fastened to his leg. One day he broke the chain
from his leg and ran off into the woods, later reaching Providence. A man on horseback recognized Hicks and tried to
capture him and take him back to jail. Although Hicks attempted to kill the man, he was overpowered by others and
brought back to Norwich, where he remained in close confinement for over a year. After his imprisonment ended he

obtained a position on the whaling ship *Phillip Tabb*. As soon as he was aboard he started a fight.

His statement continued: "I had no fear nor did I care for anybody or anything. When we reached Newport I incited a mutiny which resulted in a fight, and two men were set ashore in irons. The Captain again set sail and proceeded on the cruise. For a few weeks everything went on smoothly enough.

"I started another mutiny which resulted in two others being put in irons. When we arrived at Wahoe, Sandwich Islands, the mutineers were whipped with the 'cat' till they were nearly dead.

"While on shore I engaged in every kind of wickedness. Finally I was taken by the authorities and locked up until the vessel was ready to sail. One of the boatsteerers was then observed in conversation with me by the Captain, who abused the boatsteerer. From words they soon came to blows. The boatsteerer would have overpowered the Captain, but the First Mate interfered. Seizing a belaying pin, I felled the First Mate. Then a general fight followed. The boatsteerer and myself succeeded in giving the others a severe beating and had complete possession of the ship, for the rest of the crew were afraid of us.

"Two days afterward, on coming on deck, we found the ship was approaching land, so we released the officers who brought the ship to anchor in the harbor of Owahie, but none of the crew were allowed to go ashore. The Captain did nothing to punish us while in port.

"After a season on the whaling ground, we went to Typie Bay. The natives attacked us and a desperate fight took place. We killed a number of the natives and drove off the rest. The demon in me being fully aroused, I suggested to the boatsteerer, whose name was Tom Stone, that this would be a good time to kill the officers and take the ship, but when we got on board, we found the officers armed and ready for us.

"Another fight began and the officers were helped by the

crew, and we were put in double irons. The Captain ran the whaler into Wahoe and abandoned us ashore.

"Again Stone and I committed all the crimes possible. We were finally taken to the jail and were then put aboard the ship again. Again we deserted the ship and led the life of freebooters. We were captured and put in prison at Wahoe for the third time, but the Captain of a Dutch ship gave us berths on board.

"We sailed for the Bay of Magdalena, where I fought with the Mate and was put in irons. The Second Mate was from Boston, and he obtained for me the job of boatsteerer. One night near shore we took a boat from the davits and rowed across to land. The Captain came in and paid us off, whereupon we visited and boarded the bark *Fanny* of New Bedford.

"As the Mexican War then broke out, we went ashore for about a year in Lower California. A group of us formed an outlaw band, and we roamed all Lower California as guerrillas, pillaging and killing wherever we could. Finally we were suspected and when the United States storeship *Southhampton* came into the Bay of St. Joseph, we shipped on board of her and went to Monterey.

"It was now the time of the California Gold Rush, and we went ashore to join a group traveling to the digging. We became outlaws and were able to take many gold nuggets and much gold dust from those who were returning from the diggings. Finally we had as much gold as I could lift from the ground with one arm.

"Making our way to San Francisco, we changed the gold into coin. Six months later all our money was gone, so we shipped on board the bark *Josephine*, a Spanish vessel bound for Valparaiso. It had a vast treasure in gold dust and Mexican doubloons aboard. One night we armed ourselves, went into the cabin, gagged and bound the Captain and officers, put them in a boat with the crew, and made them push away, leaving us in possession of the ship."

Hicks and his associate sailed the vessel alone for some hours after which they set fire to the *Josephine*, scuttled her, and then with all the treasure in the jolly boat, they pulled away. Should any of the descendants of the crew on the bark *Josephine* read these words, they will learn for the first time the news of her real fate.

Favored by fine weather the two men arrived at Mazatlan, with no less than $100,000 in gold dust and doubloons. They purchased a hotel and a bowling alley and for the next eighteen months were devoted to these pursuits. Although the business flourished and they might have grown rich and lived well, the money slipped through their hands, and they soon were back in their old ways of robbing and murdering until finally they were captured.

Released from jail, the two men soon went aboard and took possession of another ship.

"We tied the crew up hand and foot, except for a boy I had protected, and one man. We took our possessions, put them in a boat, and landed upon the island of Barbados. Probably the Captain and his crew freed themselves eventually, but we never heard any more about it.

"A few days later we went aboard the English bark *Canova* bound for New Orleans. We landed at Belize with our possessions. We then shipped for Liverpool, but the ship was wrecked off Waterford and all our possessions went down with the ship. We went into Waterford penniless, but committed a robbery the result of which enabled us to reach Liverpool."

After several additional voyages, Hicks shipped on a bark bound for New York and sailed from New York on the schooner *Eliza* for Boston. His associate, Tom Stone, had died some time before, and Hicks met a man by the name of Lockwood, "whom I found to be in every respect worthy of filling the place made vacant by the death of Tom. I discovered he had led a life similar to mine, and he thought no more of stealing a purse or cutting a throat than I. In addition to his other qualifications, he was an expert navigator."

The two men made plans to take over the schooner while off Block Island. They did so the same night, killing all hands. Then, with the schooner's funds, the two men escaped in a boat.

Landing at Block Island, they explained that they had been shipwrecked, and after a long delay finally were able to ship on board a schooner for San Domingo. In the next few years Hicks and various associates time and again committed acts of piracy and violence which ended in death for others.

Finally their adventures brought them to Matagorda Bay, Texas, where they buried what treasures they had in the sand and went inland. Later, in the year 1856, they returned, dug up their gold and silver, and shipped on board a schooner bound for Boston.

Landing there, they carried out several robberies in Boston, Dorchester, Quincy, Weymouth, and Plymouth. A burglary on Washington Street, Boston, came very near trapping them, and the circumstances connected with it caused "considerable stir" at the time. The following week Hicks shipped on the slaver *Sea Horse*, bound for Africa.

"During the passage I succeeded in stirring the crew up to mutiny. After a severe fight, we succeeded in overcoming the officers and landed the vessel ashore at Congo River, took all the money aboard and joined an English vessel whose name, I believe, was the *Zacharias*. On board the *Zacharias* I started another mutiny. We fastened down the hatches with the Captain and the others asleep below, so that the officers could not make their escape, landed in the boat at Havre, France, and then took the night packet to London.

"The following year I married and came with my wife to New York on board the ship *Isaac Wright*. Captain Marshall of that craft knows me well. I went to work for a time until a longing for my old life of excitement came over me, and I returned to New York and took lodgings at 129 Cedar Street."

After many other adventures, during which time he kept

a sharp lookout for craft outward bound for cargoes of fruit, oysters and the like he came across the sloop *E. A. Johnson,* whose master was Captain Burr. The master hired Hicks at once as first mate.

"I wish to say at this time from my youth up I lived by crime. I have steeled my heart against every good impulse. I have considered mankind my natural prey, and have never hesitated to gratify my appetites, passions and desires. A dreadful punishment awaits me as a result, but let me go on to the end."

The sloop offered an easy prey. She had on board, the pirate had heard, something over $1,000, and the entire crew consisted of but two brothers besides himself.

"After engaging with Captain Burr, I went home to my wife at 129 Cedar Street. Lying down on the bed, I told her not to disturb me. She left me alone and I marked out in my mind the course I intended to pursue. Then I returned to the sloop.

"At last we put out to sea, and when we were off the Ocean House, I visited the forecastle, and got an axe, which I put in the boat hanging to the davit aft. I went to the younger Watts, at the helm, and asked him to allow me to steer a little while.

"In a few minutes I left the helm. Taking the axe, I went to him and asked if he saw Barnegat Light. He said he did not. I told him to look again, and pointed with my hand.

"He turned around and looked in my face a moment, but even if he had suspected my cruel purpose, he would have read no indication there, for I was calm.

"I pointed again. 'Look there, ain't that it?' He turned his head, and peered through the darkness in the direction I pointed. As he did so I struck him on the back of the head with the axe and knocked him down.

"The noise attracted the attention of the Captain, who soon came running up the companionway, and asked me what was the matter.

" 'Nothing,' I replied, and also asked Captain Burr if the light which I saw was Barnegat.

" 'No,' replied the Captain, 'for you should not see it for two hours.' As he spoke his head turned from me. The axe swung in the air, and killed him instantly, with the body falling down into the companionway.

"As I turned, he whom I thought I had already killed had risen and was coming aft, his arms outstretched. I struck thrice with the axe and finished him.

"Running aft, I jumped down the companionway with the axe in my hand. I stood a moment looking at the elder Watts in his berth, and dashed at him and struck out with the axe. He tried to grapple with me, but stepping back, I gave the fatal axe a full swing, and struck him again until he lay dead at my feet.

"Dead men tell no tales. I was alone. I was free to reap the reward of my work.

"I took a rope and hauled the three men to the side and got them overboard. I then threw the axe overboard as well.

"My intention was to run the sloop up the North River and fire her, but I fouled a schooner and carried away the bowsprit, so I put the money and such other articles as I could pick up into the yawl, and then sculled ashore three miles, landing just below the fort on Staten Island. My movements after landing are well known.

"My task is done. I have related all the awful details of my life with as much minuteness as I can, and now nothing is left me but to prepare to die."

* * * * *

The date for the execution was Friday, July 13, 1860. The gallows was set up on Bedloe's Island, so the greatest number of people would have an opportunity of watching the event, which was to take place on the northeast side of the island, on a green, sloping terrace, forming the earthwork of the water battery that surrounded about two-thirds of the island. The spot was about a hundred yards northwest of the boat landing and about seven feet above high-tide water.*

The *Red Jacket* had been chartered for the occasion to take the official party to the execution. When the prisoner was removed from the jail and reached the *Red Jacket*, the boat was already crowded with 1,500 persons. Gamblers, prize fighters, ward politicians, reformed drunkards and others who were not so reformed, actors, doctors, medical men, city officials, and innumerable reporters formed the great bulk of the gathering. A barroom and refreshment saloon on the lower deck did a brisk business.

It was exactly 9:30 when the cry went up, "Here he comes!" and the carriage with the United States marshal and Hicks was seen making its way out on the pier. First sighted was Deputy Marshal O'Keefe, wearing his official sword in his belt. He had on a cocked hat and other paraphernalia of the office. A moment later Marshal Rynders stepped out of the carriage, followed by Hicks, Deputy Marshal Thompson and Sheriff Kelly. The condemned man wore a white shirt, blue pants, light pumps and a Kossuth hat.

The crowd pressed to get near the prisoner, but with considerable effort the marshal and his assistants preserved order. Father Duranquet, Hicks's chaplain, was at the pirate's side all the while, and when they entered the cabin, the priest offered a prayer. Hicks requested that he be allowed a period of time alone with the priest, and for the next ten minutes they were together.

On leaving the pier the *Red Jacket* proceeded up the river, passing the revenue cutter *Harriet Lane*. Marshal Rynders now asked Hicks if he would mind postponing the execution for two hours so that the crowd aboard could sail over to see the *Great Eastern*, then in New York. Hicks answered that the marshal could arrange for as many postponements as he

---

* The scaffold consisted of two upright posts, braced and framed at the bottom, and surmounted by a crossbeam at top. Wife-murderer Coleman, and James Stephens and John Crimmings had been hanged there.

wished. Finally, after a trip up the river, and an inspection of the *Great Eastern,* the *Red Jacket* sailed back to Bedloe's Island.

As the boat neared the pier at Bedloe's Island, Marshal Rynders told the gathering that he must have perfect co-operation. Every one was to form in procession and go ashore as he indicated. Finally, at 11:10 the parade started from the boat in the following order:

Pirate Hicks had Father Duranquet on his left and Deputy Sheriff Isaacs on the right. Next came Marshal Rynders and eleven deputies and sheriffs, followed by the doctors, after whom marched the representatives of the press, fifty in number, "genuine and bogus." After them came deputy sheriffs, city officials, and then the vast horde of spectators. The police of New York completed the procession, and each group was given a place to watch the hanging.

By this time steamboats, barges, barks, oyster sloops, yachts, ships, barkentines, and even rowboats were gathered in the water before the gallows. They had come from all parts of the New England and Mid-Atlantic states. From Connecticut several craft had arrived to represent the murdered captain and the Watts brothers. From Long Island came those who had built the sloop and their friends.

Most conspicuous of all, however, was the sloop *E. A. Johnson* on which the murders had been committed. Newly painted, she stood well in toward shore, her stern less than three hundred feet from the gallows. A huge burgee flew from her topmast head on which her name was painted in large red letters. Her deck was crowded and her masts and spars were alive with human beings.

In all, there were 11,000 persons, dressed in gay holiday attire to watch the event from aboard the many craft which were decorated with lively colored flags. As the vessels maneuvered for favorable positions, the uproar was tremendous, and cries of, "Down in front," "Get out of the way," rose from hundreds of throats at once. Finally so close together did the boats get that it was almost impossible to see the water between them. The effect was that of a giant raft crowded with men.

Back at the gallows, Hicks was told that his final moment was at hand. After kneeling on the grass to pray, the prisoner then rose slowly to face the vast fleet anchored within a few feet of the shore. His eye caught the burgee of the oyster sloop *E. A. Johnson*, but he remained firm and indifferent to the very last.

Then the fatal moment arrived. Placing the rope around Hicks's neck, the executioner drew a black cap over his face. The handkerchief was waved. A moment later the axe cut through the retaining rope, and Hicks met his death. It was the last pirate hanging in New York history and perhaps the last in the United States.

The words of an unknown poet shall end this story:

> And now, an outcast's death I die,
>   My hands with gore imbued;
> The Christian's grave were mine, had I
>   The Tempter's snare withstood,
> Nor shed a brother's blood for gold,
>   To forfeit gold for blood!

XII

Death of a Portland Slaver

In my book *Piracy, Mutiny and Murder*, I told of the famous ship *Wanderer* which sailed the high seas in the period just prior to the Civil War as a slaver. Since the book appeared, I have had many requests from readers asking if any slaver, after he had been caught, was ever hanged for the crime of slavery.

This chapter tells the sad story of slaver Captain Nathaniel Gordon of Portland, Maine, who, at the time of his execution, had a mother who was still living in the city of Portland and was a prominent member of the local Presbyterian Church. Captain Gordon is the only American citizen ever hanged for the crime of slavery.

Since the abolition of the foreign slave trade in the year 1808, the bringing in of African Negroes to the United States for sale constituted piracy. Between 1808 and 1860 more than 1,200,000 slaves had reached America from Africa, and by the summer of 1860 it was estimated that as many as forty slaving craft a year were fitted out in New York, Boston, Bristol, Rhode Island, and Portland, Maine.*

---

* A famous slave ship was the clipper *Nightingale*, built at Portsmouth, New Hampshire. Suspected of being a slaver, on January 22, 1861, she was boarded off the Congo by the *H.B.M. Archer* and the *U.S.S. Mistake*, but

Nathaniel Gordon was a man of slender build, about five feet six inches in height, with a dark complexion, black whiskers and penetrating eyes. At the time of his death he was about thirty-six years of age. From his youth he had been a sailor in various capacities. Beginning as a cabin boy, he worked himself up to the position of command. If he had pursued an honest cause, he might have become wealthy and respected, for he had the energy and the ability that would have achieved success.

In all, he made four voyages to the coast of Africa for Negroes to be sold as slaves. Two of these voyages were successful, the human cargo having been landed on the island of Cuba. A third voyage was only partially successful, for it was necessary to unload the Negroes at a Brazilian port to avoid capture.

Captain Gordon sailed from Havana in the summer of 1860 on his fourth voyage as a slaver in the ship *Erie*. After he had been out about a month the crew became suspicious. Coming aft, they demanded to know where the vessel was going. Gordon explained that as the *Erie* was bound on a legal voyage and he was her captain, they had no business to ask such a question. There the matter rested until the *Erie* reached the Congo River. Anchoring forty-five miles upstream, they disposed of a large quantity of whisky on shore, and took on board more than nine hundred Negroes. Captain Gordon told the crew they would receive one dollar per head for each Negro landed in Cuba, and if they were not satisfied he could get plenty of men on shore. There was no further argument.

On proceeding to sea, they were overhauled the next day

---

allowed to proceed. She was again stopped April 23, 1861, off Kabenda on the west coast of Africa and found to have on board 950 Negroes. Taken into Monrovia, 272 men, 97 women, 340 boys, and 92 girls were put ashore. The others had died on the passage from Kabenda.

Captain Francis Bowen and his officers in charge had escaped from the vessel the night before her sailing from Kabenda, otherwise Bowen might have gone on trial and shared the distinction of the Portland captain.

by the *U.S.S. Mohican*, of the African squadron. When the
Erie was boarded, the United States officers found a cargo
of 967 slaves, consisting of men, women and children.

Immediately after her capture a prize crew was put on
board the *Erie*, and the ship was headed for Monrovia. On
the passage no less than three hundred of the Negroes died
and were buried at sea. Arriving at Monrovia the slaves
were handed over to the agent of the United States government at that point, and set free under the "civilizing
influences and institutions of the Liberian Republic."

The crew of the *Erie* was taken on board the *Mohican*
to fill the places of some of the United States sailors who had
been transferred to the prize ship *Erie*. Captain Gordon
and his two mates were sent on to New York aboard the
Erie after landing the Negroes.

About the time of the arrival of the *Erie* at New York
with the prisoners a rebellion broke out but was put down.
The prize master from the *Mohican* turned out to be a
secessionist, and in order to identify himself more fully with
the cause of the Confederacy, he set out for the South, leaving no Government witness to testify against Gordon.

The United States marshal, preparatory to the trial of the
captain, struck a panel of jurors from Columbia County.
Unwisely Gordon objected on the ground that the clerk of
the United States Circuit Court had not served the marshal
with a certified copy of the indictment, in accordance with
the statute, and the court sustained the objection. Had
Gordon submitted himself to a trial at that time, his acquittal
would have been certain, as the government had not the
evidence to convict him. Thus Gordon's objection eventually
cost him his life.

The trial was postponed, and when Gordon again came
into court a new list had been empaneled for jury service.
This group was nearly exhausted by peremptory challenges,
together with a number for cause, but finally a panel was
completed which lasted the course of the trial.

The prosecution was now faced with locating the old crew of the *Erie*. Previous to the first trial, however, the ships of the African squadron had been ordered home by the Secretary of the Navy, and the marshal found some of the slaver's old crew in New York, Philadelphia, Boston, and Portsmouth, New Hampshire.

On board the *Michigan*, at Boston, four sailors were found who had belonged to the crew of the *Erie* at the time of her capture, and they were brought to New York as witnesses. It was on their testimony that Gordon was finally convicted.*

The trial was not sensational in any way, and Captain Gordon was found guilty. After sentencing the slaver to die by hanging, Judge Shipman spoke to him at some length, uttering his words slowly and carefully:

"Let your repentance be as humble and thorough as your crime was great. Do not attempt to hide its enormity from yourself; think of the cruelty and wickedness of seizing nearly a thousand fellow-beings who never did you harm, and thrusting them beneath the decks of a small ship, beneath a burning tropical sun, to die of disease or suffocation, or be transported to distant lands, and be consigned, they and their posterity, to a fate far more cruel than death.

"Think of the sufferings of the unhappy beings whom you crowded on the *Erie;* of their helpless agony and terror as you took them from their native land; and especially think of those who perished under the weight of their miseries on the passage from the place of your capture to Monrovia! Remember that you showed mercy to none, carrying off, as you did, not only those of your own sex, but women and helpless children.

"Do not flatter yourself that because they belonged to a different race from yourself your guilt is therefore lessened

---

* When first arrested, Gordon had been lodged in the Eldridge Street jail, and he had about $5,000 with him. On one occasion he paid the sum of $50 for the privilege of a parole to enable him to live with his family in Brooklyn for a few days.

—rather fear that it is increased. In the just and generous heart, the humble and the weak inspire compassion, and call for pity and forbearance. As you are soon to pass into the presence of that God of the black man as well as the white man, who is no respecter of persons, do not indulge for a moment the thought that he hears with indifference the cry of the humblest of his children. Do not imagine that because others shared in the guilt of this enterprise, yours is thereby diminished; but remember the awful admonition of your Bible, 'Though hand join in hand, the wicked shall not go unpunished.' "

Gordon appealed to President Abraham Lincoln, who granted him a respite of two weeks from the execution of the sentence. It was made clear, however, that there was no hope of receiving further clemency. The stay was granted merely for the purpose of allowing the prisoner an opportunity to prepare for death.

A number of people protested the severity of the sentence, including one who wrote to the marshal as follows:

> New York, February 19, 1862
> Sir: If you have any regard for yourself, your family or your reputation, you will not hang that man Gordon, for it will be nothing short of murder, and the stigma of it will stick while you live. Resign sooner, by all means, a thousand times over. Do not commit murder. Cut your right arm off first.
> Yours respectfully,
> [signed]   Wm. Noble.

Gordon was almost constantly attended during his imprisonment by his wife and child. Mrs. Gordon was permitted to remain with him whenever she chose and her attendance was unremitting. A native of Nova Scotia, she was about twenty-five years of age, slight but well built, and of considerable beauty. During most of the period of her husband's confinement, she resided in Brooklyn with the family of a sea captain, who was interested in Gordon's welfare. She visited Washington on several occasions in her husband's behalf, and was entirely dependent on charity for her needs and the expense of seeking a commutation of the death penalty for him. Accompanied by the child, a fine boy of five or six years, she nobly devoted every hour at her command to Gordon's comfort and consolation. It is evident that they were much attached to each other. At their final parting, Gordon managed to maintain his self-possession, but his wife's grief was most acute.

After bidding her farewell, the captain was transferred to another cell, and his clothing was thoroughly searched to prevent the possibility of any suicide attempt. He partook of some refreshments and lighted a cigar. Then, calling for pen and ink, he sat down to write letters.

About four o'clock in the morning the prisoner was discovered in convulsions and a physician was sent for, who pronounced him suffering from the effects of a dose of poison. Gordon afterward admitted that he had taken some poisonous powder which had been furnished him and which he had concealed in a crack under his bench. The convulsions continued until about ten o'clock Friday morning, when the effects of the poison seemed to subside, and the prisoner rallied noticeably. Shortly before eleven o'clock he requested that a lock of his hair and a ring should be carried to his wife.

At eleven o'clock a dispatch was received from Judge Beebe, who had gone to Albany to see Governor Morgan. The judge announced that after his interview the Governor had sent a telegram to President Lincoln requesting a further respite for the prisoner. Great political pressure was brought to bear on the President to commute this sentence. He had already once granted the slaver a stay, and the latter's friends were confident that Gordon would not die on the gallows. Nevertheless, Abraham Lincoln remained firm, and the plans for the execution continued.

We quote from an eye-witness report of the hanging, as

published in the Portland *Daily Advertiser* of February 24, 1862:

"The traffic in mankind has received, today, a literal death blow. Between meridian and one o'clock, Captain Nathaniel Gordon suffered the extreme penalty of the law for being engaged in slave trade. . . .

"The execution took place in the yard of the city prison— generally known as the 'Toombs,' a dismal, stolid looking building, popularly supposed to be of the Egyptian style of architecture. Before eleven o'clock no inconsiderable crowd of men, women and children had gathered in the street, and were kept back from the entrance by the police. You entered between bayonets carried by United States Marines who guarded the door. In the office rooms perhaps the most noticeable man was United States Marshal Murray, dressed in a new suit of blue with two rows of brass buttons in front, bearing the United States coat of arms, and upon his left breast was a golden shield, with the words "U.S. Marshal" upon it. A cocked hat and sword completed his uniform. . . .

"All visitors present were appointed deputy marshals, and it was only upon showing a document certifying to that effect, that entrance could be obtained through the inner gate to the prison yard. This is a space in the middle of the prison, say about 45 feet wide by 75 feet in length. It is entirely enclosed by the prison walls, and from no roof or other place outside is it possible to obtain sight or sound of what occurs in the enclosure. One-third of the space was cut off by a picket fence. This was occupied by general spectators. The rest of the space was covered with planks. The gallows con- sisted of two upright beams securely fastened with a beam running across them upon the top.

"A rope swings midway between the perpendicular posts, and runs over upon pullies on the transverse beam, and descends into the executioner's box, where is situated a heavy weight, which the cutting of a rope frees so that it comes

down and jerks the doomed man several feet up in the air.
A gibbet is a bare and horrid sight. . . .

"It was about noon when the officiating minister, the Rev.
Mr. Camp, informed me that he had prayed with Gordon, but
had not conversed with him. The prisoner, indeed, had been
unable to speak for some hours, and had written on slips of
paper whatever he desired to communicate. Just after it was
discovered that he had taken poison, he exclaimed, gnashing
his teeth, 'I have cheated you! I have cheated you!' Mr.
Camp says he has all along expected that his sentence would
be commuted. His wife, no longer ago than yesterday morning, through a mistaken kindness, told him that the President
had not decided upon his case. Mr. Camp said he had never
talked with Gordon on the subject of the slave trade, as he
would have taken fire at that. At first Gordon said that his
conscience was entirely at ease, and that he was prepared to
die at any time. It was yesterday for the first time that he
thought God had forsaken him.

"Soon after twelve, Gordon was brought out from his cell
and placed in a chair, when the death warrant and the President's reprieve from the 7th to the 21st of February were
read to him. I had now a chance to observe what manner of
man he was. His frame was small, but sinewy. The pallor
of his countenance, contrasting with the black cap, was almost ghastly, and he was much emaciated from over a year's
confinement in prison. I think I speak without prejudice
when I say that his features were repulsive. . . . After the
Marshal had finished reading the documents, the prisoner still
in the chair, in a low and confused voice said:

" 'My conscience is clear. I have no fault to find with the
treatment I have received from the Marshal and his deputy,
Mr. Thompson; but any public man who will get up in open
Court and say to the Jury, "If you convict the prisoner, I
will be the first man to sign a petition for his pardon," and
will then go to the Executive to prevent his commuting the
sentence, I say that man is a man who will do anything to

promote his own ends—I do not care what people say.'

"It is needless to say that the prisoner had no grounds for this allusion to District Attorney Delafield Smith. Gordon was then led out to the gallows, the rope adjusted, the black cap drawn over his face, and he was launched off into eternity. The weight jerked the victim about four feet in the air, and he died with scarcely a struggle or contortion. His arms and legs hung listlessly, and only once, after the body had been swinging two or three minutes, the feet came slowly together and then separated to their natural position.

"It was a most ignominious end to a most infamous career. Life was extinct in several minutes. The execution was the only tenable conviction for this capital offence under the laws relating to the slave trade which has been achieved."

It was said that Gordon was at one time the possessor of over $100,000, which sum he had accumulated in the slave trade, but the expenses of his trial swallowed up all his fortune.

Thus did one wretched outrager of humanity pay for centuries of misery and suffering, as the only American slaver ever executed for his crimes.

XIII

The *Enigma*

Ninety-five years ago young Gillmore Marr of Bath, Maine, fulfilled his wish to go on a long ocean voyage, and became involved in one of the most fantastic sea stories of all time.

The *Enigma*, on which Marr set sail, was a schooner of one hundred tons, built by F. O. Moses, Esq., of Bath, Maine, and owned jointly by him and J. T. Morse, of Phippsburg, master mariner. Built to sail in relatively shallow water, the *Enigma* had a flat bottom, and had to be changed to maneuver in deep water by the addition of a very substantial centerboard.

The fateful voyage began on October 2, 1865, when the *Enigma* left the piers of Bath, heavily loaded with lumber and potatoes. J. T. Morse was sailing as master and part owner. The crew consisted of Cyrus Morse, Gillmore Marr, Joseph Anderson and Henry W. Small. Although rough weather was encountered, she reached Charleston, South Carolina, in the good time of eleven days. Late on October 17 her Charleston part of the cargo had been discharged and she sailed the following day for Mobile. All went well until the twenty-second, when a sudden terrific gale hit the area and soon became a hurricane.

In spite of the howling wind, high seas and breaking waves, the *Enigma* was weathering the storm, and everyone aboard felt that she would ride it out without trouble. At the height of the storm the captain sighted land, which he soon recognized as the Abaco Islands in the Bahamas. The *Enigma* was kept on course with a meager amount of sail, and drove ahead hour after hour through the gale.

All that day, the storm continued, and by nightfall they were still afloat. As darkness fell Captain Morse believed that the worst was over—when it is probable, in fact, that they were unknowingly approaching the center of the hurricane.

At ten o'clock all the crew retired below except for Gillmore Marr and Joseph Anderson who were on watch. As Captain Morse went down into the cabin he expressed a hope that the weather would be better when they awakened. An hour later, Anderson went below for a drink of water. As he stood in the galley, the captain called across from his bunk, "How are things going?"

"About as well as can be expected," came the answer.

Taking a piece of bread, Anderson sat down on the companion hatchway and munched away as though there were nothing to worry about. Captain Morse, now quite sure the storm had ended, offered up a prayer of thanksgiving to God for their preservation. Then he spoke to Anderson. "Keep a sharp lookout, and the other boys will be ready after another hour's sleep."

Leaning over to pat the captain's dog, Anderson then prepared to go up on deck and started for the companion hatchway. Suddenly the schooner was seized by an apparently irresistible force. The men never knew what it was, for the only one who could possibly tell what happened was Gillmore Marr, and they never saw him again.

In a split second the schooner was turned completely over. The captain, Cyrus Morse and Henry Small were thrown from their bunks almost naked, for they had taken off their wet clothes on retiring. Rushing for the companionway, they attempted to force it open, but the pressure of the water was too great, and it could not be moved. As the minutes went by, the schooner failed to right herself and the captain realized the seriousness of their predicament.

Slowly, the water began to rise in the capsized cabin. Within a short time it was two feet deep. Terrified and in utter darkness, the men wondered if they would ever see the light of day again. Then they began to think about young Marr topside and they decided that if he were still alive, he was the only one who had a chance of escaping. He could be aboard the load of lumber, if it had drifted off the schooner, but of course they had no way of knowing.

The air space in the cabin slowly grew smaller as the water crept higher and higher, and the men clung desperately to whatever they could get a grip on. Now the water began to slosh over them with every great billow which ripped through the capsized schooner. Finally the force of a wave changed the angle of the cabin so that it was necessary to clamber to the surface to get a breath of air as the craft rocked back and forth. One minute they were in water over their heads and the next moment they would be less than waist deep in salty brine.

As time passed in the darkness of the overturned wreck, the men realized the water was still slowly gaining inch by inch. Then, in the final moments of despair, Captain Morse remembered the hatchet which was always kept in the cabin. If he could only find it, perhaps he could cut a hole through the hull and escape, for he realized that otherwise it would soon be too late.

Filling his lungs with air, he dove down into a corner of the cabin and after fumbling against the bulkhead for several minutes, coming up for air three times, his hand closed over the handle of the hatchet. Returning to the surface he exhibited his find to the others, who by this time had given up hope of surviving the ordeal.

Estimating exactly where he should start cutting a hole through the partition, Morse told his men to watch out and then he started hacking away. Suddenly there was a cry of pain.

"You've hit me!" shouted Henry Small. "It's bleeding badly."

Five minutes later the wound, which was on his left hand, had been bandaged, and Small stood out of the way awaiting whatever might be ahead.

The other men took their turns with the captain in the attempt to hack a passage through into the hold. Several hundred blows later the axe went right through the cabin bulkhead, and half an hour afterward the opening was large enough for the men to clamber through. Luckily the potatoes which had filled that section of the hold had been taken ashore at Charleston, and there was substantial room to move about.

By now, the men were numbed with cold and half drowned. They crawled slowly across to where the lumber was stored and actually fell asleep on the loose planking. Still prisoners, at least now they would be able to get some rest as they awaited their fate. Later they estimated they must have fallen asleep about three o'clock in the morning. They slumbered until they were awakened by the light of dawn, when some action of the waves around the *Enigma* brought her partially back on her side. For an instant all thought she would right herself again, but in this they were mistaken.

It was lucky she did not turn upright, for the men would have been crushed to death by the lumber. Actually what did happen was that the deck load of lumber slid away from her at that moment and the masts went by the board. When one of the hatches broke off underwater, the reflected light of the sun penetrated into the hold's gloom, dazzling the four survivors with the sudden brightness.

For the first time since the capsizing the men were able to

see each other. The others noticed that the captain was bare-
footed, with only his trousers on, and was bleeding from a
score of cuts and bruises. Small's cut also still bled from
time to time.

The water started to gain rapidly once more, and the men
began to fear that they were sinking again. After several
moments of anxiety, however, the rush of water diminished
to a trickle. Evidently there was still enough lumber to keep
the hulk afloat.

By the position of the schooner, Captain Morse figured
that a part of the hull must be above the surface. They considered attempting to swim out under water through the
broken hatchway and then clamber up on the bottom, but
not one of them had the energy to try it. Furthermore, they
reasoned, there was no assurance that whoever attempted
the swim would be able to hold his breath for the necessary
period of time.

Morse decided that if he used the hatchet again in an effort
to cut through the bottom, they might reach a position on
the hull from where they could signal for help. Trapped
in the hold, they would never be able to attract attention.

It was now the morning of Tuesday, October 24, 1865,
and they set to work again with the axe. The inside hull
planks were of hardwood three inches thick, and the outside
bottom planking measured four inches. The men realized
they now had a much more difficult task than they had had
cleaving through the first opening. Their swinging position
was awkward, for they had to strike almost directly overhead. Nevertheless, Cyrus Morse, the Captain, and Anderson worked hard, but the injured Small could give no help.

All that afternoon and all night long they took turns with
the hatchet. By Wednesday they could see the light coming
through the thinnest part of the timbers. With a hatchet
now so blunt that it would not cut, they had to chip the
fragments away rather than chop through them. Hour after
hour went by in this fashion.

Finally the captain thought that he could see the suggestion of daylight above him. He then broke off a piece of timber, the size of a silver dollar. All at once, with a fearful whistling sound, the compressed air caught in the cabin began to escape through the tiny aperture. At the same moment, the men could feel the water climb as the schooner started to settle. For a brief interval the men panicked and the captain knew that he would have to act fast. He tore off his trousers and forced them into the hole, thus preventing the air's escape. The whistling noise stopped, and the hull did not sink any further.

A council of war was then held. It was decided that they would not attempt another breakthrough until there was a chance of smashing out a section large enough for them all to scramble through at once and escape. Two hours later they believed that they were ready. By that time they had cut out an area twelve inches by twenty inches, in every part of which light could be seen on the other side of the thin panel.

A battering ram was then constructed, made of several pieces of lumber tied together with a coil of rope. Acting on a given signal, they all smashed it against the section. The panel gave away at once, and the captain, directly below the aperture, was lifted off his feet by the suction which developed, and found himself being pulled right up through the hole, and out on to the bottom, where he landed with a thump! A moment later the air had all escaped.

Morse helped the others out of the hold, one by one. Each man as he emerged from the relative darkness, eagerly scanned the sea around him, but there was no sail in sight. Furthermore, there was no sign of Gillmore Marr. The schooner herself began to settle and submerged two feet. They would have drowned if they had not broken through the bottom all at once and escaped.

It was now Thursday, October 25, and they had been sixty-four hours without food or water. The captain's dog, with them all this time, was now suggested by Anderson as possible food, but the others disagreed. Although they were greatly exhausted the fresh air revived them, and they continued to search the horizon for the sight of a ship but none appeared.

With night coming, Captain Morse ordered preparations for a scaffolding of some sort to be erected as a partial shelter. Several scantlings were secured and driven into the centerboard aperture. A crossbar was then constructed some four feet above the deck, with another raised about three feet higher.

Terribly thirsty, the men realized that they would soon die unless they had something to drink. The thought of killing the dog was again reluctantly considered, and finally the captain gave his consent. Anderson plunged his sheath knife into the animal and they all drank the blood. Anderson, who consumed more than the others, soon went out of his mind and had to be lashed to the lower crossbar.

That evening the others slept by fastening themselves to the scantlings with lines so that they would not fall overboard. The next day the sailors built a platform two feet wide above the reach of the sea, on which each man could take turns sleeping, and they could stand to signal should another sail appear.

By Friday the dog's blood was all gone, but on Saturday they captured a two-foot shark. A heavy rain set in Sunday night which gave them drinking water. The next day was hot, and by the following night the shark turned green and slimy, so they threw it away. A flying fish was caught the following afternoon. Six inches long, it proved a good meal.

On Monday they sighted a ship four miles away, but in spite of frantic waving and signaling they were not seen, and the vessel soon vanished over the horizon. By this time they were suffering terribly. Not only were their throats horribly swollen, but their tongues were black and protruding. Masses of sores covered their bodies.

The next day Anderson began to fail rapidly, and Captain Morse realized that the man could not live many more days. Not a sail was sighted, however, from Tuesday to Friday. On Friday night all thought Anderson would die, but Captain Morse did not abandon hope. As he lay down to rest that night, the captain felt that rescue must be close and he talked to the crew:

"There has been a providential hand in many things since we were overturned. I think that it means something more than we have yet experienced—our finding the hatchet; our getting out of the cabin just in time to escape death from the increasing water that flowed in upon us.

"Our good success in escaping from the hold where we could have lived but a little longer; the saving of that coil of rope; the very one of all we had on board which we would have chosen for our purpose; that rain also, and that fish—God has not given us all this success to forsake us now."

Yet Morse acknowledged his fears measured up to his hopes.

Early the next morning, Saturday, the men were overjoyed to see a sail coming toward them, and soon recognized the craft as a brig. When she changed her course, and headed directly for them, they realized they had been seen.

It was the British brig *Peerless* on a trip from Philadelphia to Matanzas. After some delay the vessel sent out a boat and took them off. Anderson, then unconscious, had to be carried, and the poor man died three hours later.

The captain was the last to leave his wreck. Taken aboard the brig, the sailors suffered from their long exposure. Their throats were now so swollen that they could hardly accept a drop of liquid. Their bodies looked like skeletons and their emaciated feet and limbs were in shocking condition.

Everything possible was done for them. First they were given warm arrowroot tea, a few drops at a time. Then the amount was increased, after which gruel was served.

It had been a miracle that they were alive at all, for while on the schooner from Monday to the following Saturday they had had only a small drink of water apiece and the fish fragments. Nevertheless, in spite of all their hardships, they slowly improved.

On reaching Cuba, the men were taken to the Matanzas Hospital where they made rapid progress and were discharged ten days later. Eventually obtaining passage to New England, they arrived home six weeks later. After a few weeks of recuperation, the captain was given a new bark, then owned by F. O. Moses, and was soon far out in the ocean on another voyage. Such is the way of the sea.

For years afterward, Henry Small worked in the shipyards at Bath. Stinson Lord, of East Weymouth, told me recently that he remembers the old man, who always held his hand in a peculiar way because of the hatchet cut. He said, "We always called him 'Pleasant William' because he was able to swear in such a pleasant, loud and clear voice that we could hear him half a mile away on a cold, frosty morning."

XIV

New Englanders in Peril

Late Monday night, February 2, 1880, more than one hundred and fifty New England mariners and almost forty New England-built vessels were unexpectedly caught at sea off the coast of northeastern United States when two storms came together with fearful intensity to create twelve hours of a hurricanelike gale which ended almost as suddenly as it had started. The severest tempest of the year on the Atlantic Coast, the disturbance was one of the outstanding storms of the decade.

Although the general area hit extended all the distance from Louisiana to Maine, the terrifying fury of the elements centered chiefly on the coast of New York and New Jersey. Details of the damage wrought indicate the strength of the gale.

Many of the summer buildings at Coney Island were smashed to pieces by the sea and wind, but the heaviest damage was seen around Long Branch, with every hotel there seriously injured. The roofs of the Mansion House and United States Hotel were carried away, and scores of windows at the Ocean House were staved in. The flooring of the pier was torn up and swept away by the sea, while the gale also wrenched off the roof and stanchions of the pavilion on the pier, a building 350 feet long. Most of the summer cottages and villas suffered damage. The telegraph wires were down in every direction, and between Jersey City and Long Branch all the meadow lands were inundated.

For twelve hours from midnight on, the storm continued its devastation. It began with snow and sleet and ended with heavy rain. The sea was the highest known for many years, dashing against the bluffs at Long Branch, and the wind at times reached the velocity of eighty-four miles an hour. It was a period of hardship and danger for the lifesaving crews on the Jersey coast, several of which rendered courageous service when five wrecks occurred within the range of four neighboring lifesaving situations.

The first unhappy casualty of the gale was the schooner *Kate Newman* which collided with the three-masted schooner *Stephen Harding* seven miles out to sea. The *Newman* sank out of sight in less than a minute, the only survivor being William Ray, who had leaped aboard the *Harding* at the moment of collision.

The *Harding* suffered the loss of her anchor and her starboard bow was staved in. Aboard her was Captain Stephen Harding, whose wife was with him on this trip, and a crew of five. A vivid picture of the collision was later given by the captain.

"We sighted the schooner dead ahead," he said. "She came right out of the darkness and stood on top of a big wave, almost over our heads. The next instant we came together. A moment later we separated, and then she was gone in the sea, leaving one of her men on our deck."

The anchor which the collision had carried from the starboard bow of the *Stephen Harding* hung by fifteen or twenty fathoms of chain over her side, and could not be cleared, causing the ship to fall off from her true course and drag to leeward. Finally, at two o'clock in the morning she struck shore about a mile north of Spermaceti Cove Lifesaving Station, New Jersey.

By now a hard snow was added to the wind and sea. At this hour the patrol of the station changed, and Surfman Charles Rex started out to the north on his regular beat. He had gone nearly a mile when he saw a light ahead. Confused in the darkness by the wind and the whirling snow, the patrolman did not know just how far he had walked. At first he thought that the light he saw was the lantern of a patrol coming toward him from the station beyond. He hastened forward, and in a few minutes realized that it came from the cabin skylight of a schooner stranded in the surf about 250 yards from shore. Coming abreast of the vessel, he noticed the red light in her port rigging, and fired his Coston signal at once to let the sailors know their peril was seen.

Then, running down into the raging surf and spray as far as he dared, he shouted to them to stay aboard and await help. He dashed back the remaining distance to the station, and called to those inside to turn out. All the crew emerged with the exception of one man, away on the south patrol, and they started for the wreck with their apparatus.

Snowdrifts were more than knee-deep along the beach and hampered the progress of the cart. The wind, steadily increasing, blew snow and sand into the faces of the men as they tugged at their load. With the greatest difficulty they made their way, and by half past three were abreast of the wreck, where at once they began operations.

Despite the darkness and the interference of the elements, the first shot from the Lyle gun laid the line across the schooner, and those aboard seized it. The whipline was soon bent on and hauled aboard, followed by the hawser, but as there was no lantern on deck, the respective tallyboards with carefully printed instructions on how to set up the gears were not observed. By guesswork the sailors fastened the hawser to the mast below the hauling lines, whereas it should have been above.

The lifesaving crew then sent off the breeches buoy three times in succession, and each time it returned empty. Unable to see it when it reached the vessel's side, the surfmen only knew when it came back unoccupied that something was wrong.

Finally, on the fourth trip, it came ashore with one of the crew, a German sailor, who reported that the captain's wife was on board, and that the ship's people planned to remain on the vessel until daylight.

As the seas were breaking higher and higher, Surfman Wilson was sent off in the breeches buoy to tell them to get ashore as fast as possible. Going on board he found that the gear had been arranged incorrectly, and in about ten minutes rearranged the lines so that they were in good working order.

The schooner then began to thump on the bottom, and soon she was swept fore and aft in the rising tide. By daylight the spray was shooting forty feet into the rigging, and the decks were submerged in breakers. Wilson sent a sailor in on the breeches buoy with the message that the next passenger would be a woman. When the buoy returned he put Mrs. Harding into it, her legs dangling precariously as it left the schooner. After being partly submerged by a mighty billow halfway to shore, the frightened woman was landed safely on the beach, and one by one the men followed. Upon landing, each turned to, hauling with the lifesaving crew, to keep themselves warm.

After the last person was sent off, Wilson jumped into the breeches buoy and was drawn ashore. Now that everyone had been rescued, Patrolman Ferry, who had come from his beat and joined the crew during their operations, set out again on his south patrol, while Patrolman Rex resumed his march to the north. The rest of the crew were left to transport the gear back to the station. The keeper, fearing that the survivors might suffer from further exposure, started at once with them for the station a mile distant where they eventually recovered.

The captain of the vessel and his wife published the following letter in the local papers a few days after the wreck:

Feb. 16, 1880

We wish to make a little acknowledgement of the benefit we have derived from the service, and a word of praise, which we consider due the members of the service in general, and of Lifesaving Station No. 2 particularly, for the very brave and efficient manner in which they, in the storm of February 3, rendered such prompt and timely assistance to those on board the three-masted schooner *Stephen Harding* of Damariscotta, Maine, on shore on the beach near the station, where she now lies, whereby the lives of all on board were saved: and we wish to thank the members of the station, one and all, for the kind, gentlemanly manner in which we were treated by them, even to their great discomfort, as no provision is made at the stations in the way of beds or bedding for any more than the members. A much felt necessity is some female clothing, enough for a change while those they have on are drying or until more can be procured. We think Captain Edwards deserves praise for the neatness and efficient manner in which the duties of the station are performed.

Respectfully yours,
Captain and Mrs. Stephen Harding
Salem, Massachusetts

At the same time the *Stephen Harding* stranded, the brig *Castalia*, of Bath, Maine, also struck the beach about three quarters of a mile from Station No. 3, at Seabright, New Jersey. Bound from Galveston to New York with a cargo of cotton, the *Castalia* had a ship's company of eleven aboard, including one lady passenger, Mrs. W. C. Seymour, of Ohio. Half an hour after the ship hit, Patrolman Disbrow saw the dim gleam of her port light. Going down to the water's edge he was able to trace her outline as she lay nearly broadside on, about a hundred and fifty yards from shore.

After firing the usual Coston signal for the encouragement of those on board, he ran for the station and aroused the crew. A note was left for a man then absent on the south patrol, bidding him join his comrades at the wreck when he returned. The six others set out through the blinding snowstorm with the mortar cart. The drag over the sand and through the snowdrifts, in the face of the gale, was heartbreaking, but within an hour the snow-covered group reached the spot of light which identified the stranded vessel. Through his trumpet Keeper A. H. West shouted to the sailors to be ready for a line. He then lighted a white Coston flare, which disclosed the position of the vessel, lying about a quarter to head on, pointing northwest.

While one of the men held a rubber blanket to shield his face from the driven sleet and sand, Keeper West sighted the Lyle gun. His object was to shoot the line across the deck so that it would be taken by those on board. His first shot went through the rigging between the foreyard and forestay, leaving the line on the forecastle deck, where the sailors seized it. The whipline and hawser were then hauled out and made fast on the vessel, and the work of setting up on shore was begun by the lifesaving crew.

The lanterns were soon of little use, for the snow and sleet thickly coated them. Their light faintly glimmered in the darkness, but each man knew his work. In due time the whole tackle was adjusted and the breeches buoy began to run out on the taut hawser.

Two men were then brought ashore in rapid succession, one after the other. Then came the lady passenger, Mrs. Seymour. The vessel rolled so violently during each landing that it caused the hawser to slacken, and almost everyone was hauled through the surf part of the distance, and arrived soaking wet. The lifesavers waded into the breakers as far as possible, dragged the survivors out of the water and up on the beach.

These efforts resulted in the speedy landing of the eleven

persons on board, who then set out for the station. The vessel's captain was so exhausted that he had to be supported, and immediately upon his arrival he was put to bed. All hands were cared for at the station for two days; Mrs. Seymour was taken to the keeper's dwelling. The brig outrode the storm, being a staunch vessel, and was subsequently freed.

Mrs. Seymour, a few days after the wreck, published the following letter in the newspapers:

Being indebted for my preservation from what might have been a sure and sudden death, to the courage and daring of Captain West and his brave crew of Life-Saving Station No. 3, I take great pleasure in expressing to you that but for their prompt and energetic action we could not have been saved from our stranded vessel. The wind was blowing at a fearful rate of speed.

The sea was raging almost mountain high, sweeping over the vessel's decks, threatening to engulf her at every onslaught. The night was in inky darkness, and the snow was blinding. Our boats would have been crushed to atoms, even if we could have succeeded in launching them, which was utterly impossible. We were seen by the patrol as soon as we struck, and in an incredibly short space of time. In a scene like that, with death staring us in the face, the moments seemed like hours. The crew from Station No. 3, with the life-saving apparatus were soon on the beach. They were successful in throwing a line to the ship, which was immediately made fast by the eager and willing hands on board, and then commenced the noble work those brave men were there to perform.

I was placed in the breeches buoy, and drawn rapidly and safely over the boiling, seething surf, landing without injury on the land, and escaping with only a slight wetting. I was not allowed to stand in the cold for five minutes; but wrapped in an oilskin blanket, was taken immediately to the station, where every kindness and attention that was in their power to bestow was shown me.

I assure you I never performed a more pleasant duty than

speaking in the highest praise of the prompt and efficient aid
rendered us by the brave men of Life-Saving Station No. 3.

Respectfully,

Mrs. W. C. Seymour

At about five o'clock in the morning, Patrolman Daniel
Ferns, of Station No. 5, New Jersey, on the south end of
Long Branch, saw a vessel anchored about 2,500 yards to sea.
This proved to be the schooner *Light-Boat*, of Rockland,
Maine, bound from Norfolk to New York with a cargo of
corn. He watched her lights until dawn, when he was able
to see that she was dragging her anchors and drifting in a
southwesterly direction toward the beach. He ran to the
station, and notified Keeper W. S. Green, who at once went
out with two of his men.

The schooner, beaten by the northeast gale, continued to
drag anchor until about nine o'clock, when she struck a
shoal a mile north of the station and two hundred yards from
shore. Keeper Green had passed the word to his surfmen to
be ready for the stranding, and when their shouts were heard
at the station the mortar apparatus was ready to move.
Drawn by two stout horses, it rolled easily along the bluff,
actually arriving a few minutes before the vessel grounded.
The keeper noticed that every wave entirely engulfed her
hull and her crew of five could be seen where they had
lashed themselves to the rigging.

The Lyle gun was fired, and the line flew over the main-
topmast stays. It was retrieved by the sailors, who began to
haul it on board. Meanwhile, the tailblock and whipline
were bent on to the shotline, and soon got on board, where
they were made fast to the main mast about seven feet above
the deckhouse. Unfortunately, when the hawser followed,
the sailors neglected to read the instructions, which directed
that the hawser be detached from the whipline and made
fast above it. They simply fastened the hawser to the mast,

without unbending it from the whipline, and thus prevented
the lifesaving crew from running out the breeches buoy.

Not understanding the use of the whipline, the sailors
started to haul on one of its parts, and the lifesaving crew,
seeing what they were at, could only help them by connecting the breeches buoy with that part and slacking the line.
In this awkward manner they pulled out the rescue ring, into
which the cook climbed. By using the same part the surfmen
were able to haul him across to shore. In this way, the sailors
hauling out the buoy, and the lifesaving crew hauling it in
again, the five men were delivered from their perilous position in the rigging.

This unnecessary labor lasted about an hour, and was made
harder by the heavy rolling of the vessel, which compelled
the lifesavers to haul and slack on the line every time the
schooner rolled. Of course they found it impossible to prevent the breeches buoy, coming shoreward with its living
freight, from dipping into the sea and soaking the passengers.

It was afterward found that the ropes were almost chafed
through when the last man was brought ashore. The vessel
proved a total wreck, and her captain and crew testified
that but for the aid given them by the lifesaving station, they
would all have perished.

The *George Taulane*, of Camden, a schooner bound from
Virginia to New York with a cargo of cordwood and a crew
of seven men, had anchored the previous evening off the
Highlands of Navesink. When the snowstorm began, the
thick weather so shut in around her that it became dangerous
to attempt the planned run for Sandy Hook.

Accordingly the captain stood off shore, getting the vessel
into fifteen fathoms of water. The storm grew into a furious
gale, and the schooner soon began to labor heavily under a
two-reefed mainsail.

Then it was discovered that the craft was on fire, probably from the forecastle stove. The flames spread to her deck load and for a time it was feared she would have to be abandoned. With all hands working, however, the fire was extinguished, but the run of the vessel had been lost, and despite the steady effort to keep offshore, sufficient allowance had not been made for leeway. By eight o'clock the next morning the captain looked through the storm to see that he was just off shore. The deckload started to break away, and the perils of the men on board were increased by the shifting of the lumber.

Hoping still to save his craft, the captain let go both anchors when about a mile from land. This step proved disastrous and made the rescue of those on board immeasurably more difficult. The anchors at first clawed the bottom and brought the vessel's head to the wind. Immediately afterward the strong current setting to the southward, and the force of the storm, made them drag without holding. The vessel, broadside to the gale, swung helplessly in the trough of the tremendous sea. There she lay, rolling fearfully, with the water making clean breeches over her, staving and rending, and sweeping everything off her deck. There was no time for the men to slip the cables, for they had to scramble aloft for their lives.

In this plight the vessel slowly plowed through the breakers, going along with the current. The seas ran in torrents below the deck. Finally the men saw on the beach the lifesaving crew of Swan Point, New Jersey, located near the head of Barnegat Bay. The lifesavers were following them along the shore with lines and heaving sticks in their hands.

The captain afterward said that the very sight of this determined crew gave new life to his discouraged men. The surfmen had seen the vessel nearing the beach, and when she had dropped her anchors and begun to drag along the coast, they followed her, joined by a few fishermen who were on the beach at the time.*

They knew that no boat could get off the beach in such a sea, and they took only the heaving sticks and lines, because they wisely calculated on the vessel grounding near Green Island. The patrolman at the Green Island Lifesaving Station had seen the vessel somewhat over a mile north of that station when she had dropped her anchors. Hurrying back, he had notified the keeper, Captain William P. Chadwick, who at once ordered out the mortar cart with the apparatus and, with his crew, started for the wreck. In addition to the great surf, the tide was unusually full, being four feet higher than at ordinary high tides, and the only road to the wreck was across the rough hummocks of sand, which in many places had been covered by the battering sea. Dangerous sluices had formed in which the water rushed up each minute under the pressure of the surf, and poured back again as the flood fell away.

The crews from the two stations started toward each other, and the one from Green Island was joined by a man from Swan Point, who buckled to the cart with the rest. The conditions of travel over the inundated waste made hauling by hand necessary for at least portions of the distance, but a team of horses had been taken along by Keeper Chadwick.

The sleet, driven by a terrible wind, came down furiously. Finally they came abreast the wreck at ten o'clock at night. Reinforced by Keeper Britton C. Miller and his crew of Swan Point Station who were still following the vessel, the rescue party now numbered nineteen men.

---

* The six volunteers who participated in this rescue were William L. Chadwick, Isaac Osborn, David B. Fisher, David B. Clayton, Abner R. Clayton and Abner Herbert. The crews were, respectively, Keeper Britton C. Miller, and Surfmen William H. Brower, Louis Truex, Abram J. Jones, Charles W. Flemming, and Demerest T. Herbert, of No. 11, at Swan Point; and Keeper William P. Chadwick and Surfmen Peter Sutfin, Benjamin Truex, Tyler C. Pearce, William Vannote, Charles Seaman, and John Flemming of No. 12, at Green Island.

A memorable struggle now began. Drifting slowly, the *Taulane* began to roll fearfully, her hull almost submerged in the spectacular seas which fled across it. Seven men were in her rigging and one of them hung by his arms over a rat-line with his leg thrust through below.

Keeper Chadwick at once remarked, "There is one man gone; we will never save him." Without delay the Lyle gun was planted on the summit of a sandhill and fired. Leaping from the muzzle the line described a parabola across the fly-ing jibstay of the vessel. Here, unfortunately, it could not be reached by the men on board, and had to be hauled back. All this while, the vessel continued to drag her anchors to the south.

A second shot also failed, and the *Taulane* continued drift-ing. The cart was reloaded and the men found another un-flooded hillock from which a third shot was fired. This time the line parted. Meanwhile the vessel was still caught in the southerly set of the current.

The angry waves had been gradually tearing off and smash-ing the upper works of the vessel's hull, scattering the pieces together with her deck load of cord wood. The sluices on shore, with their constant ebbs and flows, were full of splinters of wreck and cordwood billets. Every so often a sudden overburst of the sea flung through the air great sticks of wood, which knocked down several of the surfmen. It was with great difficulty that they could stay on their feet in the combination of sleet, driving sand, spray, and pelting driftwood. Not a man flinched, however, and the volunteers, as well as the crews, bore the racking labor with courage and composure. Not the least difficult of their tasks was that of keeping the lines, guns, and powder dry.

The surfmen worked down along the beach to Green Island Station and a quarter of a mile beyond. There they fired again, but the line parted. Still the crew moved stub-bornly on and it was now noon. Suddenly a shout went up, for the man who had been hanging on the ratline for such a long time had fallen into the sea and was gone. Horror struck, the surfmen still followed the vessel with unslackened persistence. Half an hour later, another man dropped lifeless from the rigging. Then, as they staggered through one of the worst sluiceways with the cart, the gun toppled off into the flood.

It was found in four feet of water. They fished it up and wiped it dry, after which the keeper decided to carry it on his shoulder! A man was dispatched back to Green Island for a dry shotline, while the crew moved on to a point three quarters of a mile below the station. There they got another chance to fire a shot, which also failed to reach the mark. The cart was again reloaded, and the march resumed. A mile below the station a surfman overtook them with the dry shotline, and with it the sixth shot was fired.

This time it was a success. The line flew between the foremast and the jibstay, sweeping the bight into the side of the vessel. The desperate sailors grabbed and fastened it to the fore and main rigging. As the schooner still continued to drift and roll, nothing could yet be done, but three or four men kept tight hold of the shore end of the shotline, and followed along the beach with the wreck in leash. At the end of another quarter of a mile, the vessel suddenly struck the tide setting north. She stopped, swung her head off shore, and worked back to her anchors under the comb of the breaker.

The time had come at last. The whipline was bent on to the shotline, hauled aboard, and made fast by the tail of the block to the mainmast head. The wreck now slued around broadside to the sea and rolled frightfully. The hawser followed the whipline on board, and the breeches buoy was rigged on. Unfortunately, the vessel rolled so hard that it was impossible to set the other end of the hawser up on shore in the usual manner, and the men decided to reave it through the bull's-eye in the sand anchor. Several of them held on to the end to give and take with each roll of the vessel, and the work of hauling the sailors from the wreck was now begun.

After two survivors were landed the vessel grounded off shore, and now rolled worse than ever. In one instance the breeches buoy, with a man in it, swung in the offshore roll, fully fifty feet in the air. The strain and friction on the hawser were so great that, despite the hardness of the wood, the lignum vitae bull's-eye, through which it ran at the sand anchor, was worn fully half an inch deep during thirty minutes of use. Within that half hour, however, all five men were safely landed. The last survivor stepped out of the buoy at half past two, and by that time the vessel was a total wreck.

XV

The *Almond Bird*

The sailors of Penobscot Bay have always bravely fought their eternal battle with the sea and one of the greatest captains of the region is Walter Scott, now living at West Islip on Long Island, New York.

Recently Captain Scott sent me a remarkable story of death and suffering at sea which befell Captain Packard of Deer Isle. Written in Captain Packard's own handwriting, the account was submitted to the Deer Isle Custom House records shortly after its occurrence.

Although it is not generally known, around the years 1870 –1880 Deer Isle was a great fishing port. Actually it "far exceeded Gloucester as a major fishing port of the Atlantic Coast," according to Captain Scott. In addition, there were many Deer Isle craft engaged in the plaster transportation trade.

I can do no better than to allow Captain Packard to tell his own tale of the thrilling experiences which he and his crew underwent in the year 1882, aboard the *Almond Bird*:

We left Rockland Sunday, January 1st, 1882, in the schooner *Almond Bird* for Alexandria, Virginia, with a full cargo of plaster in bulk. We had originally cleared from Rockland in the latter part of December and had proceeded to Windsor, Nova Scotia, where we took on our cargo. On the return voyage we had to put into Rockland to rig a new foremast and make other necessary repairs.

Before I became master of the *Almond Bird* she had been commanded by Captain J. J. Drinkwater. On his last trip, however, Capt. Drinkwater and all his crew had been taken down with malarial fever and it had been found necessary to put on another crew in order to get the vessel home. Before leaving Rockland on this voyage, therefore, I had to ship an entirely new crew.

This crew was made up as follows—seven men besides myself: First mate, William Harriman of Prospect; Second mate, Charles Chaples of Rockland; Steward, A. B. Henderson of Friendship; Seamen, Allen Small of Deer Isle, Horace Small of Deer Isle, Fred Hamilton of Rockland, and Patrick Rogan, of Rockland. Allen and Horace Small were brothers and the younger was only sixteen years of age. He ran away from home to go to sea with his brother, and his parents did not know he had shipped on a vessel. The rest of the crew were strong, able-bodied men.

Sunday, January 1st, 1882, was a fine day, and we got down off Monhegan about eight in the evening. When about half way between Monhegan and Seguin Island it shut down with a heavy Northeast snowstorm. I concluded to run for Portland for shelter, but the wind rapidly increased to gale force, so we decided to haul off and run for Cape Cod.

The wind increased to a violent fury and at eleven we took in our light sails and Spanker. At two the fury of the gale was such that a further shortening of sail was necessary and we close reefed the Mainsail and fore-sail and took in the Jib. At this time the Flying Jib washed from the boom and the vessel was laboring heavily, the sea making a clean break over her, fore and aft, staving in the bulwarks and wash-

ing water casks and everything moveable clear to the mizzen
rigging.

Shortly after the smaller of the two boats which we had
was washed away from the stern by a heavy Sea. This boat
was the old yawl boat of the schooner, and had been replaced
by a strong, new one. In the boat we lost, was the only set
of oars on board, so when the boat was washed away so
went the oars. The mate tried to save them but in doing
so was badly injured when the sea smashed him against the
stern rail.

At six Monday morning we jumped the Jib-boom and foretopmast. As the mate was partly disabled, and had taken my
place at the wheel, I went forward myself to try to secure or
cut away the Jib-boom. I was met by a comber that washed
over her knighthead and I landed in the Waist. Stunned, I
was able to regain my feet to get away from the next comber
that followed at my heels, as I made my way aft. I was
hoping to reach the Cabin for dry clothes, for freezing tem-
peratures were beginning to stick the falling Snow to the
Rigging.

Rolling heavily in the trough of the sea under double
reefed mainsail and fore-staysail, our jib-boom gone, washed
under the bow and pounding her hull our situation became
more and more perilous, every moment.

The vessel being deep laden, the seas mountain high which
she was unable to ride, came sweeping over us, striking the
top of the house with terrific force. A mountain of water
washed away the shutters of the cabin aft and filled everything full below. Finally about seven we shipped a tremendous sea, which stove in the remainder of the bulwarks,
broke in the after Hatch and we were now face to face with
the worst.

We got spare canvas, sails, and boards. With these we
endeavored to stop the water which was pouring down in
torrents into the hold, but we were unable to do so, the sea
washed over us while attempting to batten down the hatch

in this way. At this time we were about half way between Boone and Thatchers Island, some thirty miles off shore.

Seeing that all our efforts were in vain, and that we should be compelled to leave the vessel to save our lives, we cleared away the only remaining boat, and made ready to launch her. Every moment we expected to feel the vessel sinking under us. There was no time to lose.

In the early part of the morning watch, between twelve and four o'clock, the boy Horace Small had his wrist broken when a heavy sea swept the decks. He lay disabled in his berth below, suffering untold agony. We got him out of the forecastle and placed him in the boat. But such was the haste with which we had to work that we had no time to get him properly dressed, and he had no oil clothes. We had no time to get suitable provisions, and all that we could take with us in the boat was some hard bread in a small barrel, a quart of rum, and four quarts of oatmeal.

We had no water. We threw into the boat a few bed clothes, and by watching the breakers we were able to launch the boat although she shipped water which kept two men bailing. Within ten minutes after we left the vessel she sank and we watched the last trace of her main-topmast go under.

Here we were crowded into a twenty-foot yawl drifting before a gale. We looked straight up to see the top of giant combers that threatened to crash down upon us but the old Yawl would race on the seas in time to avoid the giant following us. The boat was supposed to be equipped with sails but as we had used the Mainsail in our effort to cover the damaged Hatch, we now found ourselves with only a jib and no oars. Before we left the vessel the mate had made a drag of a windlass brake and three planks. We had long line in the boat and bending this on the drag we used it for a sea anchor.

In this way we drifted all night and until three the next day, which was Tuesday afternoon.

Tuesday morning daylight was breaking after a night of suffering from extreme cold and hunger. Wind and sea were moderating. Patches showed the sun breaking through. Snow had eased to light flurries. Under-tow seemed like mountains around us. In less then two hours the wind had abated to a calm and as the snow eased up we sighted a fishing schooner in the distance, the first sail we had seen since we left the ill-fated vessel.

Filled with eager hope of an early rescue, we made every effort to reach the stranger or to make ourselves seen by her. It was now nearly calm and we found it impossible to make any headway with our makeshift sail, having no oars. We attempted to supply the deficiency by splitting up the barrel which contained out shipbread and lashing together the Staves. We also split a new thwart which happened to be in the boat by use of handsaw and wedges, and with these insufficient substitutes for oars we paddled with desperate eagerness for three or four hours, struggling to reach the schooner.

We succeeded in getting within about two miles—so near that we could see a man on the stranger's deck. We were already beginning to congratulate ourselves on the prospect of speedy deliverance, when a breeze sprung up and the schooner sailed away without having seen us. Our hearts sank within us by this turn of events. We could not afford to be discouraged. We must hold hopes that another sail would be sighted now that the sky was clearing.

About three in the afternoon the wind shifted to the westward. We got the drag in, and tying a bed blanket to the jib which we had in the boat we made a makeshift sail. All day long we sailed on, keeping about a northeast course. Toward night it breezed up heavily to the northwest, and we were obliged to use our drag again. This January northwest wind was the beginning of untold sufferings for us all. The pangs of hunger were fast weakening us. In our small space we tried to move around to stave off the numbness that was fast penetrating our flesh.

The icy spray dashed constantly over the boat and freezing as it fell. Soon the interior of the boat and everything it contained was covered with a glassy sheet of ice. The flying spindrift coated our shoulders as we tried to keep our backs to the wind to protect our faces from freezing.

So chilled and numbed were we by the cold that when it became necessary to take in our sail we had to saw through the foot of the mast just above the thwarts, being unable to ship it from our weakness, and fearing if we attempted to do so we might stave the planks off the boat.

We lay to that night under our drag until about four Wednesday morning. It would be impossible to describe our sufferings. The numbness of cold, pangs of hunger. No one knows the terror of thirst until they come face to face with a situation such as ours. Parched throats, your Lungs on fire, lips cracked like dried earth, tongue so swollen that it became difficult to breathe. Any delivery from this situation would be most welcome.

The situation was now almost beyond description. Fortunately our drag kept the boat head to the seas, but not withstanding this the heavy seas continually boarded her, and at this point it took the utmost efforts of all hands to keep her free by constant bailing.

I watched the slowing down of my shipmates. I pleaded with them to try to keep moving. It was seldom that I got an answer. I pleaded with them not to go to sleep. Although very drowsy myself I fought off sleep, knowing it would be fatal.

The Deer Isle boy, Horace Small, lay in the bottom of the boat unprotected by any oil skins although we covered him up the best we could. His coverings were covered with a coating of ice. He groaned at times from the pain of his broken wrist. His brother did everything possible for his comfort. As this boy lay there I never saw a greater display of courage.

By this time we began to realize the danger of starvation, unless we were speedily rescued. The oatmeal which we had brought with us being raw, uncooked, was uneatable as our dry throats would not permit us to swallow it. The hard bread we had brought with us became so wet with salt spray that we dared not swallow it, for it would increase our thirst. We made the rum last until the first part of Wednesday evening by taking only a spoonful at a time.

Fresh water now seemed to be our greatest need. Some of the crew were so thirsty that although they were warned of the terrible consequences, they persisted in eating salt-water ice. The Northwest wind was fast dropping out but the biting cold was almost unbearable. Finally Chaples, the Mate, and seaman Hogan had eaten so much salt-water ice that their minds began to wander and I realized that insanity was not too far distant for them both. They would have to be watched.

I was fortunate enough to find under the thwart a lump of Snow about as large as my fist, which was very little impregnated with salt. This I ate and I have no doubt that it aided greatly in keeping up my strength during those terrible hours.

About four Wednesday morning we felt we could again resort to sail. We made a new step to the mast and set it, after which we sailed on all day and all night to the westward.

That afternoon we sighted a schooner hove to—the second sail we had seen since leaving the wrecked vessel. We tried to run up to her, but after an hour the wind freshened and she bore away without our having attracted her attention.

This second failure had a very depressing effect upon us. That same night about eleven a hermaphrodite brig passed across our bow close to us. We hailed him, but our weak voices must have made it impossible for him to hear us. We saw a man with a lantern moving on deck and we thought it a signal that he saw us. But he kept on his course and was soon out of sight. We were so close that we could see the lights in her cabin windows.

That night the first of our number succumbed to the terrible hardships which we were all compelled to undergo. This was the sixteen-year-old Deer Isle boy, Horace Small, who died about ten Wednesday evening in his brother's arms. Numbed by the cold the boy had fallen asleep which is most always fatal.

Two men went violently insane from eating too much saltwater ice. The second mate in his delirium seized the saw and before he could be prevented sawed both his hands, inflicting terrible wounds. The young Irishman, Patrick Hogan, died first of the two, about an hour after the death of the boy.

The second mate who was a large powerful man, died in delirium about two Thursday morning, thus we were left five living men and three dead bodies, in a small open boat, buffeted about by icy wind and seas that buried us with spindrift. Our boat was half filled with ice and it was no time before the bodies laying in the bottom of the boat were frozen in a block of ice. The scene was a horrible one, and most terrible of all to the survivors because of its horrid suggestions of their possible fate. The second mate's body was free of the ice block so we threw his body overboard. The others were frozen to the bottom boards and could not be released.

At daylight Thursday morning we saw three fishermen not too far away. The windward one of these we were unable to reach; the next we thought did not see us, and so we kept off for the leeward one, who was putting out his trawls. He saw us and moored his trawls and started in our direction. We were too weak to do much, but the feeling of relief which filled our hearts when we saw the boat's bow headed in our direction cannot be described.

The fisherman proved to be the schooner *Cora Lee*, Captain George A. Saunders of Pigeon Cove. A dory was sent out to take us in tow and soon we were alongside. They got us aboard and into the cabin, changed our clothes, gave us nourishing food gradually until we had gained some strength and quieted nerves.

Despite our remonstrances they left their trawls to their fate and started at once for Pigeon Cove. When within two miles of shore Captain Saunders with two men rowed into the cove to arrange for accommodations for us.

They secured comfortable quarters for us at the home of Mrs. Annie Pierce, procured medical aid and a nurse.

We had kind friends and good nurses. In behalf of the crew our thanks to the members of the Masonic Lodge who, besides furnishing watchers for us every night, did much more for our welfare. The town's people in a body were so typical of that State of Maine kind-hearted neighborliness, we five survivors pledge to love and remember always, those from Pigeon Cove who rescued us, and to those who opened their hearts, dropped all their home chores to devote many long hours in our behalf, we are deeply grateful.

XVI

The *Fannie Bailey,* a Wreck
from Portland, Maine

The State of Maine has done far more than its share in the building of beautiful ships. Rockland, where both my father and mother were born, and where the I. L. Snow Shipyard launched so many schooners and vessels of other designs, will always mean to me a city of ships. Almost all those beautiful creations of Maine shipbuilders have vanished from the seas, but many of the men who built them and scores of sailors who sailed on them, are still alive.

The story I have to tell in this chapter is of a schooner which hailed from another Maine port. On her stern the *Fannie A. Bailey* proudly carried the name of Portland.

The 272-ton schooner sailed from Windsor, Nova Scotia, with a cargo of plaster destined for Philadelphia. Captain Hume, whose wife and child had sailed with him, had a crew of six. Only one man besides the captain was from New England, Thomas Shields of Newport, Rhode Island.

By the night of June 3, 1883, the schooner had reached a point off the Delaware River, and was actually in the vicinity of the North Bar of Hereford Inlet, about two miles east of the Hereford Inlet Station.

A southerly gale had hit the area, and it was accompanied by a fog so dense that the captain could only guess as to his whereabouts. He decided to put the *Bailey* under "easy sail," and lay off and on throughout the night, so that he could wait for daylight and possible clearing weather.

At half past five in the morning of June fourth the monotonous crashing of the heavy seas, which had continued through the night, was suddenly interrupted by a shock which made the vessel tremble through all her hull, and the sailors realized that the *Bailey* was aground. Again and again the pounding ran through the schooner, until it seemed certain that the masts would go by the board. The hull struck the bottom so violently that a piece of the keel broke off and floated up alongside. All the time a mad rain of spray was showering upon the decks.

To add to the confusion and horror, the fog prevented anything being seen beyond the immediate surrounding of breakers, which by this time were almost overwhelming, and the effect for those on board was the same as if the vessel were pounding to bits on some reef far out to sea. The place of the stranding, the Hereford Shoals, was about two miles from shore, and the same distance east of the Hereford Inlet Station on the coast of New Jersey.

The Captain kept his head, but the mate panicked with fright, and before long almost every other member of the crew showed his fear. They soon started the rumor that the vessel was going to pieces. The yawl was thought of as a possible means of escape, and the sailors proceeded to hoist the boat away from where it was stored on deck over the main hatch.

The captain entreated them not to abandon the vessel until compelled to do so, and explained that assistance would come from shore when the fog lifted. When Hume went below for a few minutes, in an attempt to calm his wife and child, however, the frightened sailors dropped the yawl astern, piled their baggage into it and jumped in themselves. The mate had been the first one to leave.

Only one man stayed with the captain—Tom Shields, the sailor from Newport. Upon coming up from below, Hume saw the men about to push away from the schooner, and yelled at them to stop. The mate became ashamed of himself and clambered up on deck to attempt to persuade the captain of the wisdom of their action.

Seeing that the desertion of the vessel was a foregone conclusion, Hume finally gave in. He was afraid to be left without any means of escape for himself, his family, and Tom Shields and reluctantly yielded to the mate's persistence. His wife and child were then lowered over the stern into the boat, and the captain was about to follow them when he noticed that the fog was lifting. He then saw, "like a dark smear in the distance," the edge of the beach, and also noticed a discouraging line of breakers, which told him very plainly that a landing could never be effected in a yawl-type boat. He explained to the others that it would be suicide.

A few moments later the fog dispersed still further, and Captain Hume could now distinctly see the lifesaving station against its background of dense woods. He called to the men, telling them what he had seen, and implored them to come on board, but they still refused. He then ordered the mate to have the boat come up slowly so that he might take back his wife and child. The mate obeyed, ordered the yawl up, and slid down the painter into her so that he could help to lift the woman and the baby aboard the *Bailey*.

At that very moment, a great towering wave with a breaking crest came roaring in. Smashing into the yawl, the comber spewed its occupants out into the water, and the boat capsized. The sailors, Mrs. Hume and her baby son, were now all floundering in the tumultuous seas.

Horror struck, Hume ran along the deck for the only other craft aboard, a small nine-foot auxiliary boat which was

utterly unfit for service in such a sea. Stripping to his under-
wear, he was assisted by Shields in getting the boat over the
side.

Luckily, it landed right side up. The captain leaped into
it and started to row frantically for his wife and son. Beating off the sailors thrashing about in the water with his oars,
he finally reached the little boy. By this time the lad was
nearly insensible. Reaching down, he grabbed the boy, placed
him in the bottom of the skiff, and then rowed to his wife,
who was pulled in by superhuman effort.

Rowing desperately toward the ship, Captain Hume
dropped a line for one of the sailors he noticed on the way.
The line parted, and the man began to drift out to sea, and
soon drowned. Two other men also perished at the time.

Approaching the side of the *Bailey*, the captain saw safety
within his reach. Hume caught a line from Shields and
worked the boat up astern. Then he managed to bend the
line around his wife's body so that she could be hoisted
aboard.

Suddenly a relentless, breaking wave hit the boat, smashing into the very center of the craft, and carried it with its
helpless occupants toward shore, leaving Mrs. Hume dangling
at the end of the line. Fifty yards away the captain came
to the surface, and searched the water desperately for his
son. Eventually he was forced to give up, and neither the
boy nor the boat was ever seen again!

Mrs. Hume meanwhile had been hauled aboard by the
mate, and with a heavy heart her husband swam back toward
the *Bailey*. Reaching the side of the schooner, he shouted
for a line, and was soon pulled up to safety.

The captain found his wife stretched out on the deck, still
unconscious. He began at once to administer first aid to her,
but it was not until an hour later that she showed signs of
regaining her senses. When she was finally carried down into
the cabin, she was still unable to speak and remained in this
condition for three more hours. The *Bailey* had struck at

about half past five, and within the next hour three of her crew and the captain's son had perished.

June was the time of year when the stations on the Atlantic coast were closed for the season, as required by law.* The keeper of the station, however, Christopher Ludlam, who lived across the bay which separates the beach from the mainland, rose early that morning. Finding the weather foggy, he walked down to the boat landing at Mayville on the bay side, so as to command a view of the beach when the atmosphere cleared.

At about nine o'clock the fog lifted, and Keeper Ludlam saw the *Bailey* beyond the distant beach. He knew by the way she was canted over that the craft was aground. He put off at once in a gunning skiff, rowing across the bay to the station, where he expected to find his men. There was an arrangement that they should assemble there whenever a wreck was seen. On the way across, he came upon Keeper Holmes, of Tatham's Station, who had been out in a boat fishing with his brother Charles. They had also seen the wreck.

By half past eleven the three men reached the shore, where they met Mr. Hewitt, the lightkeeper, and Dr. Tompkins, a former army surgeon who resided in that neighborhood. Dr. Tompkins had a team, and quickly harnessed his horses to the surfboat carriage to draw it to the water's edge.

Only four of the five men present were oarsmen, but although several members of the station force were on their way, it was desirable to set out at once, even with a short crew, before the flood tide came and made the sea worse. Help was given by a local carpenter, Ellsworth Hewett, who gallantly volunteered to row an oar, and the boat put off with the five men. By keeping in the channel and sheering off as much as possible from the broken water, the surfboat crew

---

* Had the Hereford Inlet Station been open, however, the patrol could not possibly have seen the vessel through the two miles of dense fog between her and the shore.

achieved the two miles out to the wreck in half an hour by dint of the sturdiest rowing.

They found the schooner heavily slanted over on her port side, with her head to the ocean, in the midst of a wild swirl of raging water. She was broken in two and at times the sea flew over her in a flood from stem to stern. The people on board were clinging to the weather quarter, which was the highest part out of water. Riding by its painter alongside the wreck, the yawl had been righted and bailed out by those on board.

It was fortunate that the surfboat came when she did, as the survivors were planning to get ashore by the yawl, an effort that would probably have been fatal.

With difficulty the lifesavers kept the surfboat from being swept under the counter and damaged by the flume of water which was roaring along the sides of the hull like a millrace. Holding alongside, the keeper sang out to those on board to get down into the boat as fast as they could.

Captain Hume shouted back that his wife was in the cabin, whereupon Keeper Ludlam sprang on board, tumbled below, and waded waist deep in water across the inclined floor. There he found the poor woman, unconscious, in a berth on the upper side, and carried her in his arms back to the deck.

No time was lost in getting her into the surfboat, after which all the others leaped aboard. The surfmen pushed away and started rowing for shore. The survivors were in a deplorable condition. They had nothing left except the soaked clothing they sat in, all the baggage, even the ship's bedding, having been lost when the yawl capsized.

The captain's wife was very thinly clad. The first thing, after getting her aboard, was to wrap her in some of the surfboat crew's coats, which they stripped off for the purpose. Then came the dangerous moment of landing, which was carried off without a hitch. Keeper Ludlam, realizing that the poor woman was in a very critical condition, had her carried immediately to Dr. Tompkins' house, two hundred yards from the station, where she was treated for shock and immersion. By the next day all the survivors were sufficiently recovered to be taken over to the mainland for passage to their homes.

The bodies of the three lost sailors were cast ashore some weeks afterward, but the little child was never seen again. It is evident that all four lives would have been saved but for the overwhelming fright which made the sailors desert the vessel prematurely for the yawl.

XVII

Papa, Won't God Save Us?

At the height of a memorable winter storm, which is still known on Nantucket Island as the Blizzard of '86, Captain Alfred H. Anderson was driving the three-masted schooner *T. B. Witherspoon* under bare poles off the shores of New England, although he had no idea where along the coast he was. The winds of the blizzard were then hitting at better than fifty miles an hour, and it was the second day of the hurricane. Rapidly approaching a lee beach, the 117-foot schooner from Camden, Maine, was in serious trouble.*

The *T. B. Witherspoon* is said to have been named for a merchant who lived in the North End of Boston a century ago. Captain Anderson had received a charter to carry the load of tropical merchandise from the West Indies to Boston, and she had sailed away from Surinam in December 1885. Anderson had as mate one of the ablest sailors and navigators in the entire State of Maine, Burdick Berry. He had his wife and five-year-old son with him on the voyage.

---

* The cargo of the schooner, which was built in 1877, consisted of barrels, turkins, and cases of molasses, cocoa, sugar, spices and pickled limes, all of which, in various degrees of damage, were soon scattered up and down the shores of the surrounding area as soon as the vessel began to break up.

Little or no bad weather was encountered on the trip home until Friday, January 8, 1886. It was then that a blizzard of great proportions hit the *Witherspoon,* somewhere north of Hatteras. All that day and the next the ship was forced to run under bare poles in a southwest wind.* Captain Anderson knew he must be approaching the coast after the first day's run, but not having been able to take an observation for forty-eight hours, he was forced to guess his position at sea.

During the early hours of the morning of January 10 a revolving light was reported by the lookout, who had "raised" it between the snow squalls. In the storm neither the captain nor the mate could identify the land. Anderson thought it might be Montauk Point, at the tip end of Long Island, and held the ship to her course. She was then actually sailing directly for the island of Nantucket. As the light appeared at least five miles away, if it proved to be Montauk there would be no immediate cause for changing the course. All danger would have been passed in less than an hour. Fate, however, decided otherwise.

For several minutes Captain Anderson held the ship to her course. Then, to his terror, he hear the lookout's cry, "Breakers dead ahead!" The captain and the mate stared at each other, and the truth struck them at once. Close upon a lee shore, with a flashing light visible from time to time, the land could only be some part of the coastline of Nantucket.

"Keep her off! Hard to starboard!" shouted the captain to the helmsman, grasping the wheel with the sailor. None knew better than he the danger.

The mate ran forward, endeavoring to set the forestaysail, but even then it was too late. The ship had only partially answered her helm, and the staysail was scarcely set when with a grinding shock her keel struck the shallow rips. Time

---

* The course, while running before the wind, was northeast "or nearly so."

and again she bumped hard onto the shoals.* Finally she was firmly embedded in the sand.

The elements soon took charge of the situation. Lashed to the davits, the yawl was broken to bits by the first wave that struck it, and the same billow smashed in the ports and flooded the cabin. The sailors scurried up the ratlines into the rigging, the mate alone remaining in the cabin with his wife and little son.

On the Nantucket shore, Surfman Freeman had the dog watch of the Surfside Lifesaving Station. At the time of the wreck that Sunday morning, he was going to the westward and was the first to discover the ship. Freeman instantly lighted a Coston flare and set it up on the beach where its spluttering would let the doomed sailors know that help was coming. Running back to his station, he gave the alarm. Then, with Captain George A. Veeder and the others in the station crew, Freeman helped drag the lifeboat and apparatus to the scene two miles away.

Just at daybreak the lifesavers made their attempt to launch the boat. The first sea smashed it to pieces, and the surfmen scrambled to safety. The gun was then placed in position to shoot the projectile, with the line attached, out to the wreck. With powder and projectile ready, Keeper Veeder sighted the gun.

One of the bravest and kindest of men, Veeder realized his responsibility. Taking final account of the wind, he fired. The line went straight to the mark, was seized by the crew and pulled on board the *Witherspoon*. The lifesavers ran off the larger line with the breeches buoy attached, and in a few seconds it was made fast in the fore rigging of the schooner. A sailor quickly jumped into the breeches buoy, but when the men on shore attempted to haul upon the attending line, they discovered to their horror that the operating block had frozen. With all their strength, however, they

---

* The *Witherspoon* had hit on the Little Mioxe Rip, also called Weedweeders Shoal.

pulled, the block occasionally slipping along, until the sailor was within a few yards of the beach. Then the small line parted and the poor fellow dropped into the sea and drowned before their eyes.

Another line was shot out to the schooner, and Veeder's aim was as accurate as the first time. The sailors grabbed the line and made it fast, but by this time they were so numbed by the freezing surf that they were unable to act. Again and again the waves swept the *Witherspoon*'s deck, and within a short time three more sailors were washed overboard. Still the others could do nothing to help themselves.

Keeper Veeder knew that neither the boat nor the lifesaving raft could reach the *Witherspoon*, but he agreed to an attempt to launch the raft. Captain Charles E. Smalley and volunteers tried to get it beyond the breakers but the first wave pitchpoled the raft, sweeping every man upon it into the undertow. After the last volunteer was rescued the men realized that any further attempt to use this piece of apparatus was foredoomed to failure.*

Meanwhile two of the schooner's men were lashed in the mizzen rigging by Captain Anderson. Four men had been drowned, and one other was in the fore rigging, just above the chains, where the line from shore had been made fast.

In a short time one of the sailors in the after rigging froze to death, and the vibration of the waves hitting the wreck soon knocked him into the sea. The second sailor, lower down, was seen to settle gradually on the ropes which held him. He, too, had frozen to death. The captain came down to him, tied the sailor's clothes about him and went aloft again a ratline or two. Then Anderson turned toward the people on the beach, whose numbers had now reached several hundred for word of the sea tragedy had been spreading

---

* Those who made the futile attempt were Charles E. Smalley, Joseph M. Folger, Benjamin Beekman, Charles W. Cash, John P. Taber, William Morris, Horace Orpin, Benjamin Fisher and Everett Coffin.

around the island. He gave a farewell wave of his hand, as if abandoning all hope, and soon succumbed to the cold and exposure. His body dropped into the sea, from which it was recovered and later brought to town.

To all appearances, but one man now remained alive and he could be seen desperately clinging to the fore rigging. On shore, the watchers became frantic and yelled to the sailor to secure the line to the mast so that he could come ashore in the breeches buoy, but he did not budge.

A Massachusetts Humane Society lifeboat was then dragged to the scene. Lifesavers and volunteers quickly manned it, but luckily wiser heads prevailed and the attempt to launch the boat was never made.

The hours went by, but there was not the slightest letup in the blizzard. Finally, it was late afternoon and only an hour of daylight remained. The watchers were desperate in their anxiety for the lone survivor.

Suddenly out of the cabin and onto the deck sprang another figure. He stood at the rail amidships and the waves broke over him as he took in the situation. He seemed dazed, and unable to understand what was taking place. Fearful that he would be washed overboard, the men on the beach shouted at the top of their voices for the sailor to move, for any sizable wave could wash him overboard.

"Get back, get back," they cried, trying to persuade him to leave the dangerous position in which he stood. Suddenly he seemed to come out of his stupor, and ran forward, calling up to the man in the rigging. His companion responded and climbed down to the deck. Together they pulled in the slack of the breeches buoy line until the wind and the tide caught the bight and held it.

Cheer after cheer went up from the crowd on the Nantucket beach as they seized the shore end of the line. Slowly walking with it to windward against the tide, they then dropped it. All that remained for those aboard the wreck to do now was to take in the slack.

But before anything further was accomplished, dusk settled over the tense scene. The running lights of the *Witherspoon* were still burning, as they had been when she struck early that morning. Dusk turned to darkness, but nothing was heard from the stranded men. Still the minutes passed. Everyone on shore listened, feeling sure that the breeches buoy had been hauled aboard.

Suddenly there came from out of the darkness where the surf was hitting the shore, the thrilling words, "All ready. Pull away." And pull they did, all who could grab the line. In a few seconds, although it seemed hours, the form of a man more dead than alive was sighted, coming at them in the breeches buoy as it approached shore. Willing hands assisted the sailor from the buoy and he was carefully carried to a point above the reach of the tide, after which he was taken across to the lifesaving station and put to bed.

Again the breeches buoy was sent out into the darkness, but it was two long hours before all was in readiness for the final attempt. The snowflakes continued to stab through the blackness of the night, at times combining with the flying sand to cut the faces of those on the shore.

Finally the last man from the *Witherspoon* arrived on the shore. A minute later he was safely in the care of the lifesavers and was hurried off up the beach to the shelter of the station.

Now began the walk to town for the more than one hundred and fifty men and boys, a distance of four miles over snowdrifts in the fifty-mile gale, with the thermometer at ten degrees above zero.

On the following morning Mate Berry had recovered sufficiently to tell his story. He was the man who had been seen to come from the cabin and was responsible for the saving of the life of the other sailor and himself, the last man to leave the ship. He slowly told his graphic tale of what had taken place in the cabin after the *Witherspoon* struck the Nantucket shoal.

"The very first wave stove in the skylights and ports, and flooded the cabin. The water rose rapidly over the cabin floor until I was obliged to place my wife and little boy upon a table. I remained with them for hours waist deep in the water. In the midst of the terrible lurching of the ship my little boy, noticing the expression of fear on his mother's face, turned to me and said: 'Papa, won't God save us?'

"Both perished shortly after. In spite of realizing that they were dead, I bade them farewell with a simple statement, after looking at them both, for the final time in the cabin. 'I must leave you now,' I told them and went out on deck. It was there that I came to learn that my captain and mates, with one exception, had all frozen or drowned. There was little left for me, and I cared little for myself. The calls from shore, however, aroused me, and I set to work to pull off the line. With the captain gone, it was my place to remain to the last on the ship. So I assisted the sailor into the breeches buoy, and then hauled the line off alone. You know the rest!"

The following morning the bodies of the mother and the little boy were found in the ice upon the shore. Interred at first in the cemetery, their remains were later removed from the island.

Word of the shipwreck and the boy's final question of his father spread rapidly. First the people of New England learned of it. Then the story went throughout the United States. Later it crossed to England and eventually reached as far away as Australia. The question the little boy asked his father was taken by preachers of all denominations as their text and many beautiful sermons based on it were printed in the daily papers of that period.

But how fared it with the brave captain of the lifesavers? Unfortunately, Captain Veeder never was the same again. Years before, on February 4, 1871, he had received a medal from the Massachusetts Humane Society, for his part in the rescue of the crew of the schooner *Mary Anna*, wrecked on

Nantucket bar in the winter of 1871. With seven other young volunteers he had dragged two rescue boats over three miles of ice with the thermometer below zero, at night, and rescued the crew. Not only were the survivors frostbitten, but the rescuers carried to their graves marks of the sufferings of that terrible night.*

In the wake of such successful missions as those, Veeder never recovered from the hours of anguish spent on the beach that fatal night in 1886. Big-hearted, fearless and kind, he brooded over the fact that he and his men had been unable to do anything in this instance to save his fellow beings on that Sunday. It preyed heavily on his mind, and he gradually succumbed to the relentless memory of the tragedy. Finally he passed from this life with his mind a blank, but he took with him the love and respect of all who knew him.

---

* On February 4, 1871, the schooner *Mary Anna* stranded near the Inner Bar, Nantucket. Isaac Hamblen, George Veeder, Alexander Fanning, James A. Holmes, Joseph P. Gardner, William E. Bates, Stephen Keyes, and Henry Coffin manned two lifeboats and took along boards so they could work through the ice on shore and reach the men on the schooner. They succeeded in bringing ashore the crew of five. It was such a sensational rescue that the Massachusetts Humane Society awarded the eight men silver medals and raised a substantial sum of money for them as well.

XVIII

Wreck of the Schooner
Allie H. Belden

The terrible blizzard of wind and snow that swept over a large portion of the United States on March 12, 1888, was one of the most devastating in the country's history. Gathering force as far west as the Rocky Mountains, and progressing eastward, it soon centered in the region of the Great Lakes. Then, with accelerated fury, the gale began veering in a southerly direction. Off the seaboard in the vicinity of Cape Hatteras, the blizzard met another violent storm moving northward, and both disturbances united with fearful results.

The new blizzard was felt with greatest intensity in the Middle Atlantic states, and was especially severe around New York City. The storm left desolation throughout the entire stretch of country and coast, reaching even beyond the Canadian border.

Blowing in straight streaks through the air, the snow piled up tremendous drifts in thousands of locations. In fact, the quantity of snow that fell would of itself have made this an unprecedented storm, even had it occurred in the midst of winter, instead of March.

The boasted "triumphs of civilization" were temporarily overcome. Travel was suspended, all means of communication were cut off, and the ordinary pursuits of life in the great cities, towns, and hamlets were brought with startling abruptness to a complete standstill. Desolation and suffering were marked on every hand. Many lives were lost and property damage went into the millions. Although the complete effects of the storm can never be known, it is certain that they were the most disastrous ever experienced up to that time within the same geographical limits.

The staff of the Weather Bureau in New York had some strange experiences during the gale. With the storm making most of the weather reports from other locations unobtainable, a cable arrived from London containing information about the weather in Portland, Maine, and thus a new method of bringing in these records from overseas was started.

From a technical standpoint, the Great Snow of '88 was an unusual gale. Instead of a storm center with a circular low pressure in the center, there was a great trough of a so-called "low" between two definite ridges of "high" with almost the entire temperate zone in between. The weather chart for the morning of March 12 clearly shows the trough with isobars closely crowded together in elliptical shape south of Block Island. During the night of the twelfth the lowest barometric pressure and the most pronounced gradients occurred. The next morning's survey indicated a marked decrease in the storm's intensity; by the morning of the fourteenth, the Block Island depression was almost completely filled up. By this time the storm had changed to occasional snow squalls and light variable winds.

In Chesapeake Bay, no less than ninety-six schooners, sloops and barks were blown ashore, sunk or badly damaged. In Delaware Bay, thirty-seven craft were wrecked as were thirty-three vessels around New York Bay. In my book, *Strange Tales from Nova Scotia to Cape Hatteras*, I devote most of a chapter to details concerning what happened during the Great Snow of '88 off the Delaware coast when six vessels were abandoned and nine others were reported missing at sea.

The storm was so terrific that the tides did not resume their normal heights for more than six days after the end of the gale, while the Gulf Stream itself was driven far to the south of its usual course.

In New York City, by noon on Monday, the snow had fallen to depths of between two and five feet, with drifts piling up fifteen and eighteen feet in many parts of the city.

Shipping, generally, escaped with fewer disasters than might have been expected, which possibly can be explained by the fact that on most of the Atlantic seaboard the wind was off shore. At Delaware Breakwater, however, where the harbor was full of anchored vessels, the havoc was unparalleled.

The schooner *Allie H. Belden* of Portland, Connecticut, was wrecked during the blizzard at half past two in the morning about eight hundred yards northeast of the Lewes Station. She had sailed from Deer Isle, Maine, with a load of granite, stopping at Boothbay to pick up a deck cargo of ice.

Shortly before midnight of the eleventh the wind veered within seconds from the southeast to the northwest. Accompanied by rain, sleet, and snow, it then proceeded to blow with hurricane force.

A large number of vessels were anchored behind Delaware Breakwater, and most of them were not prepared for this unexpected and violent change. They were either swamped at their moorings or driven ashore. The whole fleet had suddenly been thrown into the wildest confusion, with chains sundered and masts shattered.

Stirred into turbulence by the wind roaring through the pitch blackness of the night, the ocean was enough to appall the stoutest heart. Many of the terrified crews on board the vessels barely had time to escape from their berths and scrambled on deck or into the rigging for safety. It seems little less than miraculous that so few lives were lost.

When morning dawned the havoc was discernible in all directions, as far as the eye could reach through the still driving snow. Nearly every craft that had been at anchor the night before was either sunk, stuck fast to some shoal, or stranded on the beach. Fourteen schooners and two steamers were assisted in one way or another by the lifesaving men, with many others cared for by wreckers.

As soon as day began to break on the morning of the twelfth the keeper of Lewes Station mustered his crew to make an attempt to reach the beach where he knew full well that the services of his men would be needed. The force of the gale was so great, however, and the sand and sleet hitting their faces so cut and buffeted them that one by one they gave up and dropped to the ground, obliged to crawl on their hands and knees back to the station.

Half an hour later there was a partial lull, and the snow stopped long enough for surrounding objects to be seen. The surfmen again set forth, their attention being directed to the schooner *Allie H. Belden,* fast aground a few hundred yards off shore. The sea was then making a clean breach over her, and her crew could be seen clinging to the rigging. As this craft seemed to be in the most imminent danger, steps were at once taken for the rescue of her people. The beach apparatus was placed in position. Notwithstanding the fury of the gale, the line at the first shot was landed over the vessel within reach of the captain, but the wind was so furious that he was unable to hold it and it was blown adrift. It was then hauled ashore, a dry one was substituted, and this was fired across the jibboom. The sailors, aloft in the rigging with the sea breaking heavily over the hull, could not get to it and it was finally washed off.

Another line was then made ready. At this stage a thick

snow squall set in. The seas again began flying across the beach, and the line soon became wet and stiff frozen. On being fired once more, the line parted. Two further attempts to communicate with the schooner also failed.

It now became evident that the vessel's crew could only be saved by means of a boat, though the prospect of launching and forcing a craft through the tremendous surf was anything but encouraging. It could not possibly have been accomplished by the station men alone when they first arrived on the scene. But by this time many people had assembled on the beach who were willing and eager to lend their services. The lines were taken to the station and placed near the stove to thaw. The crew, now assisted by a strong force of men, obtained the self-bailing surf boat and carried it to a point opposite the stranded pilot schooner *E. W. Tunnel*, which lay close to the beach.

Those on board threw a line ashore which was made fast in the bow of the surf boat. The lifesavers, together with several pilots, and a wrecker, were hauled out through the breakers alongside the *Tunnel*. The boat was then cast loose, but as soon as she drew away from the schooner and was caught by the wind, she veered off to leeward and, despite the united efforts of the oarsmen to maintain headway, was beaten back on the beach. After this five of the stoutest and most daring of the young pilots made a vigorous attempt in one of their own boats to reach the distressed craft, but they were similarly driven ashore.

Nothing daunted, however, a fresh crew of pilots took the places of their exhausted comrades, and by almost superhuman exertions succeeded in reaching another stranded schooner, the *E. L. Dow*, far to leeward of the *Belden*. Here they bailed out their boat, which had shipped a great deal of water. After resting, they again pushed on, but when almost within fifty yards of their goal the boat struck the bar, where the seas instantly boarded it and they were forced to push off and return to the starting point.

The station crew, assisted by two volunteers, took their boat and waded with it well to windward. With a desperate struggle they managed to get safely away from the beach, but the men were so exhausted by their previous efforts that the craft had to be anchored to allow them time to regain their strength.

By alternately rowing and anchoring, thus holding on to every inch that was made, the lifesavers inched their way out alongside the *Belden*. It was now half past two in the afternoon, nine hours from the time the rescue efforts had begun. The lifesavers took the captain, mate, and two seamen from the rigging. The crew was exhausted from having clung to the shrouds for twelve hours. It was learned that two of the schooner's men, Moses H. Small of Dennis, Massachusetts, and the cook, whose name was not known, had some time before succumbed to exposure and fallen overboard.

The survivors, all of whom were more or less frostbitten, were speedily conveyed to the station, where Dr. Hall, of Lewes, who had generously placed his services at the disposal of the keeper, did everything in his power to help them. The captain, mate, and crew were sheltered and comfortably cared for by the surfmen until they had recovered sufficiently to start for their homes.

The heroic efforts put forth by the lifesavers that day to rescue the imperiled sailors are worthy of the highest commendation. Three of the surfmen were badly frostbitten, yet they did not once shrink from the task before them. Resolutely they continued at their posts until those who remained on the ill-fated schooner were brought off. The fact that the undertaking was at times confronted by apparently insurmountable obstacles did not in the least dishearten them. Nor can too much praise be bestowed on the pilots and others, who, by their intrepid work, helped to make the rescue possible.

The following letter was subsequently received at the office of the General Superintendent:

Lewes, Delaware, March 20, 1888

Dear Sir:

Having been wrecked in my vessel at Delaware Breakwater in the late gale of March 12, I wish to commend the crew of the lifesaving station at the above-mentioned place for their brave, cool and courageous work in saving the lives of my three men and myself. I feel that I can not with my pen describe my feelings of gratitude to the U. S. Life Saving Service.

Very respectfully yours,

John L. Crowell, 2d.

Master of wrecked schooner *Allie H. Belden.*

Out in the *Portland* Gale

In several of my books I have presented various aspects of the terrible *Portland* Gale. *The Vengeful Sea* (published in 1956) contains a list of one hundred and ninety victims who went down on the *Portland*, as well as a list of craft lost or damaged in that gale. The *Portland* sailed from Boston on Saturday night, November 26, 1898, with at least one hundred and ninety persons on board, not one of whom survived the storm. The side-wheeler sank with all hands off the Cape Cod shores Sunday night, November 27, 1898.

For more than twenty years I have been attempting to get accurate information regarding three craft which were out in the gale, the *Jordan L. Mott*, the *Lester A. Lewis*, and the *Gloucester*.

Because of the untiring persistence of Laurence Macdonald of Cambridge I have been aided in getting the story of the *Gloucester*, and Mr. Alphonse Wager of Provincetown, son of Surf Patrolman Frank C. Wager, gave me verification in March 1960, of the story concerning the other two craft.

Contrary to what has become a widespread impression, the *Portland* was not the only steamer which left Boston on that November day in defiance of the elements. There was one other, the steamer *Gloucester* of the Merchants & Miners Transportation Line. Guided by the firm and steady hand of Captain Francis M. Howes, one of the ablest mariners on the Atlantic coast, the *Gloucester* weathered the gale, and although encountering almost overwhelming odds she reached her destination at Norfolk, Virginia, on schedule.

The *Gloucester* is said to be the only ship which passed in safety through Vineyard Sound on that night. Captain Howes' seamanship had long before placed him foremost among American navigators, but his handling of the *Gloucester* in that awesome storm won him practically universal commendation.

Howes met the perils unflinchingly. He knew his boat, he knew his course, and by the instinct born of experience he "shoved her ahead," despite the fact that there was nothing but his knowledge of the sea to guide him. He increased the highest speed the *Gloucester* ordinarily attained by three knots and kept the vessel plugging along.

Confident that he knew his bearings, the captain decided that he would run the boat as he had always done, but at a speed which, if she struck, would send her well up on shore where all might be saved. The marvel of it was that his reckoning, made without almost any of the familiar buoys or lights, was absolutely accurate, while the theory of forging rapidly ahead proved equally sound and successful, as he explained the trip afterward.

Captain Howes, who was a native of Chatham, was fifty-nine years old at the time. He wrote out his experience fourteen years later so that future generations would be able to appreciate his trials that night:

> The *Gloucester* was due to leave Boston at four o'clock that afternoon. I had noticed that the wind was blowing east northeast and from 35 to 40 miles an hour, and I had my doubts about the advisability of sailing. On the other hand I didn't like the idea of lying at the dock after having once made ready.
>
> I thought if I could get some information as to what kind of

weather they were having in New York that it might help me in my calculations. So I sent a note up to our agent asking him to find out from New York for me.

Well, the information came back that the wind was east northeast with prospects for an easterly gale and with rain or snow. I had consulted my own barometer and that showed me as much, but I thought I would try it anyway.

You see I had a good ship. Furthermore she was completely filled with freight. Having the vessel thoroughly loaded is of great advantage in a heavy sea, as it does away with the possibility of the cargo shifting about. With these two most important things in my favor I decided to sail, and we left at exactly 4:15 o'clock that November 26 afternoon in 1898.

It was about 7:30 o'clock that night when we were off Cape Cod, and the wind was blowing about 70 miles an hour, that there came a snow squall. It continued to grow thicker and the wind increased. It soon became so thick that we couldn't discern any of the customary objects which in clear weather served to aid us.

I was waiting to catch the sound of the whistling buoy off Pollock Rip Shoals, and had just said that we ought to be about there when lo and behold, there she was directly in our path. As a matter of fact, I almost went over it.

Well, sir, the Pollock Rip Shoals Lightship was the only light I saw before I went through Vineyard Sound. I heard afterward that Block Island reported that the wind there blew 110 miles. We must have been in the thick of it, which, as you will see, was pretty tough navigation.

Why, I couldn't see my lookout and he was less than fifty feet away. This was partly on account of the snow and partly because the wind took the water and threw it up in great waves. As a matter of fact, the water rolled into the staterooms.

I couldn't anchor, for if I did, I'd take the risk of pounding to pieces.

The only thing for me to do was to run her according to my best calculation and as fast as I could. Ordinarily the *Glouces-ter* made 15 knots an hour, but I managed to get 18 knots out of her and kept it up.

I reasoned that if she should run ashore, the thing to do would be to drive her firm and where she couldn't pound to pieces. In that way everybody might be saved and the steamer later pulled off.

Running before the wind in a heavy sea, as the steamer was, she frequently was driven off her course, but I watched carefully and took advantage of every lull to bring her back again.

The next light I saw after Pollock Rip was the red light on the Cross Rip Lightship between Nantucket and Martha's Vineyard. I was practically certain we were in the vicinity of the Cross Rip Lightship, when suddenly I caught sight of her.

We were almost near enough to touch the lightship. I hadn't expected to come so near, and as a matter of fact if I had hit her, I would have gone right through her like a piece of cheese. Just to show how my calculations worked I'll tell you an incident. After hauling up past Cross Rip the *Gloucester* did wonderfully. Finally I called to my mate and said to him that if my figuring was correct we ought to see the West Chop Light in eight minutes, reckoning, of course, on the increased speed. It was seven minutes when we saw a glimmer of light which we knew was West Chop. I was going a shade faster than I thought.

According to my calculation, we were fifteen miles beyond Gay Head when the snow began to thin out and I headed back into the eye of the wind. I had come out west-southwest and was then going east-northeast. Under these conditions we didn't make two knots an hour.

Along in the morning we began to get dim glimpses of the horizon. I was sure that I was near Block Island and I told my mate so. Within a relatively short time we sighted Block Island.

After that I ordered the sounding, and when we got to twelve fathoms I knew we were off the shore of Long Island. I kept the *Gloucester* headed along this course. Soon we were able to see four miles, and when I saw Fire Island abeam of us I knew my calculations had been exact.

I headed for shore and, to make a short story, I arrived at Norfolk at 6 o'clock Monday morning—exactly on time. Everybody was astonished. They expected that if we weren't lost, we would at least be late, but we weren't—we got there on time.

One thing that I never forgot about that storm, which, as a matter of fact, doesn't have anything to do with my trip, was a little incident that occurred just before we sailed from Boston.

When I came in the pilot house that afternoon I saw a well-built, good-looking young man talking to our quartermaster. I was impressed by the stranger's superior appearance, but I didn't inquire who he was.

After we had returned to Boston and learned of the *Portland*'s fate, my quartermaster said to me, "Captain, do you remember the man that was talking to me in the pilot house the day we sailed?" I replied in the affirmative. "Well, that was the quartermaster of the *Portland*, whose body was washed up later on the shores of Cape Cod."

My quartermaster always thought the young man, who was an excellent swimmer, had endeavored to swim ashore, but if such was the case, he didn't have a chance for survival in the fearful billows off the white sands of Cape Cod.

Many other craft out in the terrible *Portland* Gale did not survive the hurricane as well as did Captain Howes' *Gloucester*.

While Provincetown Harbor is well known as one of the safest on all the Atlantic Coast under usual storm conditions, the winds of the terrifying *Portland* hurricane simply overwhelmed a majority of the twenty-seven schooners then attempting to ride out the gale while anchored there.

Before the storm ended ten large vessels and several smaller craft had been driven ashore, while still others either foundered at their anchors or drifted into shallow water, where they pounded on the bottom until water-logged.

No less than nine wharves blew down on the Provincetown waterfront, with twenty-one buildings meeting a similar fate. The oldest inhabitant stated that he had never seen a storm like it in his life, and every person interviewed who was out in the gale declared that it was the severest of his life.

About five o'clock in the morning patrolman Frank C. Wager was out on the outer finger of land at Long Point, one and one-half miles to the eastward of the Wood End Station. Suddenly he discovered what seemed to be a vessel driving ashore. The blinding sheets of snow made it difficult to see with certainty, but he felt so sure that what he had seen was a wreck that he hurried back to his station, to give the alarm. Isaac G. Fisher, the ever-vigilant keeper, had climbed into the lookout tower just before daylight came, and he saw Wager "coming in, running very quick." The gale was at his back and helped him on. Fisher ran downstairs instantly and turned out his crew.

The wind, which had started to blow from the east, was now east northeast and gathering force. As soon as Wager delivered his message the boat was run down to the surf on the inside beach facing Provincetown, but it was impossible to get it any farther aboard the wagon, because each time they started the wind would blow it off and begin to smash it to pieces. Therefore it was taken down to the edge of the surf. The men began to push it along, wading with the boat in the water constantly up to their knees, and often to their arms. The gale frequently lifted the boat up, so that the men had to press it down by main force, and in this way, among dangerous drift logs and wreckage, they pushed on for several hours. Finally they had reached a point about a mile and a quarter along the beach to the east northeast.

Now two sunken schooners could be seen at intervals. At the point which the lifesavers had reached they got hold of a rope attached to a fish weir and hauled their boat out clear of the stakes. Then they took the oars and tried with all their might to pull toward the vessels. It was eleven o'clock and the gale was then at its greatest height. Relentlessly the storm forced them back to the shore. They had done all that men could do, and failed, for while they had been pulling and straining the wind had altered.

They had made a gallant struggle to gain a vantage point to windward, but the change had defeated them. It was the hardest battle they ever had. The gale now swung so far to the northward that there was no other way but to drag the boat around the coastline to a point another mile and a half distant, and a quarter of a mile north of where the vessels lay. They went about their new task with undaunted spirit and as much haste as they could, but the sea and wind often took them right off their feet, and progress was terribly slow. One of them was now sent to the station to bring such articles of food as he could pick up, while the rest laboriously pushed the boat along the shore at the edge of the surf.

At length, after several hours of ceaseless toil, they reached a position somewhat to windward, ready to push out. It was then four o'clock. Bravely, they rushed the boat through the surf, but, as Keeper Fisher said later, the wind, "fairly shrieking," forced them back.

Then they dragged their craft still farther to windward, and begged the aid of four fishermen who happened to be nearby. They double-manned the oars, and succeeded in pulling off some thirty yards or more, when they were again blown to the shore. For the third time they moved still farther to windward. Another launching was made with superhuman resolution. At last the sturdy boat forced her way out through the seas, not to return until the work was done.

Keeper Fisher set his course for the nearer of the two vessels, which proved to be the *Jordan L. Mott*. She was sunk at her anchors with no part of her hull above water except the after portion of the cabin. Four men, with benumbed and stiffened limbs, crept down from the rigging as the boat approached, and when it was pulled close under the stern were taken into it by the surfmen. Captain Charles E. Dyer, master of the *Mott*, was aboard with his mate,

Harry Miller, and two seamen, Winfred Thilbrook and Patrick Cambell. The lifeless body of the captain's father was lashed in the rigging, where it was left by the keeper as everyone realized that their first duty was to care for the living.

All hands had been in the shrouds for fifteen hours, and were fast approaching collapse. The boat was therefore quickly pulled to the beach in a direction favored by the wind, and a landing was effected about 5 P.M. Although the walk to the station was short, it consumed half an hour, the captain of the *Mott* and one sailor being so weak that the surfmen had to carry them.

At the station, stimulants were administered to all, and they were clad in dry clothing and placed in bed. In a few hours they showed marked improvement, but a full day elapsed before the captain could walk alone. The rescued men remained at the station three days, when they were able to travel to their homes without cost, their expenses being taken care of by the State of Massachusetts.

On the day after the rescue, the body of Mr. Charles E. Dyer, who perished on the *Mott* and the bodies of the five men who lost their lives on the *Lester A. Lewis* were taken from the wrecks and properly cared for.

The *Lewis* had been wrecked under precisely the same circumstances as the *Mott,* and all her crew took refuge in the rigging, where they perished before aid could reach them, some considerable time previous to the arrival of the lifesaving crew at the *Mott.*

All the witnesses out in the storm later agreed that the lifesaving men acquitted themselves with fidelity and heroism. Mr. Robert M. Lavander, agent of the underwriters said that "the storm was the most disastrous I ever knew in fifty years. It was impossible, in my opinion, for a boat to have pulled to windward. From the best information I have, I believe the efforts of the lifesavers were untiring and well directed in every way. Captain Dyer, of the *Jordan L. Mott,* told me that the lifesaving crew did everything in their power to help them."

Mr. J. N. Swift, one of the town officers, said later: "I was on an eminence at the northwest side of the harbor, but, owing to the dense sheets of spray and driving sleet, I failed to discover any one in the rigging of those vessels, nor could I see the boat of the lifesavers. From what I have learned of the circumstances, and from my knowledge of Keeper Fisher and the men, I believe they unquestionably did all in their power to rescue the imperiled sailors."

Even more calamitous was a disaster in Boston Harbor, the loss of the four-masted schooner *Abel E. Babcock*. This wreck occurred on the same day, although far less is known of its details.

The *Babcock* was a vessel of 812 tons, bound from Philadelphia to Boston, with a cargo of coal. Under command of Captain Abel E. Babcock, she carried eight men.

Some time after dark during the night of November 26, after anchoring in an exceedingly dangerous place, the *Babcock* dragged onto Toddy Rocks, nearly a mile from shore, and halfway between Fort Warren and Point Allerton, Hull, Massachusetts. She was pounded to fragments, all on board perishing on the spot. No one witnessed the disaster!

Near the same place, and about the same time that the *Babcock* was lost, Coal Barge No. 4 of Baltimore, Maryland, was also destroyed. Almost brand new, the vessel had been built in 1898, and weighed 920 tons. She struck on Toddy Rocks between midnight and one o'clock November 27, and went to pieces within a short time.

Of the five persons on board, the captain and a sailor managed to reach the shore alive by clinging to a piece of the deckhouse. Climbing painfully through kelp, broken timbers, spume, and jagged rocks, the two men reached the high-tide mark, and then saw a light in the distance. Struggling through the storm, they found the gleam was in a home, and knocked at the door. They received the most hospitable treatment until, together with the occupants of the house, they were driven out by the incoming tide. They were conveyed in a wagon, procured by Keeper Joshua James, to the Point Allerton Lifesaving Station, where they stayed until the storm ended.

As in the case of the *Babcock,* nobody knew anything of the disaster except that the wreckage was discovered about five o'clock in the morning on Wind Mill Point by the west patrol of the station. Both of these vessels were broken up so quickly, and the storm was so intense, that assistance would have been utterly impossible had the situation been known.

The *Don* Mystery

The State of Maine has three shipwreck mysteries in its maritime history which seem destined never to be solved. Each of these disasters occurred in a different century. Strangely enough, I have been personally involved in attempts to solve the riddles connected with all three tragedies.

The first mystery concerns the sloop *Industry*, which was built at Packard's Rock, now known as Cushing, Maine, in the year 1770. Launched late in the fall, she sailed for Boston on her maiden voyage in November, but never reached her destination.

Captain David Patterson, II, her master, was known as an expert sailor, having previously coasted for some time with Captain Reuben Hall. Others on board for the only trip the *Industry* ever made included a Major Fales and his son from Massachusetts, George Briggs, John Porterfield, Robert Gamble, John Mastick, David Malcolm, Alexander Baird, Samuel Watson, Mrs. Benjamin Packard and her child, and Abigail Patterson. Not one of the thirteen aboard was ever seen again, dead or alive. A few days after she had sailed wreckage began to come ashore all along the coast from

Cape Porpoise to Cape Ann, but her fate was shrouded in mystery.

In March 1960, one hundred and ninety years later, I was asked by Managing Editor J. N. Cole of the Kennebunk *Star* to visit and appraise a wreck whose ribs were beginning to appear out of the receding sand at a Kennebunk beach. I journeyed there at once with Naval Architect Bror Tamm of Quincy, Massachusetts, only to find that an easterly gale which had scoured away the sand from the wreck had covered it over again. With primitive methods, interested people from the area helped us dig it out, and after several days of investigation into the hull of what was obviously an ancient craft, we agreed that the wreck probably is the *Industry*. However, the evidence is not conclusive. Further research is now going on, and until the results are announced it cannot be stated with certainty that it is the hull of the missing sloop. In any event, we shall probably never know what brought her to her untimely end.*

The second mystery craft associated with Maine history is the steamer *Portland* ** which sailed from Boston for Portland, Maine, on November 26, 1898. In attempting to reach Portland the side-wheeler was seen going by Thatcher's Island at nine thirty that same night, and probably never reached a northerly point more than fifteen miles beyond, when she was pushed back by the storm. Later she sank to her doom off Cape Cod.

In 1945 I financed an expedition which discovered the hull of the *Portland* in 144 feet of water, seven miles out to sea from Race Point, Cape Cod. Diver Al George brought up identifiable fragments of the vessel at the time. Never-

---

* A boot which was discovered near the vessel's keelson has been identified as being of the mid-eighteenth century. A brick found nearby has been called typical of the year 1760. The crockery taken from the sand near the ship has not been identified as yet. The treenails with their convex-shaped wedges made with diamond-shaped heads were not of the Kennebunk area, and the type had never been used in any shipyard of the vicinity, in the opinion of former shipyard men present.

** See "Out in the *Portland* Gale," Chapter 19, in this volume.

theless, there will always be a mystery concerning the details of her final hours.

The third shipwreck mystery connected with the State of Maine is the loss with all persons aboard the 44-foot cabin cruiser *Don* which disappeared at sea on June 29, 1941. A trip from Dyer's Cove, East Harpswell, Maine, to Monhegan Island had been planned by Albert Melanson of Rumford as an outing for residents who lived in Rumford and Mexico, Maine, two towns close to each other, and situated some eighty miles north of Portland.

The group of thirty-four excursionists were to board the motorboat at about seven o'clock Sunday morning, June twenty-ninth. However, the various delays that almost always occur in setting forth on such expeditions postponed the departure until nine thirty.*

---

* The list of those who sailed aboard the ill-fated cruiser *Don* follows:

Arsenault, Raymond; Rumford, Stephens High School senior
Bridgham, Oscar; Auburn, father of Mrs. Miller mentioned below
Brundage, Miss Ramola; Reparessa, Cal.
Carey, James, Jr.; Stephens High School sophomore
Chapitis, Miss Mary; Rumford, employed by the Kerseys
Coburn, Mrs. Edith; Rumford, employed at the insurance office of Harold McInnes
Cormier, Albert; a former clerk in Parent's Clothing Store, Rumford
Cormier, Edmund; Rumford painter, brother of Albert
Coulombe, Miss Marie Rose; Rumford, employed by the Kerseys, mentioned below
Decker, Earl; Assistant personnel manager at the Oxford mill
Decker, Helen; Mexico, stenographer in the law office of Ralph T. Parker
Elliot, Harold; Rumford, employed by the Eastern States Farmer's Exchange
Foster, Norman; son of Mr. and Mrs. Donald Foster, Auburn
Hemingway, Miss Ruth; Rumford, employed at the home of Dr. J. A. Greene
Howard, Miss Elizabeth; Rumford, clerk in the Rumford Falls Trust Co.
Howard, Elliott, Rumford; Miss Howard's brother, employed by the Sunny Ridge Tea Room
Hutchins, Harry; employee of the Rumford Falls Power Co.
Johnson, Captain Paul; East Harpswell, skipper of the *Don*
Kawlaicze, Miss Adele; Rumford, an employee of the Personal Finance Co.
Kersey, Dorcas Shand; Rumford milliner
Kersey, Jack; Rumford jeweler, husband of Dorcas
Melanson, Alban; clerk in the J. I. Dorion's Handy store

With all his party on board, Captain Paul Johnson steered the *Don* out through the channel, landing later at West Point near Cape Small. There the passengers went ashore at Reed's General Store, where some of them addressed post cards to the loved ones they were fated never to see again. Miss Beatrice Roach mailed a card to her mother which read, "Feeling fine, not seasick. But there is still 30 more miles to go, Bea."

At eleven o'clock that morning the *Don* headed for sea again; this time her destination was Monhegan Island. According to those who watched her departure, a fog which had been threatening all morning was thickening just a trifle as the *Don* disappeared down the bay. She was never seen again.

Darkness fell, but there was no word of any sort from the thirty-four excursionists who had left Dyer's Cove in such a happy mood almost twelve hours before. Relatives and friends became concerned, especially as the fog was getting denser. Midnight passed, but attempts of other craft to search for the *Don* were hampered by the lack of visibility, limiting the area in which the rescuers could cruise.

The Damariscove Island Coast Guard had been alerted, and for ten hours without rest a patrol boat searched through the foggy waters of Casco Bay for some sign of the missing

---

Melanson, Albert; Rumford, Clerk in the Rumford Falls Trust Co., orchestra leader
Melanson, Albert; Jr., son of Albert Melanson
Melanson, Robert; son of Albert Melanson
Miller, Dr. Oscar; Livermore Falls
Miller, Mrs. Oscar; Livermore Falls
Roach, Miss Beatrice; employed with the M.B.A. Insurance Agency, Rumford
Robertson, William; Mexico, Oxford mill worker
Sanders, Miss Lelia; secretary to Paul Thurston, president of the Rumford Falls Trust Co.
Skolfield, Miss Arline; Mexico, secretary to Harry J. Buncke, assistant manager of the Oxford Mill
Stisulis, Miss Anne; Rumford, an Oxford office employee
Strople, Miss Bessie; Rumford, clerk at the Rumford Falls Trust Co.
Wishart, Dr. Robert; Rumford Dentist

cruiser. In charge of the operation was Captain Milton H. Seavy, who had as his assistants during the long, tiring marine vigil Thomas M. Manchester and John W. Foss.

The hours went by, and there were no new developments. When dawn broke Monday morning it was still foggy. A telephone call to Monhegan was made, and it was discovered that the *Don* had never reached her destination. Soon afterward a complete check of all locations revealed that she was not at any harbor of refuge in the area.

All that day the search went on, with many relatives and friends making their headquarters around the eleven empty cars which the passengers had left at Dyer's Cove.

When the fog lifted briefly that Tuesday morning it was hoped that the boat might be found drifting at sea with engine trouble, but again the hours passed without news of any sort.

Suddenly, however, all hopes were shattered when the bodies of two of the women passengers, Dorcas Kersey and Bessie Strople, were discovered floating in the sea off Bailey Island. A short time later another body was sighted, that of Anne Stisulis. The remains of Elizabeth Howard were then found off Bailey Island. In all, fourteen bodies were eventually recovered.* Captain Paul Johnson's body was discovered attached to a wooden keg, firmly tied to a rope around his waist. Not a single victim found wore a life preserver, indicating that whatever occurred took place suddenly. Several of the bodies were said to have been blackened and burned as if by an explosion, but this was later disputed.

As the days went by certain revelations concerning the *Don* were made. Residents who lived near Dyer's Cove stated that the boat had been allowed to stay in the ice at her moorings all the preceding winter. Others volunteered the information that she had gone to the bottom on two

---

* Lobsterman Claude Johnson was instrumental in sighting and bringing in at least one of the victims.

previous occasions when there had been no passengers aboard.

It was also claimed that Orrin Scott of the area had warned Captain Johnson two years before that the people of the vicinity would not consider Johnson one of themselves until he put some "good gear" on the *Don*, as she was then a "patch job."

The usual theory is that gasoline in the bilge water exploded and fired the craft, and that the thick pea-soup fog which lasted off and on until July 2 prevented more bodies from being discovered.

Two statements were given at the time, one by Paul C. Thurston, president of the Rumford Falls Trust Company, and the other by a prominent resident of the community, Douglas Fosdick. Thurston believed that the gas tank had been giving Captain Johnson trouble, as the latter had been working on it almost up to the very time when the trip started. He was of the opinion that the tank had developed a slight leak that morning, which produced fumes in the cabin and gasoline in the bilge. He believed that when Captain Paul Johnson lighted a fire to cook the chowder, an explosion followed at once. Paul Thurston did not believe that the boat had capsized. He was of the opinion that the tragedy occurred a little less than ten miles out to sea from West Point.

Douglas Fosdick stated that he believed that Captain Paul Johnson had no license to operate a motorboat carrying passengers for hire. In Fosdick's opinion the boat did not explode because of gasoline. He based his belief on the viewpoint of fishermen and medical examiners, that the marks found on the bodies were bruises and not burns. "The hair on the skin of the victims was not burned off," said Fosdick.

The *Don* had been used as a rum-runner in prohibition days. She was a double-ender with precariously high superstructure.

Clothing and watches found on the bodies of victims aided

the searchers to get some picture of what probably happened. A watch taken from the wrist of Marie Rose Coulombe was found stopped at 11:42, indicating the approximate time that fateful morning when the disaster occurred.

An editorial in the Rumford Falls *Times* of July 3, 1941, concluded that "the catastrophe that overtook the ill-fated party came with appalling suddenness. One moment they were chugging serenely along in the calm waters of Casco Bay. In another they were struggling for life in those dark waters. What heroic dramas were then enacted no man will ever know. Some perhaps died before they entered the water, some survived to swim briefly about the lost boat before their strength ebbed and failed.

"On shore early Monday morning word was received that the boat was overdue, but efforts of searchers were hampered by the pea-soup thick fog banks that had rolled in covering the islands with a cottony blanket. Hope was sustained for twenty-four hours until Tuesday morning when the bodies of two women were found by a woman cottager.

"Stunned by the magnitude of the calamity, Rumford and Mexico wait helplessly for the sea to give up the bodies of the souls it has claimed. All the honors that the living can extend to the dead will be ordered by the people of these communities. The pain of the loss is sharp. The grief is deep."

A day was set apart for memorial exercises for those who had lost their lives in the disaster. On Sunday, July 6, 1941, hundreds of people gathered at Rumford's Chisholm Park for services. To begin the memorial exercises appropriate music was played by the Rumford band, after which the opening remarks were given by Justice Albert Beliveau. He explained that "it was deemed fit by public-spirited citizens of the towns of Rumford and Mexico that such a demonstration as this should take place so that we might express in public our sorrow at the sudden departure of these well-known and prominent citizens, men and women of these two towns who, because of their work, came in contact daily with most of the people."

Rev. Joseph W. Merchant gave the invocation, after which a tribute in Lithuanian, in memory of the victims of that nationality who had perished, was made by Rev. Benjamin Rybokas. His words were followed by those of Rev. Arthur Cloutier, who spoke in French. The Lord's Prayer was then sung by Miss Nathaline Foster, who was accompanied on the organ by C. W. Newell. Also speaking at the memorial exercises were Rev. Harley A. Shattuck, Governor Sumner Sewall of Maine, and Rev. Timothy J. O'Mahoney. The benediction was pronounced by Rev. Philip J. Brown.

On the same day that memorial exercises were held at Rumford, other services were conducted at the church and at the wharf on Bailey Island. A sorrowful, impressive journey was made by the Sea and Shore Fisheries boat *Maine.* As she rounded the buoy off Mark Island Ledge, flowers were dropped from the boat into the sea. On shore at the same moment, the Bailey Island flag was lowered to half mast. Taps were sounded, and wreaths and flowers were thrown from the pier into the water. The Rev. James E. Herrick then offered a short prayer from the pier, and the Fisheries boat started back to the wharf. Because of the size of the church, services held inside the Bailey Island chapel could only be attended by a few of the hundreds of persons anxious to be present.

The years went by. In 1958 came a report that wreckage had been found which might prove to be that of the *Don.* I organized a searching group to attempt positive identification of the hull, but the results of our underwater efforts did nothing to solve the mystery. Fifty-three letters concerning the disaster yielded much additional information which I had not heard before. Whether that information is accurate is another matter. I was told that a Captain Joseph R. Bernier had been down under water in an attempt to find the hull at

Bald Dick Ledge a year or two after the disaster, but had been unsuccessful.

At the present writing, August 1960, the mystery as to what may have happened has not been solved. In my opinion, because of newly revealed information, it is greater than ever.

A letter I have in my possession states that unidentified parties might have decided to sink the *Don* for reasons which to me are still obscure, and that Captain Johnson was unaware of the plot.

One letter I have gives a weird theory, after which it concludes as follows: "It's just too fantastic to believe, but I know."

Another writer says with assurance that a German U-boat sank the *Don*. This letter is based on the fact that the writer picked up a bag of "Brim" with a German inscription on it, at or near Bailey Island.

The diving which was conducted under my supervision in 1959 and 1960 has so far added nothing to satisfy me one way or another. I would be pleased to show any one my dossier of material on the *Don*. I would not possibly dare to print some of the letters I have received, because of the almost unbelievable implications. However, I will allow any reliable person to examine all the records which we have gathered together, but the reader of this chapter must be satisfied with the following quotes from four different letters:

A U-boat sent the *Don* to the bottom under the cover of fog. It had waited between Monhegan Island and the mainland for an appropriate time and victim.

* * *

A mine which had been placed at the entrance to Halifax Harbor to keep out the German submarines broke from its moorings, drifted down the coast, and blew up when it bumped against the hull of the *Don*.

* * *

There is something about the disappearance of the thirty-four people and the *Don* which is so mysterious, and so far-fetched from reality, that in my opinion the disaster will never be solved. If it is solved and the truth in all its strangeness comes out, no one will believe it anyway.

*   *   *

The loss of the *Don* will always be an enigma. I have heard so many rumors from so many sources, that I now believe that the entire affair, horrible as it is to say so, was planned from beginning to end. There are greater forces than we can understand at the back of the disaster, and the average person will never know the truth which has been known for some time by certain residents of Casco Bay.

XXI

North Shore Marine Disasters

The passing years often eliminate all but the merest glimpse of a dramatic tragedy along our Massachusetts shores, but I have thought it better to include even the barest details of such disasters than to ignore them completely. Many unusual shipwreck stories which have never appeared in print before in any form are included in this and the two following chapters. The task has involved most exacting research in a number of cases.

The mariner, approaching Boston Harbor from the north, east, or south, finds himself well guided during almost all types of weather by the buoys and lighthouses. Even the many islands and ledges offer considerable lee for the smaller craft which otherwise might meet the direct onslaught of the storms and winds.

Nevertheless, it was those same islands and ledges which made the approach to Boston both difficult and dangerous in former years. Even today, lighthouses and buoys are merely "aids" to navigation. Naturally they cannot prevent storms or entirely eliminate maritime disasters.

It might be said that the dangers of ocean or coastwise travel have more than kept up with scientific improvements, such as radar and fathometers. Tens of thousands of small craft now roam the coastal seas with such powerful engines that they can easily reach, if they are foolhardy, locations twenty or thirty miles from land in a few hours.

Down through the centuries of recorded New England history, the coastline, which includes the North Shore of Massachusetts, has been the scene of countless shipwrecks.

Almost at the very beginning of Boston's settlement, in 1631, the barque *Warwick* was hit by a southeast wind, as John Winthrop tells us, and barely escaped smashing to pieces on the rocks of the Outer Harbor. Five years later a strong northeast wind completely wrecked the *Warwick* inside the harbor, but the exact location of the wreck has not come down to us.*

On February 18, 1631, a vessel belonging to John Glover of Dorchester was wrecked on the cruel rocks of Nahant, but one by one the crew swam ashore and saved their own lives.

In May 1657, a vessel owned by Captain Thomas Wiggin of Portsmouth, New Hampshire, was wrecked on Long Beach, Lynn. All on board escaped death.

In the month of September, 1682, Captain Horton sailed from Nevis in the West Indies to Boston with a cargo of silver aboard his craft. Entering Massachusetts Bay in a blinding snowstorm, he soon lost all direction and his craft slid by the Brewster Islands late at night on November 27. Early the next morning at low water, the ship shattered near the end of what is now Winthrop Bar.

Of the thirteen sailors on board, three were washed over-

_____

* Towed later into Dorchester Bay, the *Warwick* was taken into a cove or creek in the Dorchester area, which later became known as the Barque Warwick Cove. Apparently the old craft is still buried in the mud or silt of the neighborhood. The area later became a street, which was called Barque Warwick Street as late as 1848, when it appears as such on the survey of the period. It is now known as Freeport Street, with a giant sign on the Southeast Expressway so designating it.

board and drowned at once. The other ten men were successful in reaching what is now the Town of Winthrop, but as they walked along Shirley Gut Plain toward the residence of Dean Winthrop, one by one they began to falter and fall. Only six of them reached the house alive. The other four had frozen to death. Winthrop took the survivors in and gave them food and shelter.

The great cargo of silver, however, has baffled all who have tried to find it through the more than two and three-quarter centuries which have elapsed since the ship went to its doom.

During the year 1752 a ship named *Bumper* was wrecked on what is now Winthrop Beach. Knowing that crewman John Scalley had smallpox, the cowardly captain deserted the ship. When the tide went down Captain Cussen sent his crew aboard the ship to get Scalley. They returned with the victim, who had died, wrapped in a hammock, and buried him under some rocks. Two days later the ship and the corpse were discovered by the inhabitants of Point Shirley.

Not knowing of the man's sickness, the people boarded the ship and took ashore all usable material. As a result, Bartholomew Flagg, Benjamin Pratt, Samuel Tuttle, Jr., and Thomas Patten died of smallpox, and soon the people in Boston also became infected.

On February 24, 1755, a schooner from Salem under the command of Captain Collins was cast away at Short Beach, Nahant.

On February 6, 1757, two great merchant vessels from London, valued with their cargoes at one hundred thousand pounds apiece, were smashed ashore and wrecked at Lynn Beach.

On February 8, 1766, an English brig from Hull was cast away on Pond Beach, located at the "South Side of Nahant."

A canoe from shore put out to a schooner in Lynn Bay on August 8, 1769. Aboard were six women and two men. The canoe capsized on the journey out, and two of the group, Anna Hood, 23 years old, and a seventeen-year-old youth drowned.

During the following month, on September 8, a great storm hit the area. A sloop came ashore at Nahant and several buildings were blown down in Lynn.

On March 21, 1772, a fishing schooner was wrecked on Long Beach, Lynn. The only two men aboard, Jonathan Collins and William Boynton, lost their lives in the sea.

Captain Pendelton's sloop was wrecked on Lynn Beach on January 26, 1788, but as far as is known no one was drowned.

A great storm hit the north shore on December 9, 1795. At the height of the gale the Scottish brig *Peggy*, commanded by Captain John Williamson, was wrecked near the southern end of Lynn Beach. Aboard was a cargo of dried fish, the consignment of Thomas Amory of Boston. As the brig neared the shore Seaman Hugh Cameron had been ordered into the longboat to make the tackle fast. A gigantic wave swept the ship, breaking the longboat free, and took overboard all Cameron's eleven companions, including Captain Williamson. Cameron was pushed ashore in the longboat, but the others perished. The brig soon became a total wreck.

Eight bodies were recovered, and two days later the seamen were buried from the First Parish Meeting House, where the Rev. Mr. Thacher preached a sermon from Job 1:19, stressing the verse, "And I only am escaped alone!" During the sermon sole survivor Hugh Cameron stood in the center aisle alone, a pitiful, bewildered figure.

On February 20, 1829, several Swampscott vessels were driven to sea. Five days later, one craft came ashore at Chatham, the crew still alive but suffering terribly from frostbite.

In a mighty gale which swept in from the Atlantic on January 15, 1831, a schooner belonging to Stephen Smith tore loose from her moorings off the North Shore and later battered herself to pieces against the new granite seawall then being built at Deer Island near Winthrop. She smashed down sixty feet of the new wall in the process.

In 1836 the Boston brig *Shamrock*, Captain Joslin in command, was wrecked on Long Beach, Nahant. Her cargo of sugar and molasses was declared a total loss.

The schooner *Thomas*, with a lumber cargo, her master, Captain William Sproul of Belfast, Maine, was wrecked on the Nahant peninsula at the southern end of Long Beach. When their longboat swamped, five out of seven aboard perished.

On Friday, March 30, 1847, it was reported that the schooner *James Harney*, sailing from Digby, Nova Scotia, to Boston, was ashore on Long Beach, Nahant. Her crew of six was saved.

On October 16, 1851, the British schooner *Brothers* struck Swampscott's outer ledge. The crew of seven landed safely, however, with the assistance of Edward C. Bates, who went to their rescue. The wreck then battered itself ashore near Mr. Tudor's residence at Nahant Rocks.

On November 21, 1851, the brig *Exile* of Yarmouth, Nova Scotia, was wrecked off Lynn Beach. Great loads of her deck cargo of wood came ashore. Over a thousand people gathered on the beach that night, and used the wood for bonfires by the light of which the crew eventually rowed ashore in safety. It was said later that the scene was one of "terrific grandeur."

On Sunday afternoon, January 18, 1857, one of the greatest snowstorms which had visited New England within the memory of the oldest inhabitant hit the New England coast. That morning the weather was extremely cold, the thermometer ranging between twelve and twenty degrees below zero. The wind blew up and down the streets of many coastal towns and cities with great drifts piled up throughout the area. As far as is known, most of the men "stayed indoors." Quoting from the Lynn *Reporter*, "As for the women—we got a glimpse of a petticoat crossing Spring Street . . . she went up Exchange Street with a spanking breeze . . . some pluck in women after all."

The storm extended over nearly all of eastern Canada and hit New Brunswick and Nova Scotia especially hard. In the United States, Massachusetts, New Hampshire, and Maine were especially subjected to the blasts of the gale.

The ocean in that storm was a terrible thing to watch. Although there is no more sublime view in nature than a peaceful sea, when the storm of January 18, 1857 hit the coast, the waves were lashed to a fury. On the North Shore, the beach all the way from Gloucester to Winthrop was a solid mass of ice, forming a succession of cliffs against which the waves broke at high tide.

Into such a scene, the American bark *Tedesco* sailed. Hailing from Portland, Maine, homeward bound with a cargo of sherry wine, salt, and raisins, the *Tedesco* was overwhelmed by a combination of fearsome wind and gigantic waves. Indeed, it must have been a night of terror to everyone on board, but not a soul lived to tell his story.

Whether or not the captain made any effort to save his ship will never be known. The *Tedesco* had been seen sailing between Pig Rock and Egg Rock Light in a moderate northwest breeze late that afternoon. When the wind hauled to the northeast, a furious gale began. Before the snow shut in, the residents along the shore were of the opinion that the *Tedesco* had sailed up the bay to a snug harbor in Boston.

The storm hit with terrible intensity, and all those down on the beach had to struggle to reach home. The *Tedesco* probably crashed to her doom about three hours after she was last sighted, smashing ashore on the rocks about three hundred feet east northeast of Gallope's Point in Swampscott. The snow soon piled up to such a degree that it was many hours before the residents of Swampscott could reach the beach, then strewn with wreckage, but by this time every person on the *Tedesco* had perished in the surf.

Bodies later began to come ashore on Whale Beach, from which residents brought them to the Methodist Church. On February first, two more victims were found on Whale Beach when the tide melted the snow in the area. Probably they had been thrown up by the surf and covered almost at once by the snowstorm.

A formal inquest was later held by Hiram M. Breed. At this investigation, a former mate of the *Tedesco*, Mr. Joseph Cowper, testified that a ring found on the beach belonged to the captain—Peterson by name—of the *Tedesco*. Cowper's official statement follows:

> I was in Swampscott on the 21st, ult., saw these bodies, identified them all as belonging to the barque *Tedesco*. They were all Prussians and Swedes except the steward who belonged to Long Island, New York. I saw the two dead bodies on the second, instant.
>
> I identified one as being Charles Neilson; the other body was the body of Captain Peterson of the said barque *Tedesco*. I was formerly mate of the barque *Tedesco*. I joined her in Cardiff and left her at Cadiz. I arrived in New York in the Brig *William B. Nash*. I came to Boston to join the *Tedesco*.
>
> Ten men in all were on the barque *Tedesco* when she sailed from Cadiz. I think a woman was also aboard. I was connected with the barque *Tedesco* nearly three months; all but two, the

mate and the cook, were shipped at Cardiff. I knew the mate who was on the barque *Tedesco* when she sailed from Cadiz. His name was Porte Jacobs and he belonged to Cherryfield, Maine.

On Tuesday afternoon, the owner of the *Tedesco*, Francis D. Little, visited Swampscott and also identified one of the bodies as being that of Captain Peterson. He gave orders for its removal to Portland.

A lady's purse was found containing forty-two gold five-franc pieces. This may have proved that there was a lady aboard the fated vessel, but her presence is still an unsolved mystery. A watch was also found with Captain Peterson's name on it.

After it was agreed that all the bodies that might come ashore had been found, they were given an impressive funeral at the Methodist Church and then buried in the Swampscott cemetery.

Two locations in Swampscott are named after the *Tedesco*. The boulder where the bark hit at Gallope's Point is still called Tedesco Rock. The Tedesco Country Club is known all over New England as a prominent social organization.

It was said that the captain had married a lady in Cadiz just before the *Tedesco* went to sea, but what happened to her is a question which probably will never be answered.* Her clothes, it appears, were carried on board, for portions of a dress were found on the beach. Only six bodies were ever recovered—those of five men and a boy.

It appears that the names on the shipping paper were not the names of the lost men, but were those of the crew who shipped aboard in Boston for the voyage to Cadiz where they then left the vessel. None of the original crew remained

---

* The vessel's papers were found, giving the following names of the officers and crew: H. Peterson, Captain; Edward Johol, first mate; Thomas Andres, second mate; Henry Dow, cook; Nichol Jackson; Charles Peterson; Charles Melson; Edward Jackson; Frederick Hins; Lehon Neilson; and William Neilson.

except the captain, a seaman who was appointed second mate, and the cook.

On account of some misunderstanding between the captain and the crew, all but two of those who had sailed with him from Boston left him at Cadiz. The first mate reported that he engaged a new crew, and then resigned his own place in the vessel, which was filled by a new mate.

One body proved to be that of the cook, Mr. Henry Dow, a native of Long Island, New York. With the exception of this man, the crew were foreigners. Mr. Dow was supposed to be "somewhat out of his sphere" but for what reasons he took to the sea no one knew. His people in Long Island were said to have been in easy circumstances. Well dressed, even in death he appeared as "a handsome comely man."

The *Tedesco*'s hull was eventually ground into fragments by the fury of the water and dashed upon the beach. The solid timbers were soon broken up, except for the bow and masts, and little of the once majestic vessel could be found ten days after the wreck.*

Slightly more than two years later another great storm hit the North Shore. The British bark *Vernon* had sailed from Messina, Italy, late in the year 1858, bound for Boston with a great cargo, consisting mostly of fruit. Entering Massachusetts Bay early in the morning of February 3, she encountered the tremendous blow, and shortly after daybreak was driven into a dangerous position off Long Beach, near Little Nahant. Residents of nearby communities soon noticed the *Vernon*, and by eight o'clock that morning the beach was lined with hundreds of spectators.

Shortly before nine o'clock she struck bottom. Fisherman Otis Newhall, in spite of the heavy sea then running, put out

---

* The *Tedesco* was built at Brunswick, Maine, in 1847. Valued at $15,000 she was insured for that amount in Boston. Her cargo, sherry wine and salt, was worth over $15,000, the wine being consigned to J. D. & M. Williams, and to E. Codman & Co. of Boston.

in his dory in an attempt to reach the wreck and take some of the crew ashore. Just as he launched into the breaking waves a small boat was seen to leave the bark. Newhall successfully ran the gauntlet of the first three breaking waves, but the boat from the *Vernon* was caught in a giant wave which broke into the stern sheets and capsized her.

Three men were thrown into the waves. Two of them were rescued by swimming back to the *Vernon*, where they were hoisted aboard, but the third, Mate William Bond, was caught in the breakers and carried halfway to shore. Otis Newhall, still rowing out, heard shouts from the people lining the beach, and noticed that they were pointing to a spot out in the water.

Rowing in that direction, he discovered Mate Bond making his last feeble attempts to stay afloat. Newhall skillfully maneuvered his dory alongside the struggling sailor, pulled him in across the stern, and started for shore. Watching his chances, and waiting for the smaller waves, he then took one of the breakers to run the dory high on the beach, where he was assisted in getting the mate to safety.

Zebedee Small, whose name has come down to us through the years as the winner of a Massachusetts Humane Society medal in the year 1853, now called together a crew for a trip to the *Vernon*. Launching with the help of the others, he and his crew capsized on the second wave and were forced to return. Again, he put out, and again the lifeboat capsized. Tired from his exertions, Small was forced to allow others to make the next attempt to reach the stricken vessel.

By this time it was noon. Fragments of the *Vernon*'s stern began to break off and come ashore, with lemons and oranges from the cargo littering the beach for hundreds of yards up and down the shore. Although the prospects for saving the vessel were now considered poor, all her masts and spars were still standing.

Captain Miles Blanchard, a famous sailor of his day, asked for volunteers for another attempt which he planned. Soon he chose a crew, with other volunteers ready to give the lifeboat her final push into the breakers. Standing in the stern, Blanchard grabbed his long rudder oar and the launching began. Meeting the first wave as it broke partly into the foresheets,* the crew continued to row and were soon out of immediate danger. They headed at once for the wreck. While this was going on a group of Swampscott fishermen had also decided to make an attempt to reach the wreck, and launched successfully from a nearby point.

The two rescuing boats neared the bark, where they arranged to divide the *Vernon*'s crew between them. Within half an hour every man had been taken from the shipwreck, and now the trip to shore began. Running the risk of being engulfed time and again, the lifeboat under the command of Captain Blanchard finally hit the beach, where it was quickly unloaded by volunteers.

Ten minutes later the Swampscott men landed their human freight fifty yards nearer to Little Nahant. Every one aboard the *Vernon* had been saved. The crew was taken at once to the Sagmore Hotel, where they received care and nourishment after their long exposure to the elements.

At low water the following day the bark was high and dry. The remaining cargo was partially salvaged, but the bark herself was never repaired. The cargo had been consigned to Messrs. Daniel Draper and Son, Boston, and consisted of 448 cantars ** of brimstone, 109 barrels and 65 bags of canary seed, 50 bags of filberts, 100 boxes of almonds, 4940 boxes of lemons and oranges, and 27 cases of manna. The *Vernon* had been a fine looking bark of 265 tons, and belonged to Pictou, Nova Scotia.

For many years afterward the people of Lynn, Nahant, and Swampscott dated all events in relation to the year when the wreck of the *Vernon* came ashore. An artist's conception of

---

* The open space just forward of the first thwart, as compared to the stern sheets, the space abaft the stern thwart
** An Italian unit of weight representing 111.1 pounds.

the shipwreck, a picture which had a fabulous sale at the time, is part of this volume.

* * *

On Sunday, January 13, 1856, occurred an event about which people on the North Shore talked for two generations afterward, the wreck of the *Irene*. On Saturday night, January 12, Keeper Hugh Douglass at Boston Light noticed that the wind was beginning to come up. He remarked at the time that it was likely another northeast storm was on the way. By midnight six inches of snow had fallen, but when dawn came it was raining hard. By this time the wind had reached gale intensity and many ships at sea were in peril. Shortly after daylight, Captain Douglass noticed that a schooner had crashed against the dreaded Shag Rocks, half a mile from the lighthouse. The schooner was the *Lewis* and her captain, Captain Crowell, had perished with all of his crew.

At eight o'clock that same morning, five miles away, the great ship *Irene* of 1,188 tons, commanded by Captain Williams, crashed on Winthrop Bar. The crew cut the masts away and she slid across the bar, hitting the beach between Great Head and the Paul Revere Copper Works, at Point Shirley. A large part of her cargo was strewn up and down the beach, and thousands of spools of thread were picked up as the tide receded. Among other articles of cargo, the *Irene* carried 179 tons of salt, 15 crates of earthenware, and 30 hogsheads of soda. By noon there were more than ten feet of water in her hold, and it was feared she was doomed.

Lying stern on, the *Irene* presented a tragic sight, and hundreds of people journeyed to Winthrop to view her. The next day the wind died down, and the waves subsided enough for two sloops to run in at high tide and load what remained of her cargo. Tuesday morning the two craft, the *Noddle* and the *Sampson*, arrived at Boston with full loads. The remaining cargo was moved from between decks. The

ship, considerably lightened, was pulled off Point Shirley
Beach on Sunday morning, January 20, 1856, by the steamer
S. A. Stevens, and towed up to Boston with the help of the
tug *Neptune.*

The *Irene* had been built in Essex, Connecticut, in 1851.
A year and four days after she was freed from the sands of
Point Shirley, she ran aground on Long Island, New York,
and became a total wreck. But there were many residents
over in Winthrop who remembered her for a generation, as
they were still using thread from her cargo and eating from
dishes gathered from the crates strewn along the shore by the
gale of January 1856. Some idea of the severity of the storm
may be realized when it was discovered that the buoys guarding vessels from Grave's Ledge and Harding's Ledge were
both washed away, and the Lightship anchored off Minot's
Ledge was unable to flash her customary warning signals.

Skin divers of a future generation may be confused when,
and if, they are fortunate enough to discover at the bottom
of the sea off Winthrop, Massachusetts, a collection of old
Spanish guns. A great snowstorm which began on the night
of January 13, 1874, completely buried all the towns and
cities along the North Shore. Out on the ocean, attempting
to reach Boston Harbor during the gale, the schooner *Minnie,*
of Nova Scotia, was being buffeted by the gale. She crashed
on Short Beach during the night and became a hopeless
wreck. The unusual cargo of about twenty ancient guns
from old Spanish forts of the West Indies was never recovered. The schooner went to pieces rapidly, but Captain
Shaw and seven sailors were saved.

A storm which began on Monday night, March 26, 1879,
grew to blizzard intensity before midnight. When dawn
came it was seen that no less than four vessels were in distress
off Winthrop Beach. Never before or since in the history
of Winthrop have so many ships been in trouble at once.

Two of the vessels, whose names were not ascertained, were able to avoid being stranded by anchoring in the shallow water where the waves were breaking. During a lull in the storm both ships slid into deeper water and were freed.

The other two craft were not so fortunate. Both from Maine, they had run into the gale off Portland. The brig *Katahdin*, heavily loaded with shooks for the West Indies, crashed on the beach at Ocean Spray, while the schooner *Ida L. Ray*, loaded down with iron rails for New York, piled up over Seal Rocks and was soon high and dry on the beach. Both crews, rescued by members of the tug *H. A. Belknap*, were brought up to Boston. The captain's wife was among those taken from the *Katahdin*. Later in the week the two vessels were pulled off the Winthrop shore, placed in drydock in Boston, and eventually they were put back into service.

A howling blizzard swept up the Atlantic coast on January 9, 1886, trapping the *Juliette*, a heavily loaded granite schooner just inside the Graves. Captain Leach made an effort to run for the inner harbor, but the giant combers swept his vessel against the cruel rocks of Great Fawn Bar, Deer Island, a mile from the Winthrop shore. The schooner keeled over on her beam end and soon went to pieces. Three of the crew were drowned, and the other three were seen clinging desperately to the wreckage. News of the shipwreck spread quickly, and within a short time a crowd of men and boys were wading waist deep in the snow of Gut Plain, Point Shirley, watching the craft rolling back and forth in the surf.

They saw a tug going out to the wreck, and then witnessed a great rescue when three inmates of the penal institution on Deer Island rowed over to the wreck and took the survivors off, for which they were rewarded by a reduction in their sentences.

Back on the Winthrop shore wreckage drifted up on the beach. Wallace Wyman picked up the logbook and a trunk, and later obtained one of the sideboards. Many months afterward Wyman found a boot, which came ashore with a human foot still inside.

During the early morning hours of a foggy day in March 1899, the freighter *Norseman* drove aground on Tom Moore Rocks off Marblehead. A tremendous sea was raging at the time, and it was feared that the vessel might go to pieces. Lifebelts were quickly passed around, and Captain Rees ordered a rocket shot off. At the same time he blew a distress signal on the *Norseman*'s whistle.

At daylight a crew from the Massachusetts Humane Society's station rowed a lifeboat out to the scene, 250 yards from shore, but Captain John H. L. Giles, in charge of the surfboat was unable to establish contact with those on the steamer because of the heavy surf. As soon as Giles decided that he could not take off any of the 102 men aboard, he returned to shore. News of the shipwreck spread rapidly, and soon the rocks of Marblehead were covered with people.

When the sun came out to disperse the fog, a line was shot across to the stranded *Norseman*, and in a short time the breeches buoy was in place. At eight o'clock that morning, less than five hours after the wreck, the first passenger rode high above the breaking waves to land safely ashore. Another gun was fired across the ship, and another breeches buoy was attached. With the rapid service of the two lines, all the crew and passengers were ashore within a few hours.

Plans were then made to save the *Norseman*. Great crowds gathered daily on the rocks, conjecturing about the possibility of getting her off. Camera tripods were set up in every suitable location, and hundreds of pictures were taken. A few days later the combined efforts of the tugs *Juno*, *Mercury*, *Pallas*, and *Confidence*, all from Boston, freed the *Norseman*. It was indeed a thrilling spectacle as the victorious vessels started for Boston with the crippled steamer in tow.

Massachusetts lobster dealers frequently take relatively small craft down the coast to Maine where they buy a cargo of lobsters for the Boston market and bring it up the coast. Charles Johnson, owner of a three-ton launch, and Hervey Leo, both of Beachmont, Massachusetts, left Cape Porpoise, Maine, on the afternoon of October 20, 1908, bound for Boston with a heavy shipment of lobsters. They were never seen alive again. The next morning fishermen found the boat sunk, outside and to the northwest of the breakwater which forms the harbor of Rockport, Massachusetts, with the stern just above the water.

Apparently the two lobstermen were trying to make harbor at Rockport because of rough weather. A strong wind had sprung up during the night, and an exceptionally heavy sea was rolling by midnight. Without decks or coverings except for a small engine house aft, the lobster launch was not suited for the open water under any conditions of weather, and her heavy load made the trip from Cape Porpoise suicidal.

In the opinion of the keeper of the Straitsmouth lifesaving station, within whose official jurisdiction the casualty occurred, the boat struck either the breakwater or a submerged rock, damaging herself so badly that those on board were unable to beach her before she settled. Her engine, when examined after the tragedy, indicated full speed ahead. Neither of the bodies of the lobstermen was ever recovered, so far as is known.

It was brought out at the official inquiry after the disaster that many of the fishing boats doing business off the coast did not carry lights, and this may have been true of the launch involved in this accident. The boat went down a mile from the lifesaving station, too far away for any one in the lookout to have seen her unless she had displayed signals.

The tragedy which befell thirteen young boys from Lynn, Massachusetts, left a lasting impression on all those who were in any way associated with it. On the night of March 29, 1917, the twenty-three foot motor boat *Moxie* left Stone's Wharf in Lynn at about 9 P.M. Less than two hours later, shortly before eleven o'clock, Winthrop residents walking along the beach heard shouts for help coming from the ocean. Telephone calls were sent to the Nahant Coast Guard Station. Unfortunately, the boat there was out of order, so the Nahant Station telephoned to Hudson Robertson, the owner of the *Moxie*, asking him to go out in search of the persons in trouble. Robertson went down to the wharf, but found his boat missing. This was the first he knew that the boys had taken her out.

Meanwhile the Winthrop residents on the shore had lighted huge bonfires to guide those in trouble, but their cries grew weaker and weaker, finally dying away altogether. My brother Nicholas assisted in building the bonfires and shouting encouragement to the boys.

Gus Johnson of Beacon Street, Winthrop, now launched a small dory from the beach, but there was such a heavy ground swell that it capsized, and Johnson barely reached shore alive. After vainly staying up until the early morning hours, the crowd on shore gradually dispersed, hoping against hope that the lads had been saved.

The thirteen boys never returned to their Lynn homes, however, and the realization soon came that they had all probably drowned in the surf off the Winthrop shore. On the afternoon of April 6, just as our country was declaring war on Germany, my chum Tom Johnson and I began to walk toward the beach to see if any sign might be found of the missing boat *Moxie*. To our surprise we found that the bodies of the boys were washing in on the beach. In relatively short time the parents were notified, and I will never forget the pitiful, heart-wrenching scenes which took place as the identifications were made.

XXII

South Shore Marine Disasters,
1600-1859

As explained at the beginning of the previous chapter, many
of the accounts in this volume of the sea tragedies which
have occurred along the North and South Shores of Massachusetts are not in print anywhere else. The following
two chapters constitute a maritime disaster history of the
South Shore.

The first known shipwreck in this area was at Harding's
Ledge. This early marine tragedy is not recorded, but we
know that it took place long before 1697, when another
craft, the *Providence,* crashed to bits on the South Shore
ledge.

We know of this disaster because of a petition to recover
impost duties. The ship *Providence* was a new vessel, under
the command of Michael Gill. Having made only "one voyage from Boston to Barbados, and coming hence on the 28th
of September," the *Providence* "capsized by an accident"
and was soon "broken to pieces and much of her Cargo lost"
on "Harding's Rock nigh unto Nantaskett. There was butt
a small quantity of Rumm saved by being driven on Shoare

which through the badness of the Caske had much salt water mixed therewith and repairs were att considerable charge for Salvage thereof."

The petition to remit the rum impost tax was granted by the Massachusetts Council and House, and signed by Penn Townsend, Speaker of the House and Isaac Addington, secretary of the Council. Whether or not any person was saved will probably never be known, unless additional information comes to light.

On May 2, 1702, a violent storm lashed the South Shore, and caught the brigantine *Larke*—her master, Captain Daniel Noyes—off the lee beach of Plymouth. The high waves relentlessly smashed the vessel shoreward and she soon piled up on the beach. More than half her cargo of Madeira wine was lost in the wreck and when Bostonian Andrew Belcher and others appealed that the "Impost be remitted," the Council and representatives, including Witch-Judge Samuel Sewall, agreed.

Less than two years later the same Andrew Belcher appealed in the case of the ship, *John* of Exon, whose master had been Zacharia Cawley. The *John* carried a cargo of wine and salt, picking up her load at the two ports of Lisbon and "Fyall," but on November 3, 1703 "by reason of the high swelling of the sea after a violent storm was unhappily cast upon the Rocks lying off Pemberton's Island within Nantasket Bay, where she bilged and fil'd with water, her salt and the greatest part of the wines being lost, only with great difficulty Seventeen Pipes and one hogshead thereof saved." Nothing is said of the crew.

It was hinted that there were too many remissions of impost involving Andrew Belcher, and about this time he was suspected of using rum from the wrecked vessels and of "trading with the enemy." Nevertheless, Belcher, who had been accused "by ill-minded Persons," was given a clean bill of health and declared "a faithful Officer in the Discharge of his Office."

On Tuesday, November 25, 1712, six men, William Sprague, Ebenezer Bonny and Thomas Baker, all of Duxbury, and Thomas Wright, Job Cole and Andrew Seaward of Marshfield were caught in a bad gale off the Gurnet, and drowned.

In England Queen Anne died on August 1, 1714, and the *Hazard* was dispatched to Boston, then looked upon as the capital of North America, with an official message from the new monarch, George I.

On November 12, 1714, a lonely beachcomber was hiking along the Scituate beach after a terrible storm, and he noticed that wreckage was coming ashore, evidently from the vicinity of Minot's Rock. Going out to the edge of the beach, he was able to retrieve fragments of timbers and cargo. From material which could be identified, it was ascertained that the wreckage came from the *Hazard*. All aboard at the time had perished but part of her story was revealed by one of the passengers who had been put ashore at Nantucket Island before the disaster.

She carried instructions from the new King for the operation of his colonial government and, according to historian Hutchinson, "the loss of the sloop, *Hazard*, left the government without orders to proceed, as all the orders were lost on the Cohasset shores." Technically, the *Hazard* was not a sloop, but a ship, known in those days as a Government sloop.

Later, another Cohasset hiker found the missing papers,* which, according to a contemporary description, were received as follows: "The Proclamation of His most Excellent Maj's King George expressed by His Majesty's Sloop the

_____
* They are recorded in the *Massachusetts Council Records*, Volume 6, page 283.

Hazard drawn up especially for this Province was solemnly read, and published by the High Sheriffs of the County, followed with loud acclamations of God save King George and expressions of Joy."

There may have been expressions of joy about King George but there is not a single word concerning the more than thirty persons who perished in the tragedy. Hazard Rocks mark the location where the disaster is believed to have taken place.

I told the story of Anthony Collamore in my book, *Legends of the New England Coast.* I have since learned that when Collamore was buried at Scituate the interment was witnessed by his third child, Sarah, who later married Robert Stetson, grandson of Cornett Robert Stetson, one of the earliest settlers of Scituate and founder of the Stetson family in America.

Robert and Sarah Stetson had a son, Isaac, born, March 15, 1696. Isaac became a fisherman. On November 7, 1718, he sailed out through the mouth of the North River. A gale caught him, and his vessel went down off the Fourth Cliff, but details of the tragedy are lacking.

Thus Sarah had her second tragic connection with the sea. In both cases broadsides were written. The broadside concerning Isaac is confusing, and has the title *Isaac Stetson.* Part of it is called an "anagram" and was written by the Rev. Nathaniel Pitcher, a minister of the First Parish Church at Scituate.

> " 'Tis Cast on Sea.—A! Son it's Ceast
> On Sea being Cast, his Life is Cast Away,
> A! Son it's Ceast, Thou finish'd has thy day."

In the same broadside there is "*A Sorrowful Poem* upon that *Desirable Youth Isaac Stetson* of *Scituate,* who was Cast away in a sloop near the Mouth of the North River in Scituate." The title alone shall suffice.

On Sept. 22, 1722, during a storm which resulted in "thunderous billows, raging winds and waves" hitting the Scituate shore, Mrs. Hannah Robinson, forty-one years of age, and her daughter, sixteen, drowned at sea. The details are missing although there is a broadside concerning the affair in the form of an elegy, flowery in nature but with only a few facts in the sixty or so lines it contains.

A great summer storm hit New England on August 28, 1728, and at eleven o'clock that Wednesday night, a brigantine owned and commanded by Captain Joseph Anderson crashed ashore at Scituate. The lives of all on board were saved only "after abundance of Fatigue and difficulty." The vessel was a total loss, with very little of her cargo saved.

Slightly more than a year later, on October 10, 1729, a large ship, commanded by Captain Wellington of Bristol, England, and sailing to Boston from Lisbon with a cargo of salt, ran aground on Marshfield Beach in a terrible gale. Six men, more venturesome than the others, decided to attempt reaching shore before their ship went to pieces. Although warned by the others that there was very little hope in the ten-foot breakers then smashing ashore at what is now Rexham, the six sailors started away from the ship.

The first wave swept harmlessly by, but the second, with a high breaking crest, overwhelmed them. Five of the six mariners drowned, but the sixth swam feebly back to the ship where the others pulled him aboard. Thus seven of the crew of twelve were still alive.

Meanwhile the great cargo of salt began to dissolve, allowing the lightened craft to beat in closer to shore, where she broke up. All seven survivors floated high on the beach aboard one of the larger fragments of wreckage and were saved.

In December 1740, a violent gale created great havoc and

desolation for the fishermen and residents of the South Shore area. The storm brought death in the sea for all eleven aboard a Captain McCloud's ship when the craft ripped apart on the ledges at Scituate. In another disaster Captain Tilden and his crew narrowly escaped death at the entrance to Scituate Harbor, but managed to survive.

Other locations suffered terribly. Captain Underwood's craft hit the rocks at Rainsford's Island and soon bilged, while down at Nantucket, Captain Griffith's ship met disaster.

Another sloop was dismasted out to sea off Hull, but its owner and captain, Lovell by name, was able to get safely ashore with his crew. The ship was entirely destroyed.

The "summer storm" of 1759 hit the South Shore on June eleventh. It was announced in Boston that the schooner of Captain Inglish, sailing for Boston from North Carolina, had smashed ashore on the Marshfield Beach, but the crew and part of the cargo were saved. On the same Marshfield shore, a relatively short distance away, an unknown schooner was entirely broken to pieces and every man aboard drowned. At the time of the announcement no one knew where the schooner came from, what her name was, or how many persons lost their lives aboard her, and the details are not available today.

On Christmas Day, 1760, it was reported in Boston that during the previous week a hard gale of wind had stripped all the sails from a heavily laden lumber sloop "from the Eastward." Abandoning the craft, the survivors had rowed ashore at Marshfield, where they landed safely.

On September 8, 1769, a violent storm hit the South Shore, and Captain Stutson's sloop stranded at Cohasset. An unknown schooner also piled high on the beach at Marshfield, but nothing further is known of this gale.

On Friday, October 19, 1770, one of the most violent and destructive storms of the entire century began. By noon the next day it was hitting the coast with unprecedented velocity. The tide was extremely high, and floated vast amounts of salt hay from almost every coastal town south of Boston. The wind blew down trees, stores, barns, and sheds, and tore up fences. All along the South Shore scores of vessels were wrecked, and the loss of life was great.

At Boston, most of the wharves were inundated, much lumber was floated away, and quantities of sugar, salt, and other stores were destroyed. The water came up King Street (now State Street) as far as the head-tavern of Admiral Vernon, into Dock Square, above the level of the drawbridge, and into the streets nearest the seaside in the northern and southern portions of the town. The water ran not only into the cellars but into the shops and rooms of dwelling houses, compelling several families to retire to their upper chambers.

A day or two after the storm was over, a chest was discovered floating in the bay off Scituate. It was brought on shore, and found to contain a number of papers, among them private accounts of Hezekiah Blanchard of Boston for 1759, and copies of several orders from Secretary Addington to a committee of the General Court bearing dates 1706, 1707, and 1708, for printing some bills of credit for the province. Where the chest came from, and to whom it had belonged, was a mystery never solved.

A ship from Glasgow, but "last from Newbury," commanded by Captain Dunn, was lying at anchor in Nantasket Road when the storm began. The cable that held her parted and she was driven upon the flats in Braintree Bay. The masts were cut away, however, and she was prevented from driving further ashore.

All the small vessels at Hingham were pushed on shore, and one or two of about forty-five tons' burden were floated upon a wharf, which the usual high tides never covered.

Between Nantasket and Hingham a small fishing boat was sunk. The pump which it carried, a mast that had been cut away, and a boat or canoe came ashore.

The body of a fisherman washed on the beach, but it was not identified. The victim was a large man, about six-feet tall, and wore thick boots and an under and outer jacket. In his trousers' pocket was found a fish hook, and a small knife with two letters cut in the handle.

At Nantasket, Captain Higgins of a sloop bound to Connecticut was obliged to cut away his mast and bowsprit; and the captain of another sloop was forced to do the same. A ship bound to Africa, commanded by Captain Bennet, was the only vessel at Nantasket that successfully rode out the gale.

The day before the storm a small fishing schooner sailed from Salem, and was cast away in the blow at Scituate, the five persons on board being saved.

At Plymouth, many of the stores were blown down, and considerable other damage was done by the wind. Sixty-one vessels were driven ashore there, and about fifty lives were lost in the area.

One of the vessels was found to be from Rhode Island en route to Boston, commanded by Captain Ellis. Another was a new schooner of about twenty or thirty tons' burden, built wholly of black birch, which was cast away at Monument Point. The vessel, crew, and everything on board were lost. Bodies of two of the men were found on the sand near the wreck. In the jacket on one of them was found a small leather pocketbook, which contained some papers, very much torn, one being a bill of sale of the schooner *Defiance* from Lemuel Lattimore and Lucretia Lattimore, and directed to their mother at New London.

At the back side of Eastham, on Cape Cod, a vessel, commanded by Captain Scott, and bound from Turk's Island to Boston, laden with salt, was driven ashore. A Rhode Island sloop, which was homeward bound from a whaling trip was wrecked at nearly the same place. Another sloop, belonging to Plymouth, was driven ashore at Race Point. All the people on these vessels were saved. A whaling schooner, belonging in Wareham, was beaten to pieces on a sand bar at the entrance to Chatham Harbor, the crew and all aboard being saved. At Tarpaulin Cove, on Martha's Vineyard, a brig from Providence, Rhode Island, and a schooner from Newport, both returning from whaling, were also cast away.

On the night of January 22, 1771, a Captain Cooper's vessel was cast away on the Marshfield shore. Although all the members of the crew were saved, the vessel, which had sailed from Boston the previous day, was a total loss. During the same year a cargo vessel from Bermuda crashed ashore at Marshfield, but details are lacking.

In the year 1793, on February 12, the 300-ton ship *Gertrude-Maria*, bound from Copenhagen to Boston, was wrecked at Cohasset. Carrying a cargo estimated in value at $40,000 and commanded by Captain Hans Peter Clien, she was wrecked on a ledge among the Cohasset rocks known as Brush Island.

After entering the bay, the commander had been unable to realize the danger of his situation. For several days he could not ascertain his position, because of clouds which obscured "the sun by day and the moon and stars by night." Coming into Boston Bay he found that a great blizzard was hitting the coast, and the ship soon was at the mercy of the storm. Maneuvering vainly off Cohasset, the vessel first hit a small rock, where she suffered only slight damage. Then she piled up on Brush Island, the sides of which are covered with pointed ledges. The angry surf smashed her again and again with great violence, and finally she began to go to pieces.

A contemporary writer, the Rev. Jacob Flint, wrote a careful account of the shipwreck, and he tells how two men with a boat attempted to reach shore, but the craft was dashed to pieces. One man was drowned, and the other swam back to the wreck.

At length, by putting out a spar from the stern of the wreck, the survivors all landed on the island, where the waves could not reach them. Here they waited in the snow-storm, chilled and wet, without shelter.

Early the next morning inhabitants of Cohasset discovered the sailors and set about to rescue them. A boat was brought to the beach, a mile overland. Manned without delay, she was plunged into the boiling surf at great danger to the oars-men. She reached the island and brought off three of the sufferers.

Another attempt was immediately made, but the storm came on again with renewed intensity, and the waves in-creased in size. One mighty billow crashed into the lifeboat, crushing it to pieces against the rock.

Reverend Flint tells us that "two other boats were soon brought from a distance, and the dauntless exertions of the boatmen were renewed, till the sufferers, twenty-one in number, were all safely landed on the shore. Thence they were conveyed to the houses of Elisha Doane and other gen-tlemen, where they were carefully warmed, clothed and fed, as their frozen and perishing condition required. At these houses they remained, taking the wine and oil, ministered by the hand of compassion, till their wounds were healed and health restored."

In the meantime, as Reverend Flint tells us, a search was made for their property, now scattered up and down the coast. "An account of articles of the smallest, as well as of the greater value, was given to the master of the ship; inas-much that when all was collected, that could be saved, and sold at auction, its amount was $12,000.

"When the captain and his men, all members of the Royal Danish Navy, were provided with another vessel, and ready to leave the town, their hearts were swollen with grateful emotions toward those who, under God, had delivered and cherished them in their perils and distress."

Several days later Captain Clien sailed from Boston. When he landed at St. Croix he published there an affecting account of the care he had received from the people of Cohasset.

Upon his arrival in Denmark, he told the king such a wonderful story concerning his rescuers that it induced the monarch to order the College of Commerce to send to Cohasset in His Majesty's name four large gold medals, and ten of silver, with the likeness of himself impressed on one side and with Danish words on the other, signifying "Reward of Merit—Noble Deeds."

With the gold medals came directions that they be given to four men: the Rev. Josiah C. Shaw, Elisha Doane, Captain John Lewis, and Captain Levi Tower. The silver medals were awarded to other citizens who had been most active in giving relief to the sufferers.

"Honorable notice was likewise taken by the Humane Society, of the commendable humanity here manifested to strangers in distress, and a pecuniary donation was granted to the deserving agents. The governor of the Island of St. Croix manifested also the high sense he entertained of the benevolence of the peoples here, by his extraordinary kindness, on that account, to a gentleman from Boston," states Reverend Flint.

Some time later Daniel Hubbard, a merchant of Boston, was taken dangerously sick and put into the harbor of St. Croix, with a view to obtain medical aid and other assistance. At first he was refused admission, for his landing was "prohibited by the laws of the place, lest he should communicate his sickness."

But as soon as it was made known to the governor that Hubbard was from Massachusetts, he was taken ashore, and the best medical aid and every assistance and courtesy were granted him. When he recovered all compensation was refused. The governor explained that he was influenced in his conduct by the humanity and great kindness Captain Clien and his crew had experienced when shipwrecked at Cohasset in 1793.

During a great storm in February 1802, two pilot boats were washed ashore at Braintree; a schooner crashed on the Cohasset rocks; and four sailors lost their lives from a vessel named *Florenzo* at Marshfield.

On January 28, 1805, a thirty-eight-year-old Irish ship-owner-captain named Andrew Farrell sailed from Boston with great hopes for a profitable voyage on his ship *Hibernia*. Once she was out in the bay a terrible easterly gale hit the ship. Soon the captain and crew were watching with desperation for a landmark, as the *Hibernia* was being pushed toward the South Shore.

Finally the vessel smashed onto Plymouth Beach. One by one the sailors were swept off to their doom in the great surf, until only two were alive. When the storm subsided these two survivors were able to get ashore for help, but it was too late for Captain Farrell and five of his crew. Later six bodies came ashore. Placed in coffins, they were interred in Plymouth's Burial Hill Cemetery, where the inscription still stands to their memory. It reads as follows:

ANDREW FARRELL

of respectable connections

IN IRELAND

OWNER AND COMMANDER

of the ship *Hibernia*

Sailed from Boston Jany 26

And was wrecked on Plymouth Beach

Jany 28, 1805:

His remains
With five of seven seamen
Who perished with him
Are here interred.

"O piteous lot of man's uncertain state!
What woes on life's eventful journey wait—
By sea what trecherous calms; what sudden storms;
And death attendant in a thousand forms."

On November 7, 1807, the ship *Cordelia* entered Massachusetts Bay. Nearing the end of a long successful voyage, Captain Dorr had a wonderful set of china aboard to give to his wife. Countless other "small cargo" consisting of silks, tea, and curios were also on the ship. The *Cordelia* had been built by Jonathan Sampson in 1805 at the North River Bridge Yard in Hanover, and registered 252 tons. Named for the builder's daughter, the ship was two years old, and was owned by Boardman and Pope of Boston.

A storm which had been developing that November morning suddenly became worse, and Captain Dorr found that he was unable to tell where his ship was. Soon he was in shallow water, but before he could anchor, the *Cordelia* crashed on Long Ledge, Scituate, and immediately began to break apart. The entire crew reached shore safely in the longboat, but the only thing saved from the disaster was a tureen cover belonging to Captain Dorr's china set.*

On Wednesday evening, November 20, 1811, the brig *Success*, of Salem, captain Tobias Lear Porter, was driven on shore in a gale of wind at Brant Rock. She was from St. Petersburg for Boston with a cargo of hemp, iron, and duck. Upon striking at Brant Rock she immediately bilged. The vessel was lost, but most of the cargo was salvaged. The cap-

---

* The *Cordelia* had rammed against Long Ledge with such violence that as late as 1890, eighty-three years after the disaster, "a piece of her timber" was still to be seen, firmly wedged in the rocks of the ledge.

tain, mate and four seamen perished while attempting to swim to shore, two seamen only being saved.

Another wreck of the period occurred on January 24, 1822. The new schooner, *Dennis*, with Captain Dennis commanding, sailed for Newburyport from Cape Cod, but anchored in Nantasket Road, because of a threatening storm. Heavy ice formed and, caught in a floe, the vessel pushed onto the beach at Hull. A short time later the schooner *Leo*, piloted by Captain Foster from North Carolina, parted her cables and went ashore near the *Dennis*. Both were eventually freed.

On January 19, 1824, the brig *Federal George*, her master Captain Davis, sailing from Philadelphia for Boston, crashed ashore on the Scituate Beach about two and a half miles north of Scituate Light at a location "a little to the south of Widow Collins," according to the old journal of Shadrach B. Merritt of Scituate.*

The *Federal George* began to break up, but 175 casks of wine, six hogsheads of molasses, and a hundred chests of tea, together with a shipment of leather were saved.

Several days later a new storm hit the coast. Another vessel, the schooner *Alert*, forty-five days from Rochelle, hit the same beach within a few rods of the *Federal George*. Carrying a cargo which included 113 pipes of brandy and four cases of wine, she smashed apart with such force that she was not worth repairing.

On February 1, 1830, another great storm hit the coast, but except in two wrecks details are lacking. The schooner *Champion*, hailing from New York, came ashore at Scituate. In the same gale, at the foot of the Fourth Cliff in Scituate, a

---

* Mrs. Addie Cushing Colman of Greenbush has made a copy of this shipwreck story.

schooner with grindstones from Grindstone Island, Nova Scotia, foundered offshore about a hundred yards from low water. The survivors reached land in their longboat, but the grindstones went down in twenty feet of water and the schooner soon broke to pieces.*

In the year 1844 a terrible shipwreck occurred at Egypt Beach, Scituate. Eventually eleven bodies came ashore on Deacon Benjamin Bladenburg Litchfield's property. Among the effects which washed in were a number of garments which belonged to a young girl. The remains of the child were never found, however.

The bodies of the other eleven victims were placed in rough pine boxes prepared by Deacon Litchfield, and a mournful cavalcade of ox teams carried the remains to the Meeting House Cemetery, where they were interred in one large grave, the plot having been donated by trustees of the Center Burial Grounds. Services were conducted at the grave by the Rev. Daniel Wight, Jr., whose ministry lasted from 1842 to 1858.**

At nine o'clock on the evening of August 16, 1846, the forty-six-ton mackerel schooner *Maine* was out to sea some sixteen miles off Boston with Captain Joshua Litchfield in

---

* Years later Alfred Damon of Marshfield was fishing over the area on a perfectly calm day, and sighted the huge grindstones down on the bottom. Within two weeks he had brought several of them up to the surface, and later they were bought by thrifty Marshfield farmers.

** More than seventy-five years were to elapse, however, before the grave was marked. Some time around the year 1923, John Ferbuson, Charles Andrews and John Fitts arranged for a boulder to be removed from Scituate Common to the grave, located twenty-five feet from the present Trinitarian Congregational Church.

The marker planned for the stone was never placed on it, but instead a memorial was chiseled into the rough surface as follows:

IN MEMORY OF THE SAILORS
WRECKED ON EGYPT BEACH 1844
BODIES REST HERE

command and a crew of ten.* There was a deep fog, and the watch could see nothing as a strong wind began to blow. According to Keeper Reamy of Graves' Light,** who had been told the story by his father, a huge ocean packet, the *Hibernia,* had left Boston two hours before. The wind was just what the vessel wanted, for she was one of those old-fashioned side-wheeled steamboats that were fitted with masts and sails to augment their steam power. She swept forward, driven by the paddle wheels and the gale through the thick fog.

Suddenly there was a crash and a heavy thud near the bow of the *Hibernia,* and then one of the paddle wheels began to crunch the masts and the shattered frame of the little fishing schooner *Maine.* The crew of fishermen was swept under by the great wheel like bits of rubbish in a millrace. In a moment the collision was over and nothing could be heard in the darkness but the shrieking of the gale through the rigging.

The captain of the packet together with his startled officers and men rushed to the rail and looked into the sea. There was nothing to be found but angry waves. The engine was stopped, and the sailors were ordered to take in sail, while the black smoke blew in their faces.

"It's no use to stop and search for those poor jacks," said the captain. "I once ran over a sailing vessel in the English Channel and in five minutes I had a lifeboat on the spot, but not a man could be found. That was in the daytime and here it is a black night, and it will be an hour before we can get a boat to where we struck her."

The mate had a different opinion. "It is our duty, sir, we

---

* They were Mesech Litchfield, Benjamin Litchfield, Martin Wheelwright, Isaiah Lincoln, Francis M. Lincoln, Alfred F. Wood, Joseph Bowker, Luther Litchfield, Henry Richardson, and Ezekiel Lincoln.

** The late Octavius Reamy, who, with his father Milton Reamy, was keeper of both Minot's Light and Graves' Light told me this story, one day on my visit to him at Graves' Light, as he pointed out the location where he believed the collision had taken place.

must go!" There is no word that strikes so strongly to the heart of an Englishman as "duty," and the mate won his point. A lifeboat was lowered; but it swamped in the rough water before a crew could get into it. One end of the craft was hooked up to release the water, and the mate called for volunteers to go with him, as the speed of the *Hibernia* was reduced to one knot. Swinging themselves into the boat, they started off into the blackness. The steamer reversed her engine and backed up slowly over the course she had been running.

Meanwhile, the fishermen who had not been killed in the collision caught hold of spars, planks or whatever floated near. They called out for each other and found that there were six out of the eleven still floating in the water, holding on for dear life.

It was a miracle that any escaped being crushed in the debris. The skipper, Joshua Litchfield, of Beechwood, was probably injured seriously, for after holding on for some twenty minutes he loosened his grip and was seen no more.

The other five began to plan for what fate might await them. They dared not get too close to each other for fear that in the spasm of drowning, one might catch another and both would perish. They floated in the cold water, cheering up one another with what scanty hope they had.

Then they began to shout, thinking that possibly a boat might have been lowered from the packet. Their voices were so weak in the gale that they awaited a lull in the wind, at which time they all called out together as loudly as they could. A half hour went by and then another. The hope of seeing a boat from the packet was about given up, and yet occasionally they would raise their voices again.

Meanwhile in the boat the mate and his crew were rowing anxiously with the wind as their compass. It was hopeless to call out against the blow but they hoped the wind might carry to them the cries of any survivors. And so it was, for presently a voice was heard off in the darkness, and they bent to their oars. Then they shouted and waited, but there was no answer.

After a while another voice came more plainly than the first, and then they sighted the five exhausted sailors and got them aboard. They searched for others, but found none. Hunting for the crushed schooner, they discovered no further signs of her and it was not until several days later that debris came ashore.

Back toward the steamer they rowed. One poor watersoaked fisherman lay in the bottom of the boat chilled to the very bones, too weak to recover circulation. An oarsman worked off his own shirt from his back while still keeping stroke and wrapped it around the man.

The sailors were taken aboard the packet, and the captain turned her bow toward Halifax, Nova Scotia. There the survivors were able to secure passage to Boston.

Before they reached home their people had become convinced that all were lost. A Provincetown fishing boat had picked up the body of one man near the Cape, and bringing it home had placed it upon the wharf for some one to identify. It happened that a young man from Beechwood was there in Provincetown, and he recognized the remains of Joshua Litchfield, the skipper of the ill-fated *Maine*. It was the very day of Litchfield's funeral that the rescued five returned. The dead skipper had reached home first, and the living had come to tell their sad story of the sea.

On June 11, 1904, fifty-eight years after they had been overrun by the *Hibernia*, the five survivors met in the general store of Daniel J. Bates at North Scituate. It was a crackerbarrel reunion.

Luther Litchfield, 81, had become a Scituate farmer. Joseph Bowker, 80, had moved to South Dakota. Isaiah Lincoln, 78, had become a bell diver. Francis M. Lincoln, 77, had given up the sea and moved to Hingham. Alfred Wood, 73, had become a North Scituate shoemaker. They were never to meet again.

On March 28, 1849, the brig *Sea Bird* of Searsport went aground just north of the mouth of the North River. The crew was saved, and the brig was later taken off by the steamer *R. B. Forbes* and towed to Boston.

One of the great South Shore shipwrecks of all times was the loss of the brig *St. John* on October 7, 1849, when 143 persons perished on the ledges off Cohasset. I have already told the entire story in *Storms and Shipwrecks*.

During the Minot Light's storm of 1851 the following vessels met grief: brig *William*, brig *Elizabeth*, schooner *Trenton*, and the Russian brig *Wellamo*. The *Elizabeth* smashed ashore just south of the North River mouth.

It was two o'clock when the *Elizabeth* hit the shore, and in the terrific surf the seven members of the crew attempted to reach safety. Their boat capsized, however, and six of them drowned. One man, Captain Kilborn, was saved by the combined efforts of Captain Otis Baker, Augustus F. Sherman, and William Porter, all of Marshfield. Later the hull of the *Elizabeth* was sold to the highest bidder as it lay on the beach.

On April 21, 1852, a derelict floated ashore at Humarock Beach about a half mile north of the river mouth. She was found to be the brig *Marcus* of Bangor, carrying a cargo of sugar-box shocks. Not a soul was aboard, but later it was discovered that the crew had abandoned her in a storm at sea. On April 27 the brig was floated and taken to Boston by the steamer *John Taylor*.

Early one morning in February 1853, the great London packet, *Forest Queen*, came ashore on Second Cliff Beach, Scituate. There were forty immigrants aboard the packet, which had an assorted cargo of gold watches, rum, gin, pig iron, and steel. A thick snowstorm was blamed for her misfortune. Shortly afterward the sun came out brightly, and the passengers were landed on the shore. Then the ship began to break up.

Later the snowstorm again hit, and then the cargo began washing ashore. Strange scenes were enacted. One man found so many stone gin jugs that he attempted to walk away from the beach with a jug on each finger, but the boys at the wreck fired stones at them, and he reached high-water mark with each finger ringed by a jug handle and nothing else. One man found a quantity of indigo and readily found buyers at $1.50 a pound. Others had passed this loot by, not realizing its great value.

The hull was in about twenty feet of water and provided work for divers for many years to come. Whether or not it can still be identified at the bottom today is a moot question. Most of the cargo, however, was brought to the surface years ago, including cases of cochineal, valuable skins, lead blocks and casks of wine.

Strangely enough, within a day of the *Forest Queen* wreck, another unidentified vessel piled up ashore within a short distance of the London packet.

The wreck of the schooner *Mary Martha* occurred immediately to the south of Scituate Third Cliff on March 5, 1853. She was sailing from New York with a heavy cargo of corn and flour, and the captain's wife and family were along.

The time of the wreck was one o'clock in the morning, but it was not until dawn that residents along the shore realized a vessel was in trouble. A lifeboat was hurriedly manned and sent out into the high breakers. Reaching the wreck, the rescuers realized that the captain's children would have to be tossed into the lifeboat. One by one the youngsters were thrown across the water, and all were caught successfully. Finally everyone, young and old, was rescued that morning by the Scituate lifesavers.

For some reason certain storms are forgotten soon after they have caused great damage and suffering. Possibly this is because a later tempest may have been so outstanding that the memory of the earlier storm was obliterated. In my opinion, such was the blizzard of 1853, which unexpectedly struck the South Shore early in the morning of December 29. As a result of the overwhelming snowfall no one could use any South Shore highway for forty-eight hours, for in many places the snow was ten feet deep.

Immediately after the storm Captain Choate of the ship *Independence* said that it was the worst gale in his twenty-two years of experience, while almost every mariner ashore at the time from Boston to Provincetown said that it was the most severe in a quarter of a century. The winter of 1853, up to the moment of this unexpected snowstorm had been relatively mild, at least from the mariner's viewpoint, but when it hit the blizzard made up for all the good weather within a few hours.

The areas around Boston were submerged by the snow, which fell thick and fast and within a few hours made all progress except on snowshoes impossible. The temperature fell below zero while tides came in higher than they had for years.

No trains could get through because of the deep drifts, and none was reported south of the Braintree junction. At Milton one train was stuck in a drift for more than thirty hours. Finally, after a hard struggle, the Old Colony sent a special train from Boston consisting of two cars, two engines, and a snowplow, which managed to reach North Braintree.

During the storm a report came up from Hull, sent by Moses B. Tower, that the gale had struck there at two o'clock in the morning, and that vessels were coming ashore heavily encased in ice.

The Boston-to-Yarmouth packet *Maria* left Boston on Wednesday, December 28, at noon, but when off Marshfield Captain Hallett did not like the weather and returned to

Boston just in time to escape the worst of the blizzard.

The brig *Mary E. Pierce*, from Washington, North Carolina, bound for Boston with lumber, was found high and dry on Scituate Beach. Her captain said that when he was rounding Cape Cod he was in the company of seventy-five craft of all types, every one of which must have gone ashore in the storm either at "Barnstable Bay, Scituate, Marshfield or Duxbury." There was also a fore-and-aft schooner ashore at Cedar Cliff, Scituate, and another unknown craft aground nearby.

Other craft lost during this period include the brig *T. P. Perkins*, December 3, 1853; the brig *Whitaker*, December 4, 1853; and the schooner *Woodwell* of Eastport, December 29, 1853.

On February 3, 1854, the bark *Amanda* was caught in a snowstorm seventy-five miles out to sea from Boston Light. Bearing south, southwest, Captain Daniel D. Baker of Marshfield ran in toward Massachusetts Bay at night. On Saturday, February 4, he was still off Cape Cod, and when it stopped snowing he located both Highland Light and Race Point Light.

That night the spray froze on the deck, freezing the helmsman's feet so that he had to be put in his bunk. By Sunday, February 5, there were six inches of thick ice on the deck of the *Amanda*.

Finally, with a light southwest wind, the course was shaped for Boston Light. Soon the snow began to fall again, with the wind backing from southwest to southeast and reaching gale force. Scituate Light was then sighted through the storm, and the *Amanda* stood off from shore for the night. Then the caking of ice became so heavy that the ship was unmanageable.

Dawn found them off Brant Rock. A moment later the ship struck a rock, sliding off shortly afterward. The starboard anchor was thrown over, but the chain fouled and snapped. Hitting heavily on the beach, the last voyage of the *Amanda* was over.

Captain Baker looked ashore to recognize the old fence at Branch's Island, Marshfield, as his residence was a short distance away. At low tide he went ashore to find John L. Hatch on the beach with his wagon. It was comparatively easy for the others in the crew to clamber to safety, but for the captain's wife it took a little longer. A male passenger also made the precarious journey to shore. Later the cargo of fruit, dates and figs was sold and the bark was auctioned off to the highest bidder.

For some reason the name *Elizabeth* has unhappy connotations when mentioned in connection with the sea. Over fifteen craft of that name have been listed as lost within a few years, at least seven of them along the South Shore. One of the strangest occurrences was the finding of that name carved on a tree trunk near which were skeletons of men who probably were in the crew of a craft named *Elizabeth*.

An American ship *Elizabeth* was stranded in 1859 at almost the exact location later occupied by the Italian freighter *Etrusco*. With this accident occurring so soon after the tragic loss of the *Sally Badger* with all hands, the *Elizabeth* attracted the attention of hundreds of South Shore residents.

Her story begins on February 26, 1859, when she sailed in toward Cape Cod carrying a gigantic cargo of 3,500 bales of cotton. A heavy snowstorm soon set in and her captain, Tobias Lord by name, was unable to chart a safe course because of the storm.

Hour after hour went by. Captain Lord figured that by two o'clock that afternoon he must be beyond the dangerous Peaked Hill Bars off the tip end of the Cape, and gave orders to wear ship and shape a new course for Boston Light.

Darkness fell and the storm continued. During a lull at about nine o'clock that night the captain detected the gleam of what he thought was Boston Light, and headed for the beacon, actually Scituate Light, which he was destined never to pass. An hour afterward the great ship was brought up short on a rocky ledge. The next wave pushed her over the barrier and the career of the Maine-built ship was ended.

Watchers along the shore soon called out the local Scituate members of the famed Massachusetts Humane Society. They launched their surf boat into the raging breakers, rowed out to the doomed craft, and rescued all aboard. Captain Lord stated that there were twenty-two in the crew and three passengers, Mr. Elder, his wife and their son.

The news of the disaster was dispatched to Boston by telegraph. On hearing of the wreck Captain Morris of the *R. B. Forbes* started overland for Scituate. Arriving at the scene at low water he noticed there was a large rock through her bottom and she had about twenty feet of water in the hold. Fragments of her bottom, keel, and garboard streak washed ashore. All her masts were then still standing.

By six o'clock the following evening thirty-nine bales of cotton were removed from the *Elizabeth*. The running rigging was unbent and shipped to Boston by the schooner *Sarah Young*. The cargo was gradually removed from the ship, but on March 1 the wreck was still in the same position.

Optimistic predictions were made that by the next high tide she would be floated. At that time she had fifteen feet of water in her at low tide and the seas ebbed and flowed through her timbers. On March 3 it was announced that she would be floated at the next spring tide. Two days later two hundred empty casks were placed in the forward part of the ship and it was planned to put two hundred more in on March 6 and get her off.

On March 8 a score of men were working desperately with pitchforks getting rid of a veritable sea of loose cotton from a hundred broken bales amidships. On March 9 the *Elizabeth* lay in a deep hole, her stern offshore and heavily laden with cotton. It was feared that if she was moved she would strain amidships. At two o'clock the next morning, she floated free of the beach, but hard luck hounded her. An hour later she parted her cable offshore and came back on the beach. This time she was never to leave.

On March 11 the underwriters visited her and declared that she was unfit to be repaired and she was to be sold as she lay.

All the cotton was taken out of the hold, and the stripping of the ship started immediately. After her masts and gear had been removed, she was sold to the highest bidder, who cut her up the following summer.*

With the coming of the Civil War the first signs of the eventual decline of the sailing vessel were seen. We end this chapter in our survey of shipwrecks along the South Shore with the story of the wreck of this *Elizabeth*.

---

* Years later, in 1956, when bulldozers were preparing a canal for the stranded *Etrusco*, several timbers from the ill-fated *Elizabeth* were uncovered.

XXIII

South Shore Marine Disasters, 1859-1960

Although during and directly after the Civil War, great strides forward were made in the development of maritime safety regulations, there were still shipwrecks from time to time along the South Shore.

The first to be described in this chapter was that of the *Agnes R. Bacon.* This 129-foot schooner was off the shores of Marshfield during a bad gale on February 10, 1885.*

By midnight a hurricane was blowing, and the *Bacon* hit the Marshfield Beach near Beetle Rocks ninety minutes later. Captain Stanley, of the Fourth Cliff Station, informed by his surfman of the stranding, called out his crew. A terrible task faced them. Not only did they have to carry their apparatus three and a half miles south, but they were forced to cross the North River and proceed overland until they were oppo-site the wreck.

The breeches buoy was shot out to the doomed schooner

---

* Her official number was 105289, her signal letters J.N.F.H. Her breadth, 32.0 feet; and depth, 9.7 feet. Her gross tonnage was 395.62; her net tonnage 375.84. Her hailing port was Bridgeton, New Jersey.

and made secure. Then, one by one, the sailors were rescued. Captain Haley was the last to leave his vessel, thus
carrying out the traditions of the sea.

After the storm subsided Captain Haley and the underwriters visited the *Bacon* and decided that she was a total
loss. She was soon dismantled and stripped on the beach as
she lay.

Most wrecks and strandings, unless they have some unusual
item connected with them, soon fade away in public remembrance.

One such case which could have been New England's
greatest shipwreck was that of the steamer *Pavonia*. This
fine Cunard liner, under command of Captain Woolfenden,
smashed aground on High Pine Ledge, off High Pine on
Gurnet Beach in October 1886.

There was a severe storm, and the wind and surf combined to make the situation a desperate one for the five hundred people aboard. The captain thought that he was between
Nahant and the Graves Ledge and ordered the *Pavonia*
backed off the reef, an attempt which had sent one hundred
persons to their death aboard the *City of Columbus* in 1884.

Successfully freeing herself, the *Pavonia* now stood to the
southeast and went aground again, but still did not take
in water. Ten minutes later, however, a serious leak developed. The captain told the following story of the incident.

"The whole thing was brought about by my mistaking the
South Shore for the North Shore. I had been sounding all
along since five o'clock in the morning, taking soundings
every half hour. On Thursday I had obtained a good latitude and knew just where I was. When I passed Stelwaggens
Bank there was eighteen fathoms, and I supposed that I was
on the northern edge.

"It was 8:15 yesterday morning that we first sighted land,
which we thought was Nahant. I looked for Egg Rock
Light; but the mist was so thick that I could not make out

anything distinctly. When we had backed some distance, we stopped and bore away for where we supposed Boston Light lay. At 9:50 we struck the ledge, and for some time the vessel bumped heavily.

"The passengers then became somewhat alarmed, but no great stir was created. At 11:40 the engines were started astern for five minutes, and then ahead at full speed. The vessel seemed to start and quiver and then slid off into deeper water. We were then heading northeast. Soon after getting off, a boat came from the lifesaving station and informed us where we were. We then proceeded ahead and anchored near Boston Light, where we transferred some of the passengers on board of pilot boat No. 8.

"After we had anchored we found that we were making water all the time, and we decided to go inside if it were possible, for with the darkness and the wind, the high running sea and the rain, it was almost an impossibility to transfer the passengers to other boats which were lying there. We slipped our chain with sixty fathoms of cable; and with a long cable out over our stern, the *Underwriter* started to tow us in. The water in our forward compartments had brought the bow deep down into the sea, and the stern was high out.

"The tug was obliged to tow us in stern first, as we were headed stern in, and all the tugs in the harbor could not have hauled us around with that wind blowing. We passed in between the ledges to anchor in the roads. These ledges are only about a fifth of a mile apart; and with the darkness and high wind it was a miracle that she was brought in without striking."

Captain Woolfenden also said that the two holes torn in the *Pavonia*'s bottom were on the port side, one on the bow and the other a little forward of amidships, under the saloon. Both the compartments were full of water.

With the bow down and her stern up the ship soon grounded in the mud off Boston Light, and the passengers were removed by craft from the city. Despite the risk of transferring so many people over the side and down ladders into the boats, all were taken off safely.

As Boston had no dry dock long enough for the *Pavonia*, emergency repairs were performed at the Atlantic Works, and she returned to Liverpool, England, for complete overhaul. She reached there in about ten days and was repaired in a little over four months.

Before the *Pavonia* set out for Liverpool, Robert Bennett Forbes, a prominent marine personality of the day, suggested means whereby these repairs might have been made in Boston. He proposed backing her into a dock stern first, building up the timber box between her smooth sides and the stone wall of the dock and allowing the stern to overhang her forty extra feet. Then, and I quote Mr. Forbes, "At a moderate cost Simpson's Dock could be excavated at its upper end, by an active gang of men, in forty-eight hours."

It was on June 25, 1888, that the bark *Chattanooga*, built in 1864 at Calais, Maine, was approaching Boston during a dense fog. Carrying a heavy cargo of salt from Puerto Rico, the 135-foot vessel was in charge of Captain Lewis, who had ten men in his crew.

A light northeast breeze was blowing, but in the fog the bark was veered from her dead reckoning course by a strong southerly current. Finally she fetched up on the beach near Hewitt's Point, Marshfield, some three miles south of the Fourth Cliff Lifesaving Station.

It was then two o'clock in the morning. As the lifesaving station was unmanned except for the keeper, Captain Fred Stanley called two of his regular crew from the neighborhood as soon as he noticed the *Chattanooga*. He then asked for five other volunteers to assist in the rescue attempt.

By nine o'clock the fog had practically cleared, and after telegraphing for a tug, Stanley launched his surf boat into the moderate seas. Reaching the bark, he talked with the skipper of the *Chattanooga*, who owned a share of the vessel.

Captain Lewis told Stanley that he would travel up to Boston and confer with the other owners, and he asked Stanley to take charge of the craft until his return.

It was then about 10:45 A.M. Soon the *Chattanooga*'s stern filled and sank. Captain Stanley took everyone, including one passenger, ashore with the baggage, for he realized that the career of the bark had ended. Landing on the relatively smooth beach, Stanley obtained a wagon to transport the survivors to the railroad station, where they were all given a free pass to Boston.

Taking his surf boat back to the station, the captain then went aboard the wreck with his two surfmen in a small boat. The three lifesavers stayed on the bark until the night of the twenty-seventh, when Captain Lewis returned, announcing that a tug would soon arrive to float the *Chattanooga* off. She soon broke up, however, and her keel is still offshore near the position where she first hit at Hewitt's Point.

Several other wrecks of the period are important enough to mention at this time. The first was that of the *J & J Locke*, which on November 25, 1888, broke adrift in Gloucester Harbor. Her crew were rescued by another craft, and the *Locke* drifted across to Turner's Beach, where she turned bottom up. She was from Boston, and had a general cargo of flour, kerosene, and merchandise.

On January 9, 1889, the *W. Parnell O'Hara*, a fishing schooner, struck at Second Cliff, but was later taken off by a towboat.

At two o'clock in the morning on March 5, 1889, surfman Thomas J. Maddock was returning from the northerly point of his patrol to the Scituate Lifesaving Station at North Scituate. Suddenly he saw a bright red light, apparently directly ahead of him, some distance down the beach.

Starting on a run, Maddock soon came close enough to see

the black outline of a ship. Lighting his Coston flare to signal that assistance was coming he hurried down the beach to the station five hundred yards south and alerted the crew.

Captain George H. Brown started with his men for the scene of the disaster, and on arrival opposite to the wreck set up the rescue apparatus and signal lanterns.

The night was extremely dark. No moon or stars were visible, and because of the overcast it was agreed that the firing of a Lyle gun and the use of the breeches buoy would be too dangerous. Captain Brown then ordered the large lifeboat at the station to be made ready. Pushing the craft into the surf just as the largest breaker of a series started to recede, the men conquered the challenge of the next giant comber and then rowed desperately to the lee of the wreck one thousand yards off shore.

Time and again the billows smashed into the lifeboat but the crew bailed desperately to keep afloat. Finally they reached the vessel, which they found to be the brig *T. Remick* of Damariscotta, Maine, her master Captain Fossett. The crew of the brig were transferred to the lifeboat and the trip back to the beach began. After several narrow escapes Captain Brown followed the crest of a breaker in toward the sand until the keel grounded.

Five minutes later both rescuers and rescued were above the reach of the angry sea. After a brief rest the entire group started back for the North Scituate Lifesaving Station.

There, the survivors were given hot coffee and put to bed. The next morning Captain Fossett gave his story:

"We left Surinam January 27, 1889, with 260 hogsheads of molasses, 40 hogsheads of sugar, 40 barrels of empty bottles, 18 barrels of pickled limes, and 200 bags of cocoa.

"After a relatively uneventful voyage we sighted and passed Highland Light on March 4, at six thirty in the evening. Then we shaped our course for Boston.

"I plainly heard the fog whistle at Race Point as we sailed by and thus I knew that all was well. I had not the slightest idea that we were off our course, for the only thing I was fearing was the Graves Ledge.

"At ten minutes past two yesterday morning while running with free sheet, and just as we had taken in the mainsheet a little, I suddenly felt her scrape bottom. At that very moment the lookout forward called: 'Breakers directly ahead.'

"Immediately I shoved down the helm, but it was too late, and without a moment's warning we were hard and fast on the beach. At once we displayed signals and in a very short time they were answered by Patrolman Maddock.

"The only cause of the disaster that I can think of which would take us fifteen miles off our course must have been the southerly drift of the current."

The brig *T. Remick*, of 349 tons, was built in 1871 at Damariscotta. She had come in directly in front of Mitchell's Hotel, Scituate, bow on, and at low water was high and dry. There are no records as to whether or not she was salvaged.

On September 20, 1889, a salt schooner named *Active* was stranded at the harbor's mouth in Scituate. The cargo dissolved and the schooner floated off at high tide. She was later repaired and made seaworthy again.

The Belgian steamer *De Ruyter*, sailing from Antwerp to Boston, came ashore at Lighthouse Point, Scituate, March 6, 1890, at about six o'clock in the afternoon, having misjudged her position in the storm.

The distress signals from the *De Ruyter* were soon answered by both the volunteer surf boat from the Massachusetts Humane Society and the regular Lifesavers. Patrolman Joseph Peter Murphy of the North Scituate Station was the first to discover the stranded vessel. Although his station was three miles to the north, he ran the entire distance back to call out his men. Leonard Raymond meanwhile collected a crew at Harbor Village who tramped out to the Volunteer Station and launched into the breaking waves.

Between the two lifesaving groups, everyone on the *De Ruyter* was brought ashore safely to the Lifesaving Station where they were given "gallons of coffee." *

Two tugs, the *Herald* and the *Vim*, together with the lighters *Aid* and *Maple* left Boston for the scene of the wreck at noon on March 7, although the seas were still high and rough and the immediate chances of lightering were very poor.

Wreck Commissioner A. Brooks Anderson arrived at the scene early on March 7 and took charge of the proceedings. He decided that the waves were breaking too strongly at the wreck for the lighters to remove any of the cargo aboard. The wind soon came up again, forcing the tugs and lighters to flee. The *Herald* and the two lighters headed for Provincetown in the easterly gale, while the *Vim* sailed into Scituate Harbor and was soon made fast to the town pier.

Early the next morning Commissioner Anderson reported that the *De Ruyter* was losing her hatches, was full of water, and at high tide had her stern completely submerged. There was ice glistening over the entire ship in the rays of the rising surf.

Her huge cargo included crates of window glass, barrels of paint, kegs of alum, one hundred cases of cement tiles, cases of gin, a large amount of meat in tins, and countless other articles. Within the next few days the surf went down and the lightering began. Good progress was made, and soon the *De Ruyter* was buoyant enough to be towed out into deep water and then taken to Boston.**

On May 9, 1890, a fishing schooner from Duxbury cap-

---

* During the rescue work the Lifesaving surfboat was almost smashed to pieces on some piling which a cottager had placed offshore the summer before, but Brown saved his craft.

** Because of this wreck in 1890 the Scituate citizens sent Edwin Young to Washington to suggest to the federal government that Scituate be made into a harbor of refuge.

sized a mile from shore on Chest Ledge, and Edward Edson
of Scituate had a narrow escape from drowning.

A notable wreck occurred February 1, 1894, when the
coal schooner *Minnie Rowan* hit at First Cliff. James Turner,
who watched the disaster, remembers the captain high in the
rigging clad in his great cloak. The crew from Fourth Cliff
finally rescued the men with their captain, whose leg had
been broken. Shortly after the surf boat landed ashore, the
schooner smashed to pieces. George Walbach, who lived
nearby, took the survivors into his house to recuperate.

One of the outstanding veteran lifesavers of the old school
is a Scituate resident, Richard Wherity who "signed on"
back in 1889 with Captain James at Stony Beach. The following year he was transferred to the Fourth Cliff Station
where he served for ten years.

The two-masted schooner *Magnum* hit at Fourth Cliff in
April 1894, and the crew were saved. The *Magnum* was
sold on the beach. Two years later the fishing schooner
Oceania was stranded near the Fourth Cliff but floated off
at high water.

During the Portland Gale, which saw the loss of the pilot
boat *Columbia* with all hands, Wherity had duty that took
him to Hatch's Gunning Stand. He rescued David Sears at
Fourth Cliff and they hiked in back of the breakwater to
Humarock Bridge, then a drawbridge, which was perilously
weaving back and forth under the force of the wind and the
water. Wherity got Mr. Sears across it safely, however, and
then fought his way back to the lifesaving station. It was
shortly after this that he learned of the disaster which befell
the pilot boat *Columbia*.

Her last known act had been to discharge her pilot, Captain
William Abbott, aboard the steamer *Ohio*, which later was
stranded on Spectacle Island. The storm grew worse as the
evening wore on and it is believed that the *Columbia* met

her doom in the vicinity of the Boston Lightship. None of
her crew was ever heard from again.

The turn of the century was particularly free of South
Shore marine disasters. Six years were to elapse before there
was even a stranding.

A dense, heavy fog, which had settled down along the New
England coast by Wednesday noon, February 14, 1906,
caused Captain Ridley, commander of the Leyland Liner
Devonian, to misjudge his position. During the following
night a thick snowstorm set in, and at 12:50 A.M. the *Devonian* hit shore off Third Cliff, Scituate.

Luckily, she had chosen a sandy location, where she rested
easily after striking. At dawn she was discovered by the
lifesavers of Fourth Cliff, who relayed word up to Boston
that the *Devonian* was ashore.

Superintendent Booth of the Leyland Line started by boat
for the scene, but found it was too rough, and turned back
after reaching Minot's Light. Instead he sent down two large
craft, the *Underwriter* and the *Storm King*.

Meanwhile the crew of the Fourth Cliff Station were attempting to communicate with the ship by flags. Unfortunately the *Devonian*'s answering signals were not understood,
as the crew had no code book to interpret them. Finally,
late in the afternoon, the stranded vessel managed to convey the message, "Send a tug at once."

As a tug had already been requested hours before there
was nothing the lifesavers could do but watch and wait.
Soon three tugs were sighted in the distance, each racing to
be the first to get a hawser aboard. They were the *Patience*,
the *Pallas* and the *Storm King*.

The revenue cutter *Gresham* had anchored directly astern
of the *Devonian* and effectively prevented the *Storm King*
from getting a line across. Captain H. C. Calhoun in the
Patience was able to maneuver alongside and toss his line
aboard, thus winning the race.

With the *Devonian* backing and the *Patience* pulling, the big freighter was able to stir herself, pushing away from the threatening cliffs until she was out of danger.

She had a twelve-degree list all the way to Boston, but Captain Ridley explained this was because the water ballast had been unevenly pumped out. She arrived safely, and thus ended an incident which for fourteen hours threatened to become a major shipwreck tragedy.

Several years ago I interviewed Thomas J. Flynn of Scituate, who recounted his memories of several weeks.

When the 655-ton schooner *Nantasket* hit the rocks at Cedar Point, Mr. Flynn and his friends were in "Markie Damon's barber shop, as it was a mean, nasty afternoon that day after the Christmas of 1909.

"We all went down to Cedar Point to see what was happening," Flynn told me. "The crew were being taken ashore by breeches buoy when I got there and the whole stern soon came out of her.

"The very next day Jim Wherity, Bill Flynn, and I got a dory off Pegotty Beach and we backed that dory right into the gaping hole in her stern and went aboard the wrecked lumber schooner from the inside. Incidentally, the volunteer crew landed three men and the Coast Guard landed the remaining five.

"Indeed it was a weird experience. I got some old-fashioned handcuffs and a big vise. When we landed on the beach with our spoils, we were the admiration of all the others.

"Afterward, someone else started out to the wreck but by this time the wreckmaster had stationed a man with a rifle on the shore and after he shot a few times over their heads, they gave up and returned to the beach.*

---

* The official report stated that the schooner *Nantasket* "dragged her anchor and stranded. Discovered and reported by patrol. Lifesaving crew went to vessel with beach apparatus and found that volunteers had rigged up the Massachusetts Humane Society's gear and had already landed three of her crew. Keeper then took charge and landed the remaining five safely."

"Another wreck I remember," Mr. Flynn continued, "is that of the three-masted *Puritan*. She came in during March 1896, empty except for huge whiskey barrels which in themselves had a certain value.

"I remember that finally, when the sides went out of the *Puritan*, the barrels drifted out to sea and down to the south, and then when the wind swung around to the southeast the scores upon scores of barrels changed their course and started coming ashore all the way from Humarock to the Sand Hills.

"They were the fifty-two-gallon barrels and those of us who got any were able to sell them for $1 a piece.

"Another craft about which I have vivid memories was the *Professor Koch*. On April 29, 1919, she smashed into Cox's Rock off the Scituate shore. I was here in bed at the time, which was early in the morning. Frank Fallon, who was at the North Scituate Lifesaving Station telephoned his father, John Fallon, who was a mosser * and a fisherman.

"It was his task to round up a crew to go out to the wreck in the Massachusetts Humane Society surfboat. Almost always there was a good deal of rivalry between the two groups.

"Roused out of bed about three o'clock that morning, I was bow oarsman when we left from Pegotty Beach. We rowed out and smashed into the bell buoy off the mouth of the harbor, then rowed right across to where the *Professor Koch* was hung up on Cox's Rock. In that year the Scituate Proving Grounds were all lighted up all night long for the soldiers' barracks were right there.

"The Norwegian captain, sighting the lights from far off, had thought that he was entering Boston Harbor and pushed his bow high up on the rock. The bark had left Australia several months before with two of the crew shanghaied. The

---

The *Nantasket* had been carrying a load of lumber from Georgetown, South Carolina, to Boston. The value of the vessel was $10,000, with the cargo worth $13,500.
* Collector, drier, and seller of moss found in shallow low-tide shore areas.

craft had such an evil reputation that when they found out on what ship they were, they attempted suicide and were placed in irons.

"When we reached the rock we climbed up into the forecastle. By this time the tide had gone out so far that as I stood in the peak looking down it seemed as though I was in the top of the Boston Custom House. The bottom of the vessel was covered with barnacles as big as sea clams and I put some in my pockets but they died before we could eat them.

"We went up to the galley where the cook was trying to cook some corned beef. He kept sprinkling it with soda for he said the meat was rotten. While we were aboard the lifesaving crew arrived and wondered how we got there but we never squealed on Frank Fallon.

"Lobsterman Harry Driscoll then came alongside. The crew of the *Koch,* actually starving for fresh food, begged for some herring bait to eat and he took pity on them and threw up a mess of them.

"Meanwhile, Capt. Chris O'Neill of the volunteer crew went ashore and brought them out some decent food. We later found out that the Norwegian captain had taken aboard several little pigs which he killed privately and ate for himself.

"When we got ashore the whole town had turned out. At high tide two tugs from Boston Tow Boat Company released her from the rock and started to pull her into Scituate Harbor. She grounded at the mouth. They worked night and day to patch her up and eventually pulled her to Boston.*

---

* According to Commander F. E. Clark of the United States Navy, the *Professor Koch* was a steel bark, about 1,400 tons gross, built by Russell & Company, Port Glasgow, Scotland in 1891. His statement follows: "I know nothing of her early history, but about 1916 she was bought by Captain Gustaf Erikson, "sea king" of Mariehamn, Finland, and therefore came under the Russian (later Finnish) flag. At the end of World War I, the *Professor Koch* was on the east coast of South Africa. What she was doing there is a minor mystery since she was loaded with Australian wool. However, she sailed from East London on March 11, 1919, for Boston; on April twenty-ninth or thirtieth (the date is unclear in the *New York Maritime Register*) she stranded on Long Ledge, off Scituate. Shortly after tugs suc-

"Then there was the *Minnie Rowan*. She came ashore on February 13, 1894, hitting the southeasterly end of the First Cliff. We all brought our wagons down and took the soft coal from her which we burned all the remainder of that winter.

"On February 12, 1910, the *Matiana* came in near the Cliff House. I remember her captain had one arm. She lay on the beach for quite a spell.

"I'll always remember the *Henry Withington*. It was town meeting day in 1917. I had gone down to Welch's to work and when coming home I heard the guns from the Humane Society. I started down for the beach and met Tobin with a team and asked him what was going on.

" 'Why you damn fool,' he answered, 'there's a vessel ashore right at your front door.'

"I took all the short cuts I knew getting home, and in-

---

ceeded in floating her from this dangerous position and beached her in or near Scituate harbor, with eight feet of water in the hold. At first it was thought it would be necessary to lighter the cargo, but the sailors succeeded in installing pumps and patching the bottom sufficiently to tow her off the beach and into Boston on May 5, 1919. The wool cargo was discharged, and half of it had been ruined (estimated loss $100,000). The *Professor Koch* was dry-docked and the forward part of the bottom was found considerably damaged with part of the keel torn away. Incidentally, Boston Tow Boat Co. libelled her for $150,000 for salvage; how much they finally received, I do not know.

When the *Professor Koch* was repaired, she sailed from Boston September 30, 1919, for Norfolk; from there she took coal to Buenos Aires in sixty-two days. During 1920 and 1921 she continued active in the tramp trades available to sailing vessels at that time: Buenos Aires to Antwerp (probably with wheat); back to Norfolk to load coal for Copenhagen; timber from Norway to Melbourne (a five-month passage in which she was reported "overdue"); coal from Newcastle, New South Wales, to Chile. Finally, she sailed from Iquique December 28, 1921, with nitrates, bound for Lourenço Marques, in Portuguese East Africa. Off Cape Horn, the *Professor Koch* had a bad time; although details are scanty, she apparently encountered ice (losing her rudder), and also received heavy weather damage. After reportedly drifting helplessly for seventy days, she was picked up by a passing steamer and towed into Montevideo on April 20, 1922, one hundred and thirteen days out. At Montevideo, she was condemned, sold to Chilean owners, and renamed *Constancia*. However, her new owners obviously found her not worth repairing and a year later, in 1923, she was converted to a lighter and undoubtedly resold. My last information is that, as of about 1955, she was still in service, as the river barge *Don Juan V*, owned in Buenos Aires.

deed there was a great schooner at the foot of the cliff just below our house. We got the seven members of the crew into the cottage next door where they lived for the next two days until they were sent up to Boston. They had landed on the beach with hardly any clothes and we all gave them old coats and whatever else they needed.

"Their captain, Devereaux by name, had my room upstairs in this house. I was put on as watchman of the *Withington* at $5 a day."

Early in the morning of Friday, January 29, 1909, the three-masted schooner *Helena* crashed ashore at Fourth Cliff in Scituate. Aboard were 500,000 feet of yellow pine.

Surfman John Carson saw the vessel during the last beat of his early-morning watch. By that time the rain had turned to snow. The *Helena*'s sails were set, and when Carson sighted her she was driving straight for the breakers. The wind was from the northeast and blowing a howling gale.

Hoping to attract the attention of those aboard the doomed schooner, Carson lighted a Coston flare, but there was no response. After lighting two more with no results, he abandoned his attempts and ran to the station at Fourth Cliff. The crew were all having breakfast and got into their gear at once.

Back aboard the *Helena* the sailors realized they were in serious trouble. As Mate James Murchison of Boston explained later, the *Helena* had been "running to pick up Minot's Light when we struck.

"We were under a single-reefed mainsail and three jibs when we hit and my hands were so badly burned by the ropes in trying to lower the sails, that I don't know as I'll be able to use them for quite a while. We allowed half a point for currents off the Cape but that evidently wasn't enough."

Captain Frederick Stanley, veteran lifesaver in charge of the Fourth Cliff Station soon had the apparatus set up on the beach immediately opposite the wreck. Two sailors from Providence, Louis Santiago and John Santiago, were the first to land. Then came John T. Braxton of Norfolk, Virginia, Steward Orland Crowley of Indian River, Maine, and Mate James Murchison of Boston. Captain John Cummings was the last to leave his ship, carrying out that fine tradition of the sea. After he and the others had been taken into the lifesaving station he told his story.

"It was thick as mud, there being absolutely no observation. We kept the lead going and I was pointing the vessel well up for Boston Light and the first thing I knew we had breakers right under our bow."

Members of the Fourth Cliff Lifesaving Crew were Captain Frederick Stanley, Commander Dennis F. Quinn, James O'Connor, John Carson, Mark Baker, Martin Curran, Frank Carleton, William Crafts, and Richard Graham.

Once the news reached Marshfield that the *Helena* was shipwrecked off Fourth Cliff a group of residents headed by Miss Elsie Barker and Miss Edith Mills started out for the scene of the trouble with clothes and boots for the survivors.

Built at Bath, Maine, in 1900, the *Helena* was soon to achieve much more prominence as a picturesque shipwreck than she had ever enjoyed as a working schooner. People came from miles around to watch her slowly disintegrate at the base of the Fourth Cliff. Beachcombers were anxious to acquire her quarterboards and one is still at the residence of Mr. Richard W. Hatch of Marshfield, while another which I narrowly missed purchasing was taken to New Jersey some years ago.*

One of the great South Shore tragedies immediately preceding our entrance into World War I was the loss of the

---

* Massive fragments of the *Helena* can still be identified. During the Christmas storm of 1909 several giant timbers and masts were swept up the North River. One of them, about twelve by twelve inches in size and ten feet long, reposes at the foot of the oxpath leading from my residence.

barges *Ashland* and *Kohinoor* on March 3, 1916. The two craft had started down from Boston in tow along with a third barge, the *Kimberton*, but they ran into heavy seas off Point Allerton.

The tug did not experience serious trouble, however, until five thirty that night. Quoting her captain's words, "The hawsers between the *Kimberton*, my first barge, and the *Ashland*, my second, snapped, and I was alone with the *Kimberton*. In the limited visibility I worked around and stood by, but I could do nothing. I realized that the only possible act was to return to Boston Harbor, anchor the *Kimberton*, and steam back to the area around Minot's and try to find my two other barges. But I knew it was a hopeless task from the first.

"As I ran in close to the two barges which had broken loose I noticed in the brief flash which I had that the *Ashland*'s foresail was set, and the men were getting in the hawser, hoping that they could claw off to sea. I saw no activity at all on the *Kohinoor*, and the men aboard seemed stunned by the snapping hawser. I worked my way back to Boston, anchored the third barge near Fort Warren at 8:30, and was back at Minot's at 9:30, but could sight nothing, for by that time there was a tremendous sea running."

Years later I interviewed Mrs. Emma Ellen Murphy about the shipwrecks. A resident of Pondview Avenue, Minot, she had been married to a lifesaver, Joseph Peter Murphy, for many years. Concerned about the barges in the snowstorm which had developed, Mrs. Murphy's worst fears were realized when she was told there were two of them adrift.

During a lull in the storm, their black shapes were seen a half mile out, drifting shoreward. At the lifesaving station, Captain Franzen had been injured in an accident a few weeks before, and John Murphy, his lieutenant, took charge of rescue plans.

Although the storm was fierce, the waves had not then reached the terrific size which they attained later, and a surfboat filled with volunteers and surfmen was launched from the beach. On the way out, however, the craft passed wreck-age from the *Kohinoor* and they realized that the men from the old converted schooner had probably gone down with her breakup.

A moment later they sighted a dead body floating in the water. Another man was discovered, still alive, and he was pulled aboard the surf boat at once. Later he was taken to the home of Daniel Sylvester, where he was attended by three physicians, Dr. Handy and Dr. Alexander of Scituate, and Dr. Fernald of Cohasset. The sailor was an Indian, about thirty-five, but he died without revealing his identity.

Back off the shore the lifesavers rowed out to the wreck of the barge *Ashland*, which was caught on Collamore's Ledge with giant seas breaking over her.

Inside the *Ashland*'s pilot house were Captain A. G. Edstrand, Peter Bijoni, steward Axel Nilson, the donkey man, and two sailors, Antoine Hansen and John Mattson. They had watched with terror the loss of the barge *Kohinoor*. When the lifesavers rowed out, the sailors refused to go ashore with them, and remained on the barge instead. The disgusted surfmen returned to the Minot shore shortly after-ward, and explained to the waiting crowds what had happened.

By this time it was eleven o'clock at night, and after watching the surfmen set up a shore guard for the long hours of darkness to follow, most of the crowd went home. Every hour of that long tempestuous night the storm increased in strength, until by morning a mighty surf was pounding the entire bay from Salem to Scituate. Up at the Isles of Shoals the schooner *Stranger* pounded ashore at Smuttynose Island, while other vessels were in trouble up and down the coast.

Aboard the *Ashland* the five men began to realize that their decision to remain aboard had not been a wise one. Around four in the morning the great barge was hit by such a wave that it was splintered away from Collamore's Ledge and driven hard against Smith Rocks, where it perched in precarious fashion, the target for giant waves then sweeping toward Minot Beach.

A surf boat was made ready for launching from a point opposite Mike's Ledge, but at 10:30 A.M. it was decided that the waves were much too high to broach. This caused several Cohasset fishermen to jeer at the lifesavers.

However, another Cohasset resident spoke up, "If the boys go, I'll go with them, and none of us will ever get through the breakers, and we'll all die. But I'll go."

Just then the matter was settled for everyone concerned. The crowd which had assembled on the beach watched with horror as three great breakers hit the barge in rapid succession. It could be seen that the deckhouse of the *Ashland* was torn away from the barge, which rapidly began to go to pieces.

By 10:45 that morning the five men of her crew began to be battered ashore, clinging to the deckhouse. Certain that they were going to die, they wrote farewell messages on the cabin wall. But the deckhouse, which was stanchly made, floated ashore intact and all were rescued. One of the crew members later referred to the members of the ill-fated *Kohinoor*: "If we had only saved one man from the other barge, it would have been worth everything to us,* but fate decided otherwise."

The month of February 1926, was remembered up and down the New England coast as a stormy, snowy, four-week period which included many wrecks.

Thousands of persons were destined to be marooned in Boston and similar locations, while out on the ocean one lumber schooner was to end her career in a spectacular blaze of glory during the shortest month of the year. She was the four-master *Kenwood*, bringing a great load of lumber down from Halifax to Boston. Spacious in size, she was 184.5 feet

---

* The deck house is now on the property of the Scituate Cliff Hotel.

long, 37.3 feet in breadth, with a depth of 18.6 feet.*

Her captain, John Rogers, had sailed from Halifax right into a snowstorm. When she passed and sighted Halifax Lightship at eight o'clock on the night of Sunday, January 31, 1926, it was the last beacon they saw for many days. At that time the captain set his course southwest by south one quarter south.

The northeasterly gale continued day after day, during which time it was believed that the *Kenwood* had cleared outside of Cape Cod. Actually, because of the fact that the wind kept hauling from northwest to east and back to northeast and then back to east again, she was many miles north and west of where Rogers estimated her position.

Suddenly, at about six o'clock on the night of Thursday, February 4, the *Kenwood* came into an area of relatively shallow water, actually off Scituate, and even above the shrill noise of the sixty-knot gale Captain Rogers could hear the ominous sound of breakers on a lee beach.

A moment later the schooner grounded, and the captain ordered a tar barrel set ablaze to alert those ashore. It was ignited and set free, and the men began to shout for help at the top of their lungs.

Across on the shore, Gilbert Patterson of Scituate was hiking just above the reach of the breakers to see what might have washed up on the beach. This was the fourth day of that particular northeaster, and he thought there might be driftwood or old wreckage coming in. Suddenly he was startled to see the burning tar barrel, and ran down to a position opposite the blaze. Knowing that it meant trouble, he rushed across to Dana's General Store and Post Office at Sand Hills and told his story to Harry C. Reed, the manager.

It was agreed that the Coast Guardsman who had left the Minot Coast Guard Station at four o'clock was probably still

---

* Her signal letters were K.R.J.Q. and her official number was 161192. The gross tonnage of the *Kenwood* was 929 and her net tonnage, 797.

south of the location where the barrel had been burning, and the two men returned to the beach.

Surely enough, Surfman Eddie Robischeau soon came along (heading north), and they told him the news. Rushing inside the store, he used the only telephone in the vicinity to call Keeper John Glynn of the Minot Station. Glynn told him to go out and make doubly sure that there was a wreck and then come back and call the station again.

This time the three men went out and shouted across to what they could now faintly identify as a four-masted schooner. They told the shipwrecked mariners that they would get help.

Surfman Robischeau then called the Minot Coast Guard Station and Keeper Glynn ordered out the crew, one of whom was William Hersey, until recently the oldest member of the present crew at the Scituate First Cliff Station.

Keeper Glynn called the snow plow out and asked Tom Stanley to commandeer the Humane Society Surf boat and gun at Scituate which was much nearer to the wreck than the Minot boat.

Surfman Hersey and the other men started out with the snow plow, which had great difficulty maneuvering through the twelve- and fourteen-foot drifts that had piled up in several places between Minot and Cedar Point, where the *Kenwood* had piled ashore. Time and again the snow plow was hopelessly bogged down, and after reaching Egypt it was decided that the men would have to finish their trip on foot.

Eventually they reached a garage where a Packard service car was located. Commandeering this vehicle for the remainder of the journey, they picked up Tom Stanley and one of his boys awaiting them. Starting off again with the surf boat and the gun from the Massachusetts Society Station at Scituate, they eventually reached the rocky shore opposite the wreck.

By this time the *Kenwood* had swung around with her

beam to the shore, creating a partial lee. Nevertheless, to launch a boat into a northeasterly gale hitting sixty knots was to be no small accomplishment, and those who finally formed the crew of six or seven were the best men then on the beach.

While today there still is discussion as to which men went, we know that James Curran, Tom Stanley, and James O'Connor of the Coast Guard, and Gilbert Patterson, James Barry and George F. Dwyer of the Massachusetts Humane Society Volunteers were aboard when the surfboat was slid over the rocks into the seething foam. Time has erased the identity of the seventh member of the crew, if, in fact, there was one.*

The actual launching of the surfboat then took place, with those on the beach holding a long guide line. The first wave was reached and passed and the second was also conquered. Finally the lee of the *Kenwood* was dead ahead, and the surfboat was maneuvered to a position just below her.

One by one the survivors were told to leap into the boat, and all made it except the cook, Albert Ernest. The heaviest man in the crew, he slipped and fell, injuring his leg severely. On his second attempt he was hauled into the boat and the long trip ashore in the overloaded craft began.

According to Hersey those on the beach became overanxious and when the boat approached they began to pull her directly into and across the rocks, finally ripping out her bottom and sinking her in two feet of water. The men aboard grabbed the line and were hauled to safety, while the cook was carried by willing volunteers.

The nearest cottage was taken over by the Coast Guard, and the eight members of the crew of the stranded lumber schooner were soon sitting by a warm fireplace drying off.

---

* Others either at the station or in the crew at the time include John Hinchey, cook at the station, Walter Dacey, Carl Wirkala, Charles McIntyre, Lyman Richards, and a surfman named Davis.

When the firewood ran out the furniture was broken up and burned to give warmth to the unfortunate sailors. Among those who were saved were David Murphy, Samuel Baxter, Patrick Sullivan, John Scaninem, Peter Ryan, and Henry Flynn.

When the storm began to die down that night the *Kenwood* was believed by some to be fit to sail again, but her sticks started to loosen the following week. She was sold for salvage. Eventually the cargo was dispersed and she was burned on the following Fourth of July by Stanley Stonefield and a crew.

At 3:30 on the morning of October 10, 1954, the sixty-eight-foot staysail schooner *Chauve Souris* ran aground on a sand bar at the Scituate side of the mouth of the North River, which separates Scituate and Marshfield. Those aboard were five in number: Captain and Mrs. Hans Van Nes, their son, Hans, fifteen, Andres Joachim, fifteen, and Tom Anderson, eighteen.

Captain Van Nes explained that he thought he was sailing into the entrance of the Cape Cod Canal, which is one of the most original explanations for maritime error ever given on the South Shore.

I recall wading out at dawn to photograph the stranded schooner and to meet the people aboard. The Scituate Coast Guard soon alerted Boston headquarters which sent down the buoy tender *White Heath* while Point Allerton dispatched a surf boat. After several attempts to free her had failed, the schooner was pulled off the bar by five o'clock that night.

On the afternoon of November 19, 1955, the 73-foot converted fishing schooner *Snow Maiden* was entering Plymouth Bay for what was hoped would be a brief repair job at a boat yard before her planned trip to the West Indies on a cruise. Aboard were owner-captain Frederick P. White of Norwell and five others.*

At first the wind was moderate and the seas fairly calm, but the wind increased until it blew at almost gale force. The Scituate Coast Guard Station received a call for help from the schooner and when their forty-foot boat arrived on the scene under the command of Warrant Officer Warren Miller, two crewmen were taken ashore.

Returning to the scene at about eleven o'clock that night, the Coast Guard craft developed rudder and propeller trouble, but managed to take off two more men from the stricken vessel. Meanwhile the storm grew in fury, and when a heavy dory began to wash off the deck of the *Snow Maiden*, two of her crew scrambled into it. Driven before the wind, they finally reached the town pier at Plymouth, where they clambered up on the wharf to safety.

The *Snow Maiden* soon went to pieces and her wreckage strewed the South Shore for miles.

The last important stranding on the South Shore was that of the 441-foot, 7,000-ton Italian freighter *Etrusco*. Ripping ashore over the ledges at Cedar Point on March 16, 1956, she remained almost touching old Scituate Light for the next eight months.** Finally on Thanksgiving Day, November 22, 1956, a salvage crew under Admiral Lebbius Curtis freed the huge craft and she was rechristened *Scituate*, by which name she is still cruising the northwest coast, according to last reports.

---

* John Martini of Hull; John Ware, Cohasset; Rene Stackpole of Mystic, Connecticut; David Fulton, Montreal; and Everett Wheelwright, Cohasset, comprised the ship's company.

** I devote an entire chapter to this shipwreck in my *Legends of the New England Coast*.

XXIV

The *Monica Smith* and the *General Greene*

The winter of 1959-1960 was distinguished by two great storms, one of which brought the highest tide since March, 1956. The other gale eventually battered the Coast Guard Cutter *General Greene* ashore at Spring Hill, Sandwich, Massachusetts. In addition to the two great storms, a high westerly wind on the night of Saturday, February 20, 1960, possibly contributed to the stranding of the 258-foot Swedish motor vessel *Monica Smith* at Hatches Harbor, Cape Cod.

With the combined efforts of two craft, the *Monica Smith* was pulled off the beach into deep water. We watched the final moments of this operation, and the passenger in our car, Monica Smith, stepped out onto the Donald MacMillan Pier to wave farewell to her namesake. Another chapter in the Cape Cod shipwreck history was over and within a few years the vessel's name would be forgotten by all but a few.

On Thursday, March 3, 1960, a blizzard which battered the New England coast into almost total submission left record snowfalls in scores of locations and smashed across

Cape Cod with devastating results. By the time the storm ended hundreds of telephone poles were down with thousands of miles of wires on the ground. Electric and telephone services were cut off for days and in some cases weeks. The Donald MacMillan Pier at Provincetown suffered extensive damage, while all along the shore destruction was extremely heavy.

Off the Massachusetts Bay entrance to the Cape Cod Canal the tug *M. Moran* ran into serious trouble en route to aid the *General Greene* stranded to the north of Spring Hill Beach in Sandwich, Massachusetts. Boatswain's Mate John T. Pershman, attached to the Sandwich Coast Guard Station, told me later what occurred.

"It all started when the tug lost her rudder," he explained.

"Reaching the Spring Hill shore, we could see nothing. About a mile from where we started Fernet and I located the ship about 125 feet offshore in the great breakers. Each wave hit and went up, way up, and over the mast itself. We were both scared, but went back to the beach and got the duck ready.

"We kept on, and I jammed that duck's stern right against the *Greene*'s side. One by one the crew jumped aboard with us, and we made the trip to shore. Finally there were only three men left aboard the *Greene* and I was feeling pretty good.

"We backed out to the *Greene* for the final trip and got the three remaining men, but as soon as we hit the beach another giant wave scooped the duck up and sank her right before our eyes. We all got back to the station and into dry clothes, but the duck was still in the water, wedged under the *Greene*'s side. Later it was salvaged."

Several days afterward the *General Greene* was towed and pushed off the shore by the combined efforts of Coast Guard craft at sea and tanks pushing from shore. The final act in another South Shore Massachusetts shipwreck had been completed.

Index

303